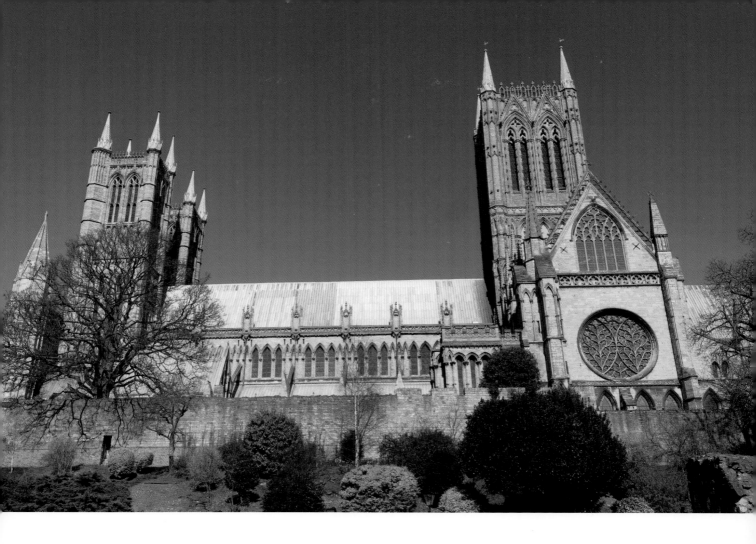

LINCOLNSHIRE
Unusual & Quirky

Andrew Beardmore

HALSGROVE

ALSO BY ANDREW BEARDMORE:

Our English counties are full of glorious countryside, historic buildings and thriving cities, towns and villages. However, lurking not far beneath their surface is a host of oddities and peculiarities that turn the apparently staid and conventional into something much more intriguing…

Derbyshire: Unusual & Quirky: Find out about Derbyshire's Gretna Green, the Devil of Drakelow, and T'owd Man, and see what Muggles and Full-Blood Princes have to do with Ashbourne's Shrovetide football!

Or how about the World Head Balancing Champion, Black Harry, Harry Potter's owls, Naked Racing and Colditz Castle; and not forgetting award-winning urinals, the man who crossed the English Channel in a bath, and the woman who lived in a bacon box!

Nottinghamshire: Unusual & Quirky: Find out which Notts villages are home to a lethal Roman curse, an eight foot trumpet and the Black Pig Dancers, and which one swapped sides of the Trent in the 16th century.

Or how about Harry Potter's gravestone, an *oven* made of gravestones, the Flying Bedstead, and Britain's "hardest pub"; and not forgetting a pub chair that increases fertility, a house haunted by an inebriated butler and an evil bishop, plus a village which put cows on thatched roofs to keep them topped up on straw!

Leicestershire and Rutland: Unusual & Quirky: Find out which Leicestershire villages had a beer-swilling fox, a wig-detecting phantom, and a parson who tied 58 bulldogs to 58 apple trees to prevent scrumping!

Or what about which Leicestershire village was hit by a meteorite, which one saw doves dictate the build of a church, and which one still fights annually over a hare pie! Alternatively, find out which Rutland village had a 14th century rector involved in serious organised crime, which one is twinned with Paris, and which one is home to a truly mind-blowing historical revelation.

Staffordshire: Unusual & Quirky: Find out which Staffordshire town has a noisy peace memorial, or which Staffordshire villages are home to Britain's unluckiest church, and the man who danced for a dozen days.

Then there's the Staffordshire constituency that returned the oldest-ever MP (aged 93), the village that suffered the largest non-nuclear explosion on British soil, and the town which saw its brand-spanking-new canal lock destroyed by the very cannon that was supposed to be heralding its grand opening! Alternatively, find out which ancient customs involve one-thousand-year-old reindeer horns, teapots, brass statues and a goose!

If you think you know these counties, read these fascinating and profusely illustrated books and think again…

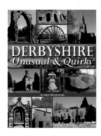 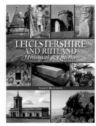  

First published in Great Britain in 2017

Copyright © Andrew Beardmore 2017

British Library Cataloguing-in-Publication Data
A CIP record for this title is available from the British Library

ISBN 978 0 85704 303 0

HALSGROVE
Halsgrove House,
Ryelands Business Park,
Bagley Road, Wellington, Somerset TA21 9PZ
Tel: 01823 653777 Fax: 01823 216796
email: sales@halsgrove.com
website: www.halsgrove.com

Printed and bound in India by Parksons Graphics

Lincolnshire – Unusual and Quirky

Welcome to *Lincolnshire – Unusual and Quirky*. This is the fifth book in a new series that calls to mind that classic series of travel books called *The King's England*, written in the 1930s by Arthur Mee, since each volume in Mee's series was suffixed with *"There have been many books on <insert county>, but never one like this…"* Well the very same tag line could be applied to this book, as some of its elements are certainly unique. Having said that, the book still has plenty to offer in terms of conventional reference, but it delivers this in a lateral and humorous format never seen before.

Essentially, then, the book is comprised of two main sections which are called *Conventional Lincolnshire* and *Quirky Lincolnshire*. The *Conventional* section kicks off with some county maps along with key facts and figures relating to the county – such as county town, population, highest point, key industries and famous sons and daughters. The facts are then followed by a history of the Lincolnshire *area* from the Stone Age to the 11th century – by which time Lincolnshire, along with most of England's counties had been officially formed – after which the last one thousand years of county history is covered, bringing us up-to-date and into the 21st century. Nevertheless, in keeping with the title of the book, the *County History* also has a number of appropriately historical "Quirk Alerts" interspersed, too; like a paragraph on William the Conqueror's landowning baker, an anecdote about a village ritual that could only be carried out by a virgin in mourning garb, and another town ritual involving the vicar, a whip and 30 pieces of silver!

The *Conventional* section then hands over to the *Quirky* section…and it is here that we really begin to earn the *"…but never one like this…"* tag line – as the whole section is driven by a quirky poem known as a Shire-Ode! Told in rhyming verse, the Shire-Ode portrays imaginary inhabitants of Lincolnshire but, as an extra twist, the poem contains dozens of place-names found within the historic county, each subtly woven into the tale – and it is these place-names upon which the *Quirky* section focuses. Firstly, the places have their location pin-pointed via a map. A series of chapters then follow in (largely) alphabetical order for each place featured in the Shire-Ode – and it is here that the strangest and most interesting facts and features about each place are explored. As a result, you get a random almanac of places that would never ordinarily appear together – along with population figures, earliest place-name recording and origins, famous sons and daughters, historic trivia, Quirk Alerts…and lots of accompanying photographs, too.

So, feel free to commence your obscure Lincolnshire fact-digging; to read about some very famous people and their Lincolnshire exploits, to read about ancient battles and, quite frankly, some ridiculous legends, too…but to hopefully have a little chuckle along the way. For example, find out which Lincolnshire village has a stone that if ever moved, will result in the escape of the Devil, which one is home to a memorial bungalow, and which church has the country's first ever carving of an ursine musician! Or discover which Lincolnshire village has a mystery White Lady, which village has a ghostly Black Lady, and which village pub landlord left money to ensure the preaching of an annual sermon warning of the perils of drink!

Then there's Lincolnshire's most bizarre custom, The Haxey Hood – so find out why The Boggins set fire to The Fool while he delivers his annual speech, and which is the prelude to a bizarre tussle between hundreds of people to direct The Sway to one of four pubs! Alternatively, simply find out what Lincolnshire words and phrases mean, such as Meggies, kek and yaffle, or find out where the oldest inhabited rectory in England is.

From a historical perspective, find out which precious Bronze Age treasure was destroyed by German bombs, but conversely, which village church had German bombs to *thank* for revealing ancient wall paintings of immense importance! Or what about which Lincolnshire town was the capital of England for around six weeks in the early 11th century, which village pub T.E. Lawrence penned his autobiographical *Seven Pillars of Wisdom* in, which village has been home to the King's Champion since 1066 and which Lincolnshire landmark became the tallest building in the world in the late 13th century. Alternatively, you'll need a strong stomach to read of the Hideous Happening in Holbeach, while you'll be amazed at the Lincolnshire horse that walked the 120 miles to Aintree, promptly won the Grand National and then walked home again!

Finally, check out *Bicker, Wrangle and Wressle*, the quirky Shire-Ode that drives the idiosyncratic *Quirky Lincolnshire* section and learn how a firm of solicitors treat their customers, Messingham about and then financially Hameringham with their Irnham, Burnham brands!

Anyway, that's the introduction completed. As you have probably gathered by now, this book is indeed "unusual and quirky"…so it's time to prime the quirkometer and pull up a pew at St Strangeways – oh, and did I mention which school regularly locked the headmaster out, which village has two churches in one churchyard, and which church has the largest single-handed clock in the world? Or what about which Lincolnshire village was home to a man after whom the Roundheads were named, which stately home's clock stopped the minute King George III died, which tiny village has a bizarre one-way system…

Contents

Lincolnshire Facts and Figures

County Status:	Ceremonial county and (smaller) non-metropolitan county (minus Lincoln)
County Towns:	
Lincolnshire (Pre-1889):	Lincoln
Lindsey (1889-1974):	Lincoln
Kesteven (1889-1974):	Sleaford
Holland (1889-1974):	Boston
Lincolnshire (Post-1974):	Lincoln
County Population:	1,042,000
County Population Rank:	18th out of 48
Cities:	Lincoln
Largest City:	Lincoln
Largest City Population:	104,221
Largest City Pop. Rank:	83rd (English); 93rd (UK)
Largest City Status:	Unitary Authority
National Parks:	N/A
Other Areas:	Lincolnshire Wolds (AONB)
County Area:	2,687 miles^2 (6,959 km^2)
County Area Rank:	2nd out of 48
Highest Point:	Wolds Top at 551ft (168m)
Longest River:	The River Trent at 185 miles (298 km) is the longest river, part of which defines Lincolnshire's borders with Nottinghamshire and South Yorkshire. However, the River Witham at 82 miles (132 km) is almost entirely within Lincolnshire.
Football Clubs:	Scunthorpe United (League One); Grimsby Town (League Two); Lincoln City (National League [formerly the Football Conference]), Boston United, Gainsborough Trinity (National League North)
Rugby Union Clubs:	Scunthorpe (National League 3 [Midlands]); Market Rasen and Louth (Midlands 1 East); Spalding, Stamford (Midlands 2 East [North]); Boston, Grimsby, Kesteven, Lincoln, Sleaford (Midlands 3 East [North])
Industries (Present):	Arable Farming (especially barley, rapeseed, sugar beet, wheat), Commerce, Cut Flowers, Fishing, Food Manufacture, Import/Export, Renewable Energy, Services, Steel (reduced), Tourism, Vegetables (especially cabbage, onions, cauliflower)
Industries (Past):	Agriculture, Baltic Trade, Deep-Sea Fishing, Steel, Tank & Military Vehicle Manufacture, Textiles, Train Manufacture, Wool
Born in Lincolnshire:	**HUM:** Darren Pattinson, Sheridan Smith **LIN:** Kelly Adams, George Bass, Jim Broadbent, George Boole, Richard Busby, Geoff Capes, William Cecil, Susanna Centlivre, Lee Chapman, Colin Dexter, Michele Dotrice, Matthew Flinders, Michael Foale, John Foxe, Richard Foxe, Sir John Franklin, St Gilbert of Sempringham, Thomas Goodrich, John Haigh, Hardicanute, Henry IV, Hereward the Wake, Patricia Hodge, Gervase Holles, Charles Hudson, Ian Huntley, Benjamin Huntsman, Jean Ingelow, Herbert Ingram, Tony Jacklin, Elizabeth Jennings, Dame Madge Kendal, Jonathan Kerrigan, Alexander Kilham, Bennet Langton, Stephen Langton, Halford Mackinder, Robert Mannyng, Neil McCarthy, Sir Neville Marriner, Thomas Miller, Fynes Moryson, Sir Isaac Newton, Paul Palmer, Nicholas Parsons, John Patrick, Simon Patrick, Joan Plowright, Henry Rands, William Robertson, Sir Malcolm Sargent, Jennifer Saunders, John Smith, Liz Smith, John Smyth, William Stukeley, Thomas Sutton, Bernie Taupin, Rod Temperton, Alfred, Lord Tennyson, Charles Tennyson, Frederick Tennyson, Dame Sybil Thorndyke, Margaret Thatcher, Chad Varah, Richard Watson, Robert Webb, Charles Wesley, John Wesley, John Whitgift, Dr Francis Willis, Luke Wright

Lincolnshire Maps

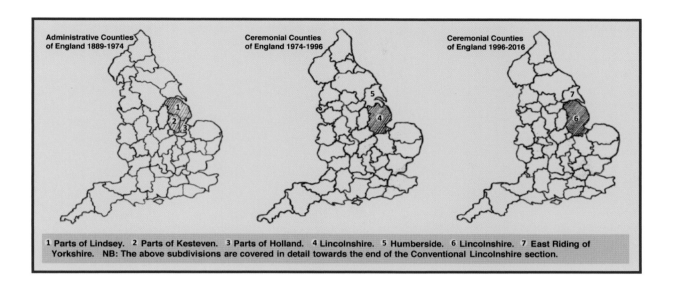

1 **Parts of Lindsey.**   2 **Parts of Kesteven.**   3 **Parts of Holland.**   4 **Lincolnshire.**   5 **Humberside.**   6 **Lincolnshire.**   7 **East Riding of Yorkshire.**   NB: The above subdivisions are covered in detail towards the end of the Conventional Lincolnshire section.

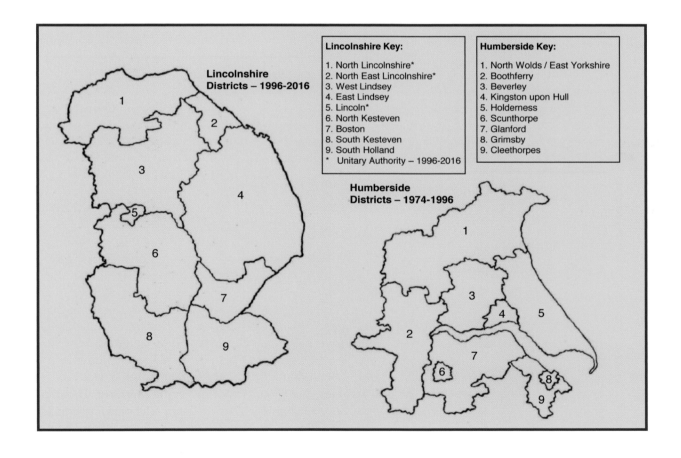

Lincolnshire Districts – 1996-2016

Lincolnshire Key:

1. North Lincolnshire*
2. North East Lincolnshire*
3. West Lindsey
4. East Lindsey
5. Lincoln*
6. North Kesteven
7. Boston
8. South Kesteven
9. South Holland
* Unitary Authority – 1996-2016

Humberside Key:

1. North Wolds / East Yorkshire
2. Boothferry
3. Beverley
4. Kingston upon Hull
5. Holderness
6. Scunthorpe
7. Glanford
8. Grimsby
9. Cleethorpes

Humberside Districts – 1974-1996

Prehistory

Like most other English historic counties, Lincolnshire dates from the 11th century, and was formed towards the end of the two hundred year struggle on English soil between Anglo-Saxon and Viking. The name means "shire or district of the town of Lincoln", and is clearly derived from the place-name *Lincoln*, plus the Old English word *scīr*, meaning "shire or district". As for Lincoln itself, the place dates back to before the Roman invasion of Britain in AD 43, when the Celtic *Corieltauvi* tribe named the place as *Lindon*, with the name deriving from the Brythonic Celtic word *lindo*, meaning "pool" – a reference to today's Brayford Pool on the River Witham in Lincoln.

Of course, the *area* of Lincolnshire goes back much further than Roman times, and the biggest influence on the current landscape of the county occurred between the various ice ages and the warm interglacial periods. The most dramatic of the ice ages, when the ice sheets advanced as far south as London, saw the entirety of Lincolnshire covered in ice several hundred metres thick. When it retreated, the clay vales were deeper, but its greatest effect was on the course of the River Trent in what is now Lincolnshire. This is because from around 1.7 million years ago, instead of heading in a north-easterly direction to Newark and then north to the Humber, the Trent flowed eastwards through the Vale of Belvoir to cut a gap through the limestone ridge at Ancaster, now known as the Ancaster Gap. From here it flowed to the Lincolnshire east coast and out into the North Sea. However, around 130,000 years ago a mass of stagnant ice left in the Vale of Belvoir caused the river to divert north along the old Lincoln River, and what is now the course of the River Witham, and this time through the Lincoln Gap to the North Sea. Then in a subsequent glaciation around 70,000 BC, what is today known as the lower Trent basin was home to vast areas of water known as Glacial Lake Humber. The "lake" was kept in check by a glacier, and when this retreated, the Trent adopted its current, northern-bound course – making it fairly unusual amongst English rivers, the majority of which flow in the other three directions courtesy of the country having mainly west, south and east coasts!

By the time the Lincolnshire of today had been shaped, two thirds of the county lay at less than 100ft (30m), with much of that lying at less than 10ft (3m). Of the other third, much of this is taken up by two very distinctive hill ranges, both running from north to

---

Quirk Alert: *Legendary Stones*

Below, we have photographs of two glacial erratics, composed of soft Spilsby sandstone, and initially deposited in their locality by the retreating ice sheets. The photograph below left is what is known as the Winceby Stone, near to the village of Winceby, 3 miles west of Horncastle. However, it is also known locally as The Devil's Stone and legend has it that if it is moved, the Devil will escape from beneath it! Meanwhile, the stones shown below right are located outside St Edith's church at Anwick, and are known as The Drake Stones. The legend of these stones is that a man ploughing a field north of the church saw his horses and plough mysteriously disappear into the ground after which a dragon (or drake) flew out. The next day, the villagers found a stone shaped like a drake's head and decided that there would be treasure beneath it. Alas, they were unable to move the stone, and it therefore remained unmoved for hundreds of years until the 19th century when local men Doctor Oliver and Reverend Hazelwood used a traction engine to drag it to the church. It was during this transportation that the stone broke into two and thus inherited the name Drake Stones.

south. The more westerly of the two is comprised of limestone heath, and is split into two parts. The northern half runs from Scunthorpe in the north, down to Lincoln, where the aforementioned Lincoln Gap occurs. The southern half then runs from just south of Lincoln, down through Sleaford on its eastern flank and Grantham on the western flank, before levelling out towards Bourne and Stamford in the south. The highest point on this range of hills is 505ft (154m), while the western side is characterised by a distinctive escarpment known simply as Cliff, or sometimes Lincoln Edge. Meanwhile, the other hill range is known as the Lincolnshire Wolds, and runs from Barton-upon-Humber in the north, heading in a south-easterly direction taking in Louth on its eastern fringe and Horncastle on its south-western fringe, and rising to a peak height of 551ft (168m) at Wolds Top. As for the lowland areas, these are characterised by the Fens in the south-east, the marshlands and coastal plains to the east, the Trent Vale to the west, and the equally flat Isle of Axholme in the north-west, much of which was under water until reclaimed by drainage engineers in the 17th century. Many of these areas are just a few metres above sea level and rely on drainage and sea defences to protect them from river and coastal flooding. The final Lincolnshire geographic area is the clay vale country in between the two hill ranges through which the River Ancholme flows.

Possibly the earliest worked flints in the area were found buried in silt beds at Kirmington in North Lincolnshire, although dating them isn't easy – but they may date from as long as 200,000 years ago during an interglacial period of the Palaeolithic (Old Stone Age) period. Numerous other Palaeolithic hand axes and tools have been found, such as those at Barlings, Risby Warren, Roxby, and Whisby, while a Palaeolithic flint core that was used to flake material in order to make flint tools was found at Salmonby and dates to between 50,000 to 10,000 years ago. The majority of these artefacts were therefore made during what is known as the Devensian phase of the Palaeolithic period, and which ran in Britain from 110,000 to 12,000 years ago. This phase is also widely acknowledged as covering the last glacial period in these islands.

Following the retreat of the ice sheets, *Home sapiens* would perhaps have hunted and gathered in Lincolnshire, most likely coming from Creswell Crags on the Derbyshire/Nottinghamshire border, a recognised settlement of these times. They would have had sparse pickings, though, as the area of Lincolnshire would have been a pretty inhospitable, treeless landscape of tundra at that time. However, as the temperature rose, seeds from further south gradually began to bring about the re-forestation of the county area, and by the end of the Mesolithic (Middle Stone Age) period, which ran from 10,000 to 4,500 B.C., the first permanent settlements would have appeared in the Lincolnshire area, while trees would have been cleared for the first farming in the area. The earliest evidence of Neolithic

The Neolithic Burgh Top long barrow is a scheduled ancient monument measuring 88ft by 44ft and 8ft high in places. Today, it shares its place with some redundant cold-war accessories!

This is the long barrow known as Beacon Plantation, a mile northwest of Swaby. It is one of Lincolnshire's best-preserved Neolithic long barrows and is also the largest, at 256ft (78m) by 62ft (19m). The barrow survives as three raised sections, with the largest being the circular mound at the southern end and which is around 6.5ft (2m) high.

(New Stone Age) farming was thanks to an excavation at Tattershall Thorpe which revealed traces of a wooden building, while Neolithic pottery and flint artefacts have been found at Dragonby, Little Gonerby and Tallington.

The Neolithic period ran from around 4,500 to 2,000 B.C. and few settlements of this period survive today thanks to modern farming. However, numerous burial sites do survive, and which usually take the form of earthen long barrows or drystone mounds, generally with flanking ditches, and which remained in use over a long period of time. These long barrows were also often used for communal burial, often with only parts of the human remains having been selected for interment, while it is thought that they acted as important spiritual sites, too. Interestingly, more than 60 long barrows in the Lincolnshire Wolds and surrounding areas had their flanking ditches continued around the ends of the barrow mound, although only a small number of these survive as earthworks. The rest are

This Bronze Age round barrow is known as Bully Hill, and can be found between Tealby and Kirmond le Mire on the course of a prehistoric trackway.

Grim's Mound, another Bronze Age round barrow located a mile or so east of Burgh-on-Bain.

only visible from the air as cropmarks or soilmarks with no evidence of a mound at ground level. Nevertheless, this regional characteristic is considered to be of great national importance.

One of the best-excavated Neolithic long barrow examples is one of a trio known as Giant's Hills just off the A1028 between Ulceby and Skendleby. Excavated between 1933 and 1934 by C.W. Phillips, Giant's Hills 1 measures 213ft (65m) by 75ft (23m), dates from between 3,500 and 2,700 B.C., and contained the complete remains of four people and the partial remains of three more. The other two barrows at Giant's Hills are actually larger than Giant's Hills 1, but nowhere near as well preserved, thanks to farming damage. Giant's Hills 2 is barely evident, amounting to a minor swelling of the ground. It was excavated in 1991, though, by Evans and Simpson who discovered that it was trapezoidal in shape and would have measured 253ft (77m) by 62ft (19m), and had a fully enclosing outer quarry ditch. As for the third barrow, this now only survives as a cropmark, but measured 249ft (76m) by 75ft (23m).

Another Neolithic long barrow can be found at Burgh Top, just south of Burgh-on-Bain on the B1255. A scheduled ancient monument, Burgh Top long barrow is a substantial and prominent earthwork measuring 88ft (27m) by 44ft (13.5m), and is roughly oval in shape. It is also clearly visible from the B1255 thanks to having a height ranging from 8ft (2.5m) to 5ft (1.5m), all of which gives it something of a whale-back profile. As for the B1255, this is thought to have been built along the course of a prehistoric trackway, so there may have been a prominent Neolithic settlement in the vicinity. Certainly Burgh Top long barrow is known to be one of a number of Neolithic and Bronze Age burial mounds associated with the valley of the River Bain and its prehistoric trackway, while other finds nearby include Neolithic leaf-shaped arrow-heads and Bronze Age flints.

Further Lincolnshire Wolds long barrows can be found at Ash Hill and Cromwell's Grave (both north of Binbrook), Ash Holt (east of Cuxwold), Beacon Plantation (north-west of Swaby), Deadmen's Graves (north-west of Claxby St Andrew's), Hills Brough Farm (south of Caistor), and Spellow Hills (south-west of Ulceby Cross). As well as the long barrows in the Wolds, many Neolithic flint axe-heads have been found here, and elsewhere, such as the uplands north of the River Witham, and in smaller numbers on the limestone upland south of Lincoln. Interestingly, most of these axes don't originate from the Lincolnshire area, with the majority originating from Cumbria or North Wales, and thus suggesting elements of trade existed back then. Of the remainder, these originated from relatively nearby Leicestershire and Warwickshire, to the extremes of England at both Cornwall and Northumberland; some even came from Ireland!

As for Neolithic henges, there aren't any that visibly survive in Lincolnshire, but aerial photographs from the 1970s did reveal an oval area of 82ft (25m) 2 miles north-west of Horncastle, that has since been named as Shearman's Wath Henge. What is now designated as a Class II henge was encircled by a 6.5ft (2m) ditch and had entrances to the south-east and the north-west. The site also has a concentric ring of post holes or pits outside the ditch, but it is thought unlikely that they once accommodated standing stones.

Towards the end of the Neolithic period, the eastern and southern parts of England were being settled by the Beaker People of Western Europe, so-named after their distinctive pottery drinking vessels. In Lincolnshire, there is evidence of these people settling again in the Wolds, but also in the Grantham, Ancaster and Scunthorpe areas, as evidenced by pottery remains and barrows. It is also barrows – round barrows in this case – that mark settlement in Lincolnshire during the Bronze Age (2,100 to 700 B.C.). Although many of these round barrows were destroyed by farming from the 18th century onwards, some fine examples still survive. These include the incongruous Beacon Hill, which took its name from a medieval beacon site, but which today is located in the middle of a Cleethorpes housing estate! Past excavations have determined that this might even have started out as a long barrow during Neolithic times, thanks to Neolithic worked flints found during the 1930s. Also found was a large plain Bronze Age urn. Intriguingly, this urn also contained four decorated smaller urns containing the cremated remains of a child. The barrow is 6.5ft (2m) high and measures 59ft (18m) by 33ft (10m) round.

Another beautifully preserved round barrow can be found at Bully Hill, north-east of Tealby, yet another ancient barrow located on the ancient prehistoric track-way known today as High Street. This barrow rises to a height of 10ft (3m) and a diameter of 82ft (25m). Meanwhile, the similarly-named Bully Hills are located at Tathwell, just south of Louth, and gain their plural name thanks to seven Bronze Age bowl barrows, six of which are aligned together on the usual south-west to north-east alignment, forming a linear chain of nearly 400ft (120m). The seventh barrow is located around 740ft (225m) to the north-east. The two central barrows are the highest at around 10ft (3m) each, with the others between 3 to 6.5ft (1-2m), while their diameters range between 39ft (12m) and 82ft (25m). Barrow 7 at 10ft (3m) high with a diameter of 52ft (16m) is something of a mystery. Finally, the nicely-named Grim's Mound can

Lincolnshire came from the valleys of the Rivers Trent and Ancholme, as well as alongside the River Witham, and include awls, axe-heads, daggers, knives, rapiers and spearheads. In particular, a hoard of Bronze Age socketed axes were found at Fiskerton, while the haul of Bronze Age axes found at Nettleham are now in the British Museum and Lincoln Museum.

> ### Quirk Alert: *Das Boot*
> Other than round barrows, the best Bronze Age find in Lincolnshire occurred in 1886 when excavations were being made for a gas-works at Brigg, during which they discovered an ancient boat. It had been carved out of an enormous oak-tree and was almost 50ft (15m) long, as well as 4-5ft wide (1.5m) and 3-4ft deep (1m), and was thought to have been capable of carrying up to 50 men. At the time, it was thought to date from the Late Bronze Age, perhaps c.1000 B.C. Alas, any chance of modern dendrochronological verification is not possible, as the boat was sent to Hull Museum…which was destroyed by German bombs during World War II!

Six of the seven Bronze Age round barrows that comprise Bully Hills, close to Tathwell. The seventh lies 225m to the north-east.

be found a mile east of Burgh-on-Bain, and again close to High Street. It measures 8ft (2.5m) high and 66ft (20m) in diameter, and the name is probably another derivation from the Danish chap, *Grimr*, after whom Grimsby was named! There are also a number of other barrows to the west of Burgh-on-Bain, either side of High Street.

Other Lincolnshire Bronze Age round barrows can be found at Burwell Wood (south-west of Muckton), Buslingthorpe, Butterbumps (a dozen small barrows near Willoughby), Cleatham Barrow (south of Manton), Donington on Bain, Folk Moot and Butt Mound (a pair of bowl barrows near to Silk Willoughby), Fordington Barrows (near Ulceby), Hagworthingham, Hatcliffe Barrow (one of Lincolnshire's largest but in the private grounds of Hatcliffe Manor House), Howe Hill (near Wootton), Kelstern, King's Hill (north of Bardney), Ludford Barrow (south-west of Ludford), Mill Hill (north-east of Claxby St Andrew and the only one standing on top of a sheer chalk face), Revesby Barrow (east of Revesby) and Ring Holt (south-west of Dalby).

As for Bronze Age objects, two thirds of the finds in

The Iron Age in Britain ran from around 700 B.C. to the 1st century A.D. The most impressive remains of an Iron Age hillfort in Lincolnshire is Honington Camp, situated around a mile to the south-east of the village of Honington and below and to the north-east of the highest point of Barkston Heath. It may, however, have been more of a defended settlement or farmstead, as these were more prevalent in the east of England compared to the Iron Age hillforts of upland England; Honington Camp certainly doesn't quite have the 360 degree view that most hillforts did. However, its elaborate triple defence system does suggest a settlement of some strategic importance, as does its location in the Ancaster Gap. The structure is rectangular and measures 492ft (150m) by 574ft (175m), and is enclosed by 82ft (25m) wide defensive banks and ditches. The enclosed part of the settlement sits on a flat plateau and the defences consist of an inner bank, a ditch, a larger central bank, another ditch and then a lower outer bank or counterscarp. The entrance was located on the eastern side.

Two other probable Iron Age camps include Careby

Camp in the south of the county, around 4 miles south-west of Bourne, and Yarborough Camp in the north, close to the North Lincolnshire village of Croxton. Careby Camp is a multivallate oval earthwork with ditches, and measures around 850ft (259m) by 750ft (229m), while the distance between the inner and outer banks is around 130ft (40m). The outer bank is barely defined, but the inner bank is around 3ft (1m) above ground level and 5ft (1.5m) above the level of its ditch. Meanwhile, Yarborough Camp is a sub-rectangular univallate enclosure, measuring 260ft (80m) by 195ft (60m). It is surrounded by banks that are 33ft (10m) wide and 3-7ft (1-2m) high, and a 32ft (10m) wide ditch. The entrance to the enclosure was on the eastern side. Both sites are scheduled monuments.

We can't be completely sure that these settlements date from the Iron Age, though, as subsequent farming and deep ploughing has destroyed a lot of the evidence – but it is highly likely that they pre-date Roman Britain, while their respective sizes suggest a measure of importance – perhaps the strongholds of local chieftains. Evidence supporting the fact that both Honington Camp and Yarborough Camp continued to be populated throughout the Roman period is supplied by a number of finds, with Roman coins found at both sites, and with the hoard of coins found at Yarborough Camp specifically dating from the 4th century. Also found at Yarborough were the remains of what could be Iron Age weapons and horse fastenings.

Other Iron Age settlements have been discovered on the Wolds at Kirmington, Ludford, Ulceby Cross and possibly Horncastle, and on Lincolnshire limestone country at Ancaster, Dragonby and Owmby, while another settlement at Old Sleaford represents the Fen edge. There is also evidence of a 1st century B.C. Iron Age settlement at Lincoln, by the modern-day Brayford Pool. This is located in the River Witham at the foot of the hill upon which the Normans would later build Lincoln Cathedral and Lincoln Castle.

Returning to Iron Age finds, and one of the finest in Lincolnshire is what is known as the Witham Shield – although it is actually made out of bronze! It was probably used for symbolic and ceremonial purposes rather than in battle, and resides today at the British Museum in London – although there are copies around Lincolnshire, like the one at the City and County Museum at Lincoln.

The indigenous population of the British Iron Age were Brythonic Celts, and Lincolnshire was home to the Celtic *Corieltauvi* tribe. The territory of the *Corieltauvi* stretched from Lincolnshire down to all but the south-western slice of Warwickshire, with the *Corieltauvi* capital in the centre where modern-day Leicester is located. The capital was later named *Ratae Corieltauvorum* by the Romans – meaning "fortified city of the Corieltauvi", with the word *Ratae* a Latin form of the Brythonic word for "ramparts". As for defining *Corieltauvi* territory in the Fens, this is very difficult, as much of the Lincolnshire Fens was under water, partic-

This view of Honington Camp demonstrates the defensive banks and ditches. However, this Iron Age structure was probably more of a defended settlement or farmstead rather than a hillfort.

Part of the defensive earthworks that once surrounded Yarborough Camp, a probable Iron Age defended settlement and which today is located a mile south-west of Croxton in North Lincolnshire.

ularly at high tide; indeed, the coastline may even have reached Bourne in the Iron Age, then stretched northward to South Kyme, and then eastwards along the southern edge of the Wolds. However, it is thought that salt production began in the Fens during the Iron Age, as the conditions were perfect here; during high tide, sea water became trapped in clay beds, and when the tide went out, it revealed large tracts of land where the trapped sea water evaporated leaving salt residue. The earliest Iron Age salt production occurred at Ingoldmells and Wrangle. These sites were followed by those at Billingborough, Cowbit, Deeping St Nicholas and Helpringham, all on the Fenland Basin back then, with their product exported all over Britain, and used for the storage of food and the preservation of hides.

Romans, Anglo-Saxons and Vikings

It is thought that just before the Romans invaded Britain in A.D. 43, the Celtic *Corieltauvi* tribe were heavily under the influence of their south-eastern neighbours, the *Catuvellauni*, whose main base was at

Verulamium (St Albans). The *Corieltauvi* certainly issued their own coinage, though, as coin moulds of baked clay and sherds of crucibles have been discovered at both Leicester and Sleaford. By A.D. 47, though, the Roman legions had defeated the *Corieltauvi*, and constructed the Fosse Way, which ran all the way from Exeter (*Isca Dumnoniorum*) in the South West to Lincoln (*Lindum*) in the East Midlands. For a few years, the Fosse Way was thought to mark the temporary frontier of the embryonic province of *Britannia*, with most areas to the south and east of that line under Roman control; they didn't advance north and west for another two decades.

The legion that controlled Lincolnshire was the Ninth Legion, Legio IX Hispana. Roman fortresses were initially constructed close to the south and western margins of Lincolnshire at Longhthorpe, in Peterborough, at Great Casterton in Rutland and just inside today's West Lindsey border with Nottinghamshire at Newton-on-Trent. The latter fort was not discovered until 1962, but it was thought to have enclosed an area of at least 30 acres (12ha/0.1 km²), not sufficient enough to house a whole legion, and which has therefore been classified as a vexillation (small) fortress that may have accommodated half a legion. The fort was positioned at the north end of a ridge that rises to around 70ft on the east bank of the Trent and which commands extensive views. Today, all that is visible is the double-ditched system on part of the north and east sides, with a number of crop marks visible from the air to the east and which probably represent two temporary camps; the western side has long-since been lost to river erosion. The fort probably had simple gates on the north and south sides, while the east side was more complex, with staggered entrances.

At around the same time, it is thought that another temporary base was established in the Witham Gap just to the east of the Brayford Pool at Lincoln, a broad and deep pool in the River Witham, and the site of a previ-ous Iron Age settlement. Indeed, the pool had lent the Iron Age settlement its name, as the *Corieltauvi* had named it *Lindon*, with the name deriving from the Brythonic Celtic word *lindo*, meaning "pool". However, the Romans re-named it *Lindum* in A.D. 48, and then set about developing the settlement. The fortifications at the top of the hill were probably developed between A.D. 54 and 60 and consisted of a square stockade protected by a square timber box rampart defended by a large V-shaped ditch. Within the stockade were rows of wooden barracks, stores and granaries. However, there wouldn't have been enough space within to accommodate the entire legion of c.5,000 soldiers, so other units would have been accommodated elsewhere in the county, probably to the south-east of the Fosse Way.

The taking of Lincolnshire was a fairly routine affair for the Romans, as the *Corieltauvi* didn't put up anything like the resistance that their north-western neighbours, the *Brigantes* did, and they certainly didn't go to the lengths of their south-eastern neighbours, the *Iceni*. The Ninth Legion were called upon in A.D. 60 to put down the *Iceni* rebellion, led by the talismanic Queen Boudicca, who had sacked the Roman capital at Colchester (*Camulodunum*) – this as vengeance in return for broken promises, the rape of her daughters and her own personal flogging. Boudicca's forces then burned and destroyed London (*Londinium*) and St Albans (*Verulamium*), and despite their technological advan-tage, the Legio IX Hispana was overwhelmed; it wasn't until the Battle of Watling Street in A.D. 61 that this early threat to Roman Britain was finally extinguished.

From this point onwards, the Romans were able to consolidate their conquered land and gradually began to push their frontier further north, with the legion then redeployed beyond the Humber. This meant that by A.D. 71, the Romans had re-named *Lindum* as *Lindum Colonia*, as the legion had moved onto York (*Eboracum*) by this stage and the fort at *Lindum* had been converted into a settlement for army veterans or retired legionar-

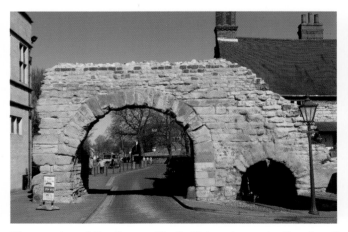

The remains of the Roman North Gate entrance to the city of Lincoln. Known as the Newport Arch, it was built at the beginning of the 3ʳᵈ century and is the only Roman arch still standing in Britain.

All that survives of the East Gate to Roman Lincoln are these remains of its northern tower. The East Gate was also built in the early 3ʳᵈ century.

ies. Unsurprisingly, therefore, the name *Lindum Colonia* means "Roman colony for retired legionaries by the pool", with the latter element of the name deriving from the Latin word *colonia*, meaning "colony".

During this early Roman period, Lincolnshire was part of the sub-district of *Flavia Caesariensis*, along with other parts of the Midlands. *Lindum* was the county's most important settlement in the district and this was reflected by its location on two of the principal arteries of Roman Britain: the Fosse Way we've already mentioned, while the other was Ermine Street, which eventually ran from *Londinium* up to *Eboracum*, passing right through *Lindum*. This included a ferry over the Humber at Winteringham (*Ad Abum*), with the latter also becoming a key Roman settlement. Further Roman bases were also established on Ermine Street to the south of *Lindum* at Ancaster (*Causennæ*) and Navenby (Roman name not known), and to the north at Owmby-by-Spital and Hibaldstow (neither Roman name known), with the latter fort set up in the late 1st century and which remained occupied until the late 4th century. Further important roads throughout Lincolnshire were constructed, with *Lindum* largely pivotal. Heading up from the south via Bourne and Sleaford was the road

known as Mareham Lane. Sleaford was home to a *Corieltauvi* mint between the 1st centuries B.C. and A.D. and there is also evidence to suggest that a road connected Sleaford to Heckington, around 4.5 miles (7.2 km) to the east, where Roman tile kilns have been uncovered. Heading out north-east from *Lindum* was a road that forked several miles further on, with the north-eastern prong heading for Ludford and the south-eastern fork to Ulceby and Burgh le Marsh. Minor roads then branched off these two roads, one to Horncastle, and another to Caistor, Kirmington and South Ferriby before joining Ermine Street at Winteringham.

The other important Roman road in Lincolnshire was Tillbridge Lane, which headed out from *Lindum* in a north-westerly direction, crossing the border over the Trent into what would later become Nottinghamshire at Littleborough (*Segelocum*), before heading for Yorkshire at Doncaster (*Danum*) and onto York (*Eboracum*). And then there was Salters' Way, which closely followed the course of the current A52 as it heads out towards the east coast, which in those days was at Donington – around 10 miles from the coast today! Other Roman settlements developed in Lincolnshire at places for which we *do* know the Latin name, such as Brant Broughton (*Briga*), Broughton (*Praetorium*), Kirton in Lindsey (*Inmedio*), Louth (*Luda*), Stow (*Sidnacester*), Tattershall (*Drurobrivis*), Torksey (*Tiovulfingacester*), Wainfleet (*Vainona*) and Willoughby (*Verometum*).

Of the previously listed Roman sites, Ancaster (probably *Causennae*) was the last Roman stronghold on Ermine Street before Lincoln, and was built on the site of the existing *Corieltauvi* settlement. Thousands of coins have been unearthed at Ancaster, including one hoard of 2000 alone, and which are said to have still been in use for trade as late as the 18th century. Other finds at Ancaster include a mosaic pavement and a fragment of Roman wall 7ft (2.1m) wide, while the remains of a pottery kiln along with pottery and more coins were found north of the village. Further finds have ended up at the museum in Grantham, including a small altar, a milestone of Constantine I and a Roman sculpture. Excavations under-

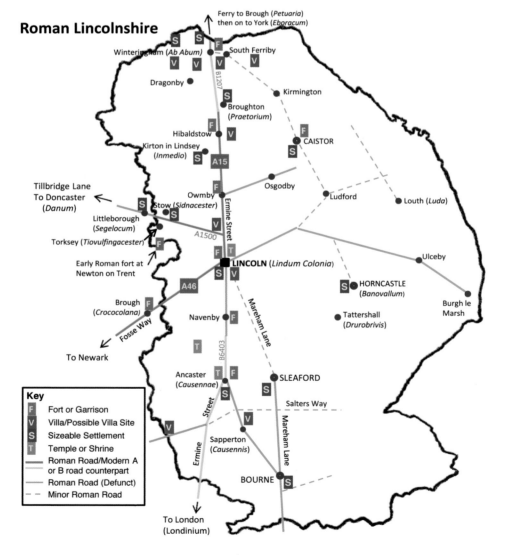

taken by Nottingham University also uncovered a Roman cemetery containing more than 250 Roman burials which included 11 stone sarcophagi. It is also thought that Ancaster was re-fortified in the 4th century along with accompanying ditches possibly as a defence against marauding Saxons.

The Mint Wall in Lincoln is the highest piece of Roman wall in England. It was once part of the Roman basilica, built c.100 A.D.

Also surviving from Roman Lincoln is this 3-metre-thick wall which was once part of a vast Roman water reservoir or castellum aquae. It was built onto the inside of the northern defensive wall and was 52 feet long (16m), 16 feet deep (5m) and held around 2,660 gallons (12,000 litres) of water. Lincoln's Roman baths were also in the north-eastern quarter of the settlement and would have used this reservoir for its water supply.

The next most significant Roman town after Lincoln and Ancaster was at Caistor, its name today (like Ancaster) deriving from the Old English word *cæster*, meaning "Roman camp or town". As at Lincoln, some of the 4th century Roman walls survive to this day, with parts visible on the southern boundary of the parish church of St Peter and St Paul, while the area occupied by the fortress is now classified as a Scheduled Ancient Monument. Excavations have determined that the defensive walls formed a polygon of around 850 by 525 yards (777 by 480 metres). It is also theorised that Roman Caistor developed courtesy of a spring with health-giving properties, while in 2010, the remains of a 4th century Roman cemetery were discovered when building the foundations for a new supermarket. Local

legend also has it that Simon the Zealot, one of the 12 apostles, came to England where it is said that he was martyred at Caistor on 10th May A.D. 61, after being crucified here on the orders of a Roman procurator called Catus Decianus.

As for Sleaford, excavations where the ancient Mareham Lane passed through the town have revealed a number of Roman finds including a large stone-built domestic residence, associated farm buildings, corn-driers, ovens and field systems, plus a number of burials. Meanwhile, at Horncastle, parts of its surrounding Roman wall survive, most notably in the town library which was built around the wall! It was constructed in the 3rd or 4th century (the Roman wall, not the library) and enclosed a site of around 5 acres in the centre of Horncastle. Interestingly, by the 19th century it was thought that the Roman name for Horncastle was *Banovallum*, meaning "wall on the River Bain", and a number of local businesses have adopted the name, as has the local secondary modern school. However, the name is not a certainty, as it is also thought that the 7th century reference to *Banovallum* in the *Ravenna Cosmography*, may well have been referring to Caistor instead. Interestingly, both towns were fortified despite neither being on a major Roman road.

As well as the roads, the Romans also constructed two impressive waterways in Lincolnshire territory. The Carr Dyke was a series of semi-natural and artificial boundary ditches which run from the River Welland at Market Deeping to the River Witham at Washingborough, just east of Lincoln. The watercourse was 56 miles long and was one of the greatest engineering feats carried out during Roman occupation of Britain. The Carr Dyke ultimately drained into and connected the Rivers Witham and Nene, and was also used for the movement of grain and heavier goods. The other waterway was the 11-mile Fosse Dyke canal, which connected Torksey (*Tiovulfingacester*) on the River Trent with the Brayford Pool at Lincoln, the latter having been developed as an inland port. These waterways thus connected Lincolnshire territory with the Midlands via the Trent (southbound) and its tributaries, and with the North also via the Trent (northbound), and the River Ouse. It is also likely that Lincolnshire goods ended up at Hadrian's Wall via the Fosse Dyke, Trent, Humber and East Coast route. As for the Carr Dyke, this also functioned as a catch-water drain – and thus began the centuries-long process of draining the Fens. The Romans also constructed hard standings and walkways across the fens, too.

Thanks to its arterial position in terms of both road and waterway, *Lindum Colonia* flourished, and became the provincial capital of *Flavia Caesariensis* in the early 4th century. Evidence of the town's wealth is demonstrated by a number of archaeological finds. These include fragments of amphorae (pottery containers for marine transport), mainly of Spanish origin and used to transport wine and other luxuries from the Mediterranean regions. Also discovered were large quantities of good quality Samian ware, often produced in Gaul, plus finds of German, Italian and Greek marble. And talking of pottery, evidence of numerous Roman kilns have been found throughout Lincolnshire too, at Dragonby, Knaith, Lea, Little London, Market Rasen, North Hykeham, South Carlton and Torksey. In terms of other industry, the Romans certainly quarried limestone at Ancaster and Greetham, while iron was produced in the south-west of the county at Castle Bytham, Colsterworth, Corby Glen, Grantham, Ingoldsby, Woolsthorpe and Wyville with Hungerton. As for the salt industry which had begun in the Iron Age, this also continued throughout the Roman period.

With the departure of the Ninth Legion in the late 1st century, new ramparts and stone walls were constructed in Lincoln, while the former military headquarters became the new *basilica* and *forum*. The town was then laid out in the typical Roman grid fashion, and gates were built into the four walls. Of these, part of the North Gate still stands today and is, in fact, the only surviving Roman arch in the country – although this particular arch is not part of the 1st century construction but the 3rd century one which followed it. Some foundations of the East Gate also survive, while the West Gate was re-discovered in the 19th century at the north-west corner of the castle bank, just north of the west gate of the current castle.

By the 2nd century, the Romans had extended the city beyond the enclosed hilltop fortress, building southwards down the hill towards the River Witham. This area was then also fortified with the southern gate placed where today's Stonebow is located, and which was the entry point to Lincoln from the south of both the Fosse Way and Ermine Street. By this stage, Lincoln was an impressive place, with fine buildings, a sewer system, public spaces with fountains and statues, public baths and imposing temples, with the water used for the fountains and the sewer systems brought into the city by an aqueduct, thought to have been positioned at the north-eastern end of the town. Meanwhile, as well as Lincoln, it is known that Ancaster, Caistor and Horncastle were also walled Roman towns, although the exact time of their build is not known.

Quirk Alert: *Grassed-On Villa*

In the early 20th century at Norton Disney, Abbey Field on Potter Hill was something of a mystery because nothing ever grew there but weeds. After a few years of persistent crop failure, the farmer decided to dig down to see if he could solve the mystery – and solve the mystery he most certainly did – because he found walls and roof tiles! The site was then properly excavated and a sizeable fortified Roman villa was uncovered, along with a defensive ditch system. Also uncovered were two magnificent Roman pavements, one of them 20 feet long and 16 feet wide, designed in small cubes of coloured stone and brick.

It was also during the 2nd century that a proliferation of villas broke out in Lincolnshire, no doubt considerably helped by the passivity of the locals. A large number were constructed on the chalk and limestone uplands to the north and south of Lincoln, usually made of stone, with tiled roofs and a regular floor plan. One of the most impressive was found at Winterton in North Lincolnshire on Ermine Street. This was comprised of a square with stone buildings on three sides, while the living area had painted wall plaster and the floors were decorated with mosaics. Part of the floor area was also heated by a hypocaust system – where the raised floor was supported by pillars constructed of layered tiles and concrete, thus allowing the hot air from the furnace to circulate under the floors. It is also very likely that one of this villa's inhabitants was found in October 1968! This happened during a project to widen the A1077, when workers found a huge stone coffin containing a skeleton of a young woman aged between 20 and 25 years of age. She was 5ft 3in (1.6 m) tall, and was evidently of high status, given the quality of the limestone coffin and the fact that she was lying on a sheet of lead. Four miles east of Winterton at Horkstow, another large and high status villa was discovered in 1796 in the grounds of Horkstow Hall, and its tessellated mosaic pavement was so impressive that it ended up at the British Museum in 1927. Today, though, it can be seen in Hull's Archaeological Museum where it has been since 1974. Meanwhile, 4 miles *west* of Winterton was another Roman settlement at modern-day Alkborough. The earthworks here to the south-west of the village were first identified by the 18th century antiquarian William Stukeley, who believed the site to be a Roman camp, latterly named as Countess Close – and where pottery fragments dating from the 1st to the 4th century A.D. have been found. A small hoard of Roman coins was also found at nearby Walcot Hall. However, the theory of a Roman camp was reconsidered following a geophysical survey taken in 2003, which although showing clear evidence of a Romano-British ladder settlement, also suggested that the earthwork was more likely to be the remains of a medieval fortified manor house.

Returning to Lincoln again, and following the conversion to Christianity of Constantine I in A.D. 313, the faith gradually spread throughout Roman Britain. The earliest evidence of this in Lincoln was found following excavations in the 1970s at the Victorian church known as St Paul-in-the-Bail, which was built on the site of the original Roman *forum*, and it is thought that a very early Christian church may have stood here by the end of the 4th century. Lincoln was certainly still flourishing under the Romans, having been elevated to one of the four provincial capitals of *Britannia* in the early 4th century. This new status was reflected in improved fortifications and the construction of a huge gate at the lower western entrance to the town. However, by this stage, Roman control over Britain was waning. Conscious of greater threats from the north by Picts and Scots, and particularly from the east by the Saxons, the Romans had improved the fortifications at Ancaster, Caistor and Horncastle, as well as at Lincoln during the 4th century. Any evidence of coastal fortification, though, has long-since been eroded away, but it is thought that there may have been a fort at Skegness and perhaps another further north at Grainthorpe, while one 15th century Court Rolls refers to the existence of a fortress at Ingoldmells.

There have been many other Roman finds in Lincolnshire, the majority of which are listed on the author's website (andybeardmore.com).

The Romans eventually left Britain in around A.D. 410, and their departure had a severe effect on Britain's economy which didn't really return to similar levels again until the late Anglo-Scandinavian period. It is likely that some form of life persisted in the towns and on the villa sites for an undefined length of time, whilst those who lived in Romano-British settlements and farmsteads must have continued their lives much as before. However, it is thought that the Roman infrastructure of government along with the bureaucratic system designed to maintain Roman laws and to levy taxes, soon disintegrated. Naturally, this had a negative effect on trading and the economy reverted overwhelmingly back to agriculture, while the towns – which had essentially been bastions of Roman government and administration – saw their importance drop dramatically in tandem with their populations. This was certainly the case where Lincoln was concerned, and in the two centuries following the Roman withdrawal from Britain, the town became largely deserted and dilapidated.

What we do know of the early post-Roman period, though, is that the country gradually became settled by the Angles and Saxons of northern Europe. The traditional view of Anglo-Saxon colonisation of England is that they settled first in Lincolnshire before making their way inland towards Nottinghamshire. They certainly used the Trent Valley to push further inland,

as is evidenced by mid-6th century heathen burial sites found from Newark-on-Trent to Burton upon Trent. However, more recent research suggests that the Angles reached Lincolnshire much earlier in the first half of the 5th century, and potentially earlier before the Romans had even departed. This viewpoint is based on the evidence of pagan burial grounds found close to Roman roads and Romano-British settlements, as well as the discovery of Germanic brooches, buckles and strap ends. However, these early Teutonic migrants were probably not settlers *per se*, but soldier mercenaries known then as the *foederati*, and deployed by the Romans to help keep the locals and any invaders in check, as well as manning coastal fortresses. So it may well have been these people who then took on the responsibility to defend the county following the Roman departure; there is certainly evidence to suggest that the north Lincolnshire coast was well defended by the end of the 5th century.

This gradual settling of Lincolnshire throughout the 5th and 6th centuries also seems to have been relatively peaceful, particularly when compared to the later Viking raids. This is evidenced by the fact that cemeteries demonstrate both Saxon and British burials side-by-side, thus suggesting the co-habitation of both communities – although as time progressed, the Anglo-Saxon ritual became the norm. It was also during these two centuries that the ancient Kingdom of Lindsey was formed in what is today the northern half of Lincolnshire. The kingdom's boundaries were all natural; the River Humber to the north, the North Sea and inhospitable marshlands to the east, the River Witham and the Foss Dyke to the south and the River Trent to the west – although the marshy Isle of Axholme on the other side of the Trent was also part of the kingdom. Given this complete encircling of water, it is no surprise to learn that the name Lindsey means "island of the tribe called the *Lindēs*", with the name deriving from the tribe name *Lindēs* (people of Lincoln) and the Old English word *ēg* (island or land partly

Looking north up the River Trent between Dunham on Trent (Notts) and Newton on Trent (Lincs). It was along this stretch that the first Anglo-Saxons travelled in the 5th and 6th centuries before settling throughout England.

A little further upstream looking across to the Lincolnshire side of the Trent. Mid-6th century heathen burial sites have been found all the way up the Trent from Lincolnshire, to Burton upon Trent in Staffordshire.

surrounded by water). The earliest recording of the name dates from c.704-714, when the place is named as *Lindissi*. The *Lindēs* tribe were also known as the *Lindisfaras* or *Lindesfaras*, and are generally accepted as being immigrants from northern Germany.

At varying times throughout Anglo-Saxon Britain, Lindsey was part of the much larger kingdoms of Northumbria and Mercia, although it does appear to have had a level of independence during early Anglo-Saxon times – this based on accounts written in the early 8th century by the Northumbrian monk and scholar known as the Venerable Bede. In Bede's *Historia ecclesiastica gentis Anglorum* of 731, the scholar describes *Lindissi* as a *provincia*, a name usually reserved for separate kingdoms. Recounting the visit of the missionary Paulinus of York in 625, Bede also mentions that he was received by the *praefectus* of Lindum (Bishop of Lincoln) called Cynebehrt, thus hinting at both Lindsey and Lincoln's elevated status – with the latter being the capital of the kingdom despite its proximity to the southern border. However, both Northumbria and Mercia had constant designs on the territory throughout these times, with the former looking to extend south of the Humber and the latter wanting to gain a foothold on the river and the Lindsey coastline.

As a relatively small kingdom, it is likely that the kings of Lindsey generally fell in with whichever of these two super-powers was in the ascendency. Nevertheless, the collection of royal genealogies known as the *Anglian collection*[1], and which was created towards the end of the reign of King Offa of Mercia (757-796) does indeed list the rulers of Lindsey and thus implies an independence of sorts. The start of the list, from the first king, Geot, to the sixth, Woden, may well be the names of kings of Anglia (German *Angeln*), the German peninsula in southern Schleswig which protrudes into the Bay of Kiel, and from which the first Angles who settled in England came. However, those kings listed from the seventh king, Winta, to the sixteenth and final king Aldfrio, are thought to be *bona fide* Kings of Lindsey.

[1]The *Anglian collection* is comprised of four manuscripts, two of which reside at the British Library, one at Corpus Christi College at Cambridge and the other at Rochester Cathedral.

This suggests that Winta was the first Anglian king to settle in England, and it is presumably after him that the places Winteringham and Winterton are named; it is also reasonable to assume that this is where he first set foot on English territory. Alas, none of these sixteen kings can be realistically dated, with the possible exception of the last, Aldfrio – this courtesy of the witness list for an Anglo-Saxon charter of the late 8th century which includes a certain Ealfrid rex. Scholars now believe that this name on the witness list should have read Ecgfrio Rex who was, in fact, King Offa of Mercia's son – and who therefore may have been made King of Lindsey in the late 8th century as the kingdom, by this time, had definitely been absorbed by Mercia.

Meanwhile, the southern half of Lincolnshire had been part of the Kingdom of Mercia since the end of the 6th century. The kingdom was centred on the Trent valley and its tributaries, and as well as southern Lincolnshire, its territories also covered much of southern Derbyshire, Leicestershire, Rutland, Nottinghamshire, Staffordshire and northern Warwickshire, with its capital sited at Tamworth. The most

Saxon Lincolnshire

Alkborough (*Alchebarge*)
Barton-upon-Humber (*Bertune*)
Bonby (*Bundebi*)
Barnetby-le-Wold (*Bernedebi*)
Old Clee (*Cleia*)
Crowle (*Crohlea*)
Bottesford (*Budlesforde*)
Cabourne (*Caburne*)
Caistor (*Castre*)
Tillbridge Lane To Doncaster (*Donecastre*)
Stow (*Stou*)
Brattleby (*Brotulbi*)
LINCOLN (*Lincolia*)
To Newark (*Niweweorce*)
Fosse Way
Coleby (*Colebi*)
Cranwell (*Craneuuelle*)
Burton Pedwardine (*Berton*)
Salters Way
Colsterworth (*Colsteuorde*)
Edenham (*Edeneham*)
Creeton (*Kretone*)
Barholm (*Bercham*)
To London

Key
T Surviving Saxon Church Tower
F Surviving Saxon Church Features
C Surviving Saxon Cross
M Early Saxon Cemetery Site
P Middle Saxon Pottery & Coin Finds
S Saxon Saltern (marks former coast!)
— Former Roman Road

This iron boss of a shield has been fixed to the door of St Margaret's church at Bag Enderby. It was found in a nearby field, and whereas some reports believe it to be Danish, Arthur Mee suggests that it is Anglo-Saxon.

Bottom Left: *St Mary's church at Stow is a cross-shaped building with a central tower, much of which dates from its original build between 1034 and 1050 under the supervision of Bishop Eadnoth II. The main exceptions are the chancel which was replaced by a 12th century late Norman one, and the tower which was replaced in the 15th century, both replacing their Saxon predecessor. As for the nave, that includes the tallest Saxon arches in Britain (right). Known as Stow Minster during Saxon times, the church was considered to be the mother church of Lincolnshire and remained so until Lincoln Cathedral was built in 1092.*

authentic source of information at this time was again from the early 8th century Northumbrian monk and scholar, Bede, who describes Mercia as being divided in two by the River Trent.

In terms of Christianity, there was certainly a Bishop of Lincoln in 625, and therefore the faith already had a basis in Lindsey. As for the previously-pagan Mercians, they also began their conversion to Christianity when, in 653, Peada, son of King Penda of Mercia, was converted to the faith so that he could marry the Christian daughter of King Oswy of Northumbria. At this time, the Mercians also invited four priests to join the kingdom as missionaries, with their leader, Diuma, based at Repton in Derbyshire. A double abbey under an abbess was built at Repton and was presided over by the person holding the title of the Bishop of Mercia and Lindsey – hence reinforcing the allegiance between the two kingdoms. In 669, Bishop Ceadda – later sanctified as St Chad – moved his see from Repton to Lichfield, and from this point onwards, Christianity gradually became the main faith of the inhabitants of

Lincolnshire. By the beginning of the 8th century, a number of religious houses had been built around the county, including those at Bardney, Barrow, Crowland, Hibaldstow, Partney, Stow-by-Threekingham and West Halton, and a little later at Louth and South Kyme.

One of the very earliest Christian establishments in Lincolnshire territory was Bardney Abbey, founded in the late 7th century, possibly by King Æthelred of Mercia (675-704). The abbey was dedicated to St Peter and St Paul and was one of the very earliest Benedictine houses in England; it was also one of the richest. We are once again indebted to Bede for much of what we know of Bardney Abbey (which he called *Beardaneu*), and he recounts the story of Æthelread's wife, Queen Osthryth, who in around 679 sought to move the bones of her uncle, King Oswald of Northumbria (c.604-642) to Bardney. Slain at the Battle of Maserfield (believed to be near Oswestry) by King Penda of Mercia, Oswald was later sanctified. However, when Queen Osthryth brought St Oswald's remains to Bardney Abbey, the monks refused to accept them as the former

Top left: This doorway at St Martin's church, Barholm, is thought to date back to Anglo-Saxon England.

Top right: St Mary's church at Barnetby-le-Wold includes this Saxon keyhole window with a crude carving of a cat above.

Above: This tomb cover in the south porch at Howell St Oswald's church is pre-Conquest and almost certainly Anglo-Saxon. Lying on its side, we can see that the top is carved with three crude crosses.

Northumbrian King Oswald had once attacked Lindsey and conquered them. The relics were therefore locked outside, but during the night a beam of light was said to have appeared and shone from his bier reaching up into the heavens. The monks therefore accepted this as a miracle and allowed the remains into the abbey. Thereafter, pilgrims flocked to his shrine, and a number of miracles are said to have occurred – believed to be because St Oswald's bones had been washed at Bardney before interment, and the ground into which the water was poured supposedly gained great healing powers. As for poor Queen Osthtryth, she was murdered by Mercian noblemen in 697, for motives that have remained unexplained, and was buried at Bardney Abbey. Five years later, Æthelred renounced the crown and retired to Bardney, eventually dying here in 716. It is believed that he was laid to rest in King's Hill, an ancient barrow in a field to the east of the abbey. As for St Oswald's bones, they remained at Bardney for almost another 300 years until 909, when in response to increased Danish raids they were moved to a new minster in Gloucester that was re-named as St Oswald's Priory in his honour.

Perhaps founded even earlier than Bardney Abbey

was another monastery, founded by Ceadda (later St Chad), at Barrow-on-Humber. Given that Ceadda died in 672, having only been "Bishop of the Mercians and the Lindsey People" since 669, and the land was given to him by King Wulfhere of Mercia (658-675), the chances are it was founded between 669 and 672. Alas, the monastery was destroyed by marauding 9th century Danes, and nothing of it remains today. Meanwhile, at the opposite end of the county, a monk called Guthlac settled at Crowland in 699. He belonged to a noble Mercian family, but after a wild youth, he abandoned his wealth and military career and devoted himself to God. After a spell at Repton Abbey in Derbyshire, he craved a life of greater solitude and arrived at Crowland in 699 where he built a small chapel. On his death there in 714, he was laid to rest in his chapel which became a place of pilgrimage. As promised following earlier council from Guthlac, King Æthelbald founded Crowland Abbey on the same spot in memory of Guthlac.

We now return to Bede again, for it was he who recorded the Battle of the Trent in 679, a battle fought at an unspecified site near the River Trent within the Kingdom of Lindsey. The battle was fought between the Mercian army led by King Æthelred (675-704) and the Northumbrian army led by King Ecgfrith (c.645-685), and which ended in victory for the Mercians. This was therefore the point in time (679) that Lindsey came under direct control of Mercia and lost its status as an independent kingdom. It then remained under Mercian rule until the Viking invasion of the mid-9th century. In his account of the battle, Bede also talks of a Northumbrian thegn called Imma – the likely founder of Immingham. Imma was apparently captured by the Mercians during the battle and, having proved a handful, was promptly sold into slavery to a Frisian merchant.

Evidence of early Anglo-Saxon settlement is sparse. They were relatively well spread out across the county, particularly throughout the fertile uplands and valleys, so there were no major concentrations of population. Without any imposing structures to mark their colonisation and occupation, we are therefore restricted to archaeological finds such as cemeteries, coins and pottery – of which the majority have been unearthed in the well-drained chalk and limestone uplands and, to a lesser extent, in the light sands and gravel of the Fens.

One of the most significant excavations of an Anglo-Saxon inhumation cemetery was performed in the late 20th century at Castledyke South in Barton-upon-Humber. The cemetery dated from the late 5th or early 6th century until the late 7th century, and archaeologists unearthed the skeletal remains of 227 individuals, probably of high status, including one who had undergone trepanation (a hole drilled through the skull to expose the brain and allow evil spirits to escape), and survived!

The other lasting evidence of Anglo-Saxon colonisation is place-names, with over 300 places in

Anglo-Saxon cross in St Cuthbert's churchyard at Brattleby.

Anglo-Saxon cross in St Peter's churchyard at Creeton.

Lincolnshire ending in the Saxon – *hām* (homestead) or – *tūn* (farmstead). As for the early Anglo-Saxon minster or mother churches, nothing remains. However, these churches – which served a large area in the days before parishes were introduced – included those at Caistor, Grantham, Horncastle, Lincoln and Stow.

By the end of the 9th century, Mercia had fallen into decline. During this time, King Ecgbert of Wessex (802-839), defeated King Wiglaf of Mercia (827-829) in 829, allegedly at Caistor, and some mounds outside the town are claimed to be the site of this victory. Egbert drove Wiglaf out of his kingdom and temporarily ruled Mercia himself for a year, before Wiglaf recovered the kingdom in 830 – albeit perhaps subject to Egbert's overlordship. It may even be that this was the point at which Mercia lost its kingdom status completely as by the mid-9th century, Mercia was ruled by ealdormen serving under the throne of Wessex. The kingdom's weakness therefore meant that it was ripe for plunder when the Danes invaded in the late 860s. The *Anglo-Saxon Chronicle* describes "a great heathen army" which landed in East Anglia in 865, and over the next decade or so, took control of the majority of England's east coast, including Lincolnshire. One Anglo-Saxon who died fighting them in Lincolnshire was Alfgar, Earl of Mercia, at the Battle of Stow Green, 870 – and after whom the Boston district village of Algarkirk is part-named.

The Danish army wintered at Torksey in 872-873, and then under Halfdan, the Danes established a base at Nottingham where he was joined by a second army led by Guthrum. This left Mercia appealing to their old enemy, Wessex, but that didn't stop the Danes invading much of their territory. Under Ivar the Boneless they saw out the next winter of 873-874 further south-west at Repton in South Derbyshire, from where they subdued the surrounding countryside and destroyed the Mercian capital at Tamworth.

As the Danes established their control over the East Midlands, further waves of settlers arrived, and Danish settlements began to develop along the navigable Rivers Trent and Witham. Again, it is difficult to assess these early settlers' impact upon the area with only sparse archaeological evidence available. The best example on Lincolnshire soil is at Goltho, on the clay vale 8 miles to the north-east of Lincoln, where evidence of a fortified earthwork enclosure has been found and which appears to have succeeded an earlier Anglo-Saxon settlement. Having said that, the fortification doesn't follow typical Danish lines, as it consisted of a rampart, with a width of 19.5ft (6m), on which a timber palisade was constructed, and which was surrounded by an 8ft (2.5m) ditch.

Of course, one area where the Danes most definitely did leave their mark was in place-names. Hundreds of former Saxon –*tuns* and –*hams* underwent a Danish suffix transformation to *bý* (farmstead, village or settlement), *thorp* (secondary settlement, dependent outlying farmstead or hamlet) and *holmr* (island, promontory, raised ground in marsh or river-meadow). Very telling is that the Danish place-name element *bý*, only occurs 10 times in Domesday Book entries for Derbyshire, compared with 22 in Nottinghamshire, 60 in Leicestershire…and 225 in Lincolnshire – a trend which emphasises Danish dominance the further east you go. A tight concentration of these early Danish settlements can be found on the southern Wolds and, to a lesser extent over the rest of the Wolds, in the Kesteven uplands and along the Trent Valley.

Quirk Alert: *Oo, ee*

A number of ancient watercourses in Lincolnshire are suffixed with the word "Eau", such as the Bourne Eau or the Old Eau at Bicker which in Saxon times ran through Bicker towards Bicker Haven. Most people reading that second word would pronounce it like the French word for water. However, some locals pronounce it as "oo" and others as "ee". Of these two, the latter actually makes sense, as the Old English word ēa, meaning "river", is a common Anglo-Saxon derivative. Other Lincolnshire Eau's are the nearby Donington Eaudyke and Quadring Eaudyke with the latter recorded as Quaderyng Eee in 1343, and which takes its name from the same water-course that flows through Bicker. As an aside, that latter spelling of a triple E reminded me of A level French and the verb to create (créer) which when used with the feminine past participle is formed as créée…which then led me to look for English equivalents – and there aren't any, as we always hyphenate – i.e. bee-eater, cross-section, bell-like, etc. End of English/French lesson!

By 877, the Danes had begun to partition eastern Mercia and it is at this point in time that the area of Lincolnshire and some of its neighbouring counties begins to take shape. However, the Danes suffered a massive setback at the Battle of Eddington in 878 where they were defeated by King Alfred of Wessex. As well as being forced into baptism as a Christian and to accept Alfred as his adopted father, King Guthrum also agreed what has been termed both the Treaty of Wedmore and the Peace of Wedmore, perhaps in around 878 – although there is confusion as to the dates, with a later "Treaty of Alfred and Guthrum" possibly dating from as late as 886. Either way, the treaty essentially carved up England between Saxon and Dane – the south and the west to the Saxons of Wessex and Mercia, and the east to the Danes – and a temporary peace was established. In the years following the Treaty of Wedmore, the area of today's East Midlands became known as the Five Boroughs, the name deriving from the Old English word *burh* meaning "fortified place or stronghold", and the strongholds in question being at Derby, Nottingham, Lincoln, Leicester and Stamford. The Five Boroughs became occupied by separate divisions of the Danish army, and the Danes introduced

their native law and customs known as the Danelaw. Each of the Five Boroughs was ruled as a Danish Jarldom, controlling lands around the fortified *burh*, which served as the centre of political power, although they were all subject to their overlords in Jorvik (York).

Despite the Treaty of Wedmore, the Danes renewed their attacks on Mercia in the late 9th century. By this stage, though, Mercian links with Wessex had been cemented further by the marriage of Earl Æthelred of Mercia to Æthelflæd, daughter of King Alfred of Wessex. On Æthelred's death in 911, Æthelflæd ruled Mercia as the 'Lady of the Mercian's' and set about fortifying Mercia's eastern borders. By 913 she had encroached deep into Danish territory, having established a *burh* at Tamworth. Along with her brother (Edward the Elder), Æthelflæd then launched her first offensive foray in July 917 and expelled the Danes from the fortress at Derby and annexed the whole region back into English Mercia. According to the *Anglo-Saxon Chronicle*, this included Derby "together with the region which it controlled", thus indicating that the county area of Derbyshire had already been established – and thus suggesting that the same applied to the other counties of today's East Midlands, albeit with Lincolnshire ruled in two halves from Lincoln (for Lindsey) and Stamford (for Kesteven and Holland).

St Andrew's church at Bonby includes two now-bricked up Anglo-Saxon doorways that were probably built in the early 11th century.

At the same time, Edward the Elder of Wessex had re-captured East Anglia as far as the River Welland, and then marched north to Stamford where he took control of Kesteven. By 918, Leicester and Nottingham had fallen to the Saxons, although this year also marked the death of Æthelflæd – at which point the Mercians submitted to the rule of Edward the Elder. By this stage, the only part of ex-Mercia still under Danish control was Lindsey. However, when York fell to Edward's son and successor, Æthelstan, in 926, Lindsey was also restored to England. Furthermore, King Æthelstan (924-927) became the first Saxon ruler since King Offa (757-796) to hold complete control of southern, central and northern England, and proclaimed himself "King of all

Britain" – at which point, the Scots and Welsh presumably raised eyebrows! Nevertheless, this political unity was marked by new coinage, and a mint was established at Lincoln in the 920s.

By 942, the *Anglo-Saxon Chronicle* records the fact that the former Five Boroughs strongholds at Derby, Leicester, Lincoln, Nottingham and Stamford had been given special Borough status. It was also at this time that Lincoln was beginning to prosper and expand economically for the first time since the departure of the Romans. New streets and buildings appeared along the River Witham and within the old lower southern Roman enclosure. Trade was also beginning to expand, both domestically and with northern and western Europe, the latter exploiting the old Roman waterway from the North Sea, up the Witham to the Brayford Pool and then along the Fosse Dyke to the Trent and the Midlands. Domestic trade was dominated by agriculture and pottery; imports from Scandinavia included walrus ivory, soapstone and the mineral known as schist, while quern stones were imported from Germany. As for the local pottery industry, the most important kilns were based at Lincoln and Stamford, with Stamford ware found as far afield as Aberdeen, but which is eclipsed by a complete Lincoln-produced jar which was found in a grave at Birka in Sweden.

Quirk Alert: *Grim Up North*

The legend of how Grimsby came to be named was allegedly first written about in the late 9th century, and revolves around Havelok, son of the King of Denmark. For after the king was assassinated, Havelok was cruelly put to sea in a boat. However, it is said that he was rescued and then raised by a poor Lincolnshire farmer called Grim or Grimr. By the time he reached adulthood, Havelok was a man with a fine physique and the courage of a lion, and proceeded to win back his kingdom. As thanks for all he had done, Havelok granted Grim great rewards, and with these, he settled on what would later become the north-east coast of Lincolnshire, and the settlement that developed here was named in his honour.

Throughout the second half of the 10th century, there had never been complete peace between the Saxons and the Danes, and the Danish attacks began to ramp up again in the 990s. During these years, King Æthelred was forced to pay tribute to the Danes, known as Danegeld, in order to prevent his lands from being ravaged – lands that almost certainly included Lincolnshire. A concerted attempt was then made by King Sweyn of Denmark in 1013, who first took Lindsey before launching an attack to the south. So concerned was he by this advance, that King Æthelred fled to Normandy and Sweyn claimed the crown of England, the first Dane to do so, while leaving his son, Cnut, in charge of the fleet and the Danes' army base at

Gainsborough. However, Sweyn Forkbeard (as he was also known), only survived for another five weeks, dying at Gainsborough, at which point Cnut was immediately elected king by the people of the Danelaw. The English Witan took a different view, though, and recalled Æthelred the Unready (as he was also known) from Normandy. Æthelred immediately led an army north towards Gainsborough, at which point Cnut (presumably unready, too), fled with his army back to Denmark. Those supporters of Cnut in Lindsey were reported by the *Anglo-Saxon Chronicle*, to be brutally dealt with by the Saxons, with the *Chronicle* stating that Lindsey was "ravaged and burnt, and all the men who could be got were killed". However, Cnut then returned in 1015 with a large invasion fleet of around 10,000 men in 200 longships. England was ravaged again, and Cnut was proclaimed king in 1016, going on to rule for 19 years until 1035, thus uniting the thrones of England and Denmark for a short time.

Quirk Alert: *Bells and Skulls*

In around 986, Crowland Abbey became the first church in England, and one of the first in the world, to have a tuned peal of bells. Furthermore, and almost one thousand years later on 1st November 1925, the then-incumbent bells became the first to be broadcast on wireless radio! Finally regarding the bells, the ropes attached to those 1920s bells were the longest in England at 90ft (27m).

Another Crowland Abbey story spanning over a millennium, concerns the skull of the 9th century Abbot Theodore. For the latter had the misfortune to be abbot when the marauding Danes attacked and destroyed the abbey in 866, killing the abbot at the altar. Abbot Theodore's skull, however, was retained as a relic, and was still on public view in the late 20th century. Alas, the skull was stolen in 1982 from its display case, but was returned anonymously 17 years later in 1999!

In terms of lasting evidence of the Anglo-Scandinavian period, there is little better than St Peter's church at Barton-upon-Humber, one of England's finest surviving Anglo-Saxon churches, with its Anglo-Saxon tower still completely intact. The church was originally turriform, when Anglo-Saxon churches were built as towers (also known as tower-nave churches). In this configuration, the ground floor of the tower served as the nave, and there was a small projecting chancel to the east. However, in some of them, there was another projecting chancel, known as the baptistery, on the *west* side of the tower – and not only did St Peter's church have a baptistry, but it is still there, intact, today. The church is now owned by English Heritage, and they have dated the baptistery to the 9th century and the tower-nave to the 10th – although others have dated it slightly later to between 970 and 1030. The tower is

NORTH LINCOLNSHIRE'S SAXON CHURCHES

The church of St John the Baptist at Alkborough has an Anglo-Saxon tower thought to date to 1052, and which belonged to a small monastic, pre-Conquest establishment which was a cell of the monastery at Spalding.

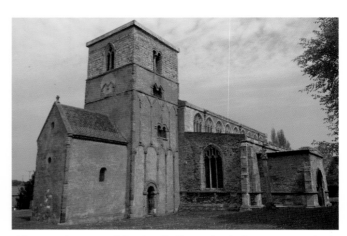

Also sporting one of England's finest Anglo-Saxon towers is St Peter's church at Barton-upon-Humber. The Saxon church was once turriform, meaning the tower once doubled up as a nave, with a small chancel to the east and another to the west, known as a baptistry, and which also survives completely intact.

The 11th century Saxon tower of the church of St Peter and St Paul, Caistor.

Cabourne's church is dedicated to St Nicholas, and also sports a Saxon tower, this one dating from the early 11th century.

typically Anglo-Saxon: walls of rendered rubble, with decorative pilaster strip work, plus long and short work, while it contains a few small windows, with either round or triangular heads. A third storey was

added to the tower in the late 11th century by the Normans, which was probably around the time that the Anglo-Saxon chancel was replaced; the current nave and chancel date from the 14th century.

The church also lies immediately east of the remains of an enclosure which contained a hall, with the surrounding ditch dating to before 900, while we've already mentioned the early pagan Saxon cemetery excavated to the south of the church, and which is believed to be linked with the enclosure. Also already mentioned is the monastery at neighbouring Barrow-on-Humber, founded in the late 7th century, and an Anglo-Saxon charter of 971 suggests that Barton became a grange attached to this monastery. Meanwhile, the earliest Christian graves here date from the 9th century, around 100 years after the pagan cemetery was abandoned.

There are another dozen or so churches in Lincolnshire that have full or part-Saxon towers. These, along with the majority of other Lincolnshire churches retaining Saxon features or stonework, are listed on the author's website (andybeardmore.com).

Quirk Alert: *Gainsborough's Trinity*

Gainsborough is home to three significant pre-Conquest events. The first occurred in 868 when King Alfred was married in Gainsborough to Ealhswitha, daughter of the Ealdorman of the Gaini, an ancient Mercian tribal group.

The second event occurred on December 25th, 1013, when Sweyn Forkbeard, King of Denmark, was proclaimed as King of England in Gainsborough, after defeating the Anglo-Saxon King Æthelred. Having been based in Gainsborough for his campaign against the Saxon's since July 1013, Gainsborough briefly became England's capital as King Sweyn took up high office in Gainsborough Castle.

However, the third event occurred some five weeks later, when King Sweyn was thrown from his horse in Gainsborough, and died there on 3rd February 1014. Shortly afterwards, Gainsborough ceased to be the capital of England as Æthelred returned to reclaim the throne.

We could feasibly add a fourth event, too – for it is claimed that King Canute (1016-1035) performed his famous, but unsuccessful attempt to hold back the tide on the River Trent at Gainsborough – knowing full well that this was the furthest reach of the Trent Aegir, a tidal bore that occurs on the Trent at certain times of the year. The Trent Aegir rises to a height of around 5ft (1.5m) and takes its name from the Norse god of the ocean.

Quirk Alert: *Oaklore*

At Aslackby in South Kesteven, the wapentake court was founded here in the 10th century, and it actually held those courts for the next 900 years until the 19th century…under an oak tree!

The fate of Stamford is interesting during the Anglo-Scandinavian period, since the other four strongholds of the Danish Five Boroughs went on to have counties named after them, but Stamford didn't. English county history was in the balance here, and given that Stamford was an important strategic fortress town on the River Welland, it must have come close to being designated the administrative town of a new county called Stamfordshire. However, it wasn't to be, and the two former boroughs of Lincoln and Stamford were united into one county. By the end of the 10th century, much of Lincolnshire's local government structure was in place, and because of its size, it was sub-divided into three parts: the Parts of Lindsey to the north, the Parts of Kesteven to the south-west and the Parts of Holland to the south-east. Lindsey was further sub-divided into three ridings, named after the Old Scandinavian word *thrithjungr*, meaning "a third part", and which gradually morphed into *thryding*. The West Riding covered the western part, including Gainsborough, Scunthorpe, Crowle and Epworth, the North Riding covered the north-east, including Barton upon Humber, Caistor, Cleethorpes, Brigg, Grimsby, and Market Rasen, while the South Riding covered the south-east, including Louth, Mablethorpe and Skegness. Each riding had its own court, as did Kesteven and Holland – although most of the day-to-day government was conducted by the 33 wapentakes of Lincolnshire – another Danish legacy which remained in place until the late 19th century, and described an administrative unit that was of the same standing as the Anglo-Saxon hundreds. At the courts of each wapentake, taxation was levied, the maintenance of peace and order was discussed and agreed, and some criminal and civil offences were also dealt with.

Undoubtedly, therefore, Lincolnshire and its internal areas had clearly taken shape long before the Normans arrived in 1066.

From the Conquest to the Wars of the Roses

Following the Norman Conquest of 1066, Lincolnshire was soon subjected to the same ruthless overhaul of ruling class and high clergy that was to be repeated in most other English counties. In other words, out went the previous Anglo-Scandinavian incumbents, to be replaced by Norman gentry and bishops. A large number of Lincolnshire manors actually went to William himself, as he automatically inherited the royal manors which had previously belonged to Edward the Confessor. He also acquired manors from dispossessed Saxon thegns like Morcar, Earl of Northumberland who, having initially submitted to William then went and took up arms against him – at which point, William seized Bassingham, Boothby Graffoe, South Kyme and Wellingore; the rest of Morcar's Lincolnshire lands were farmed out to William's loyal Norman lords. In fact, by the time he'd finished re-distributing the land, there were 90 landlords in Lincolnshire and only one of them (Kolsveinn) wasn't Norman. As for William's other Lincolnshire manors, these included the grand manor of Grantham, which brought with it Barkston, Belton, Braceby, Denton, Dunsthorpe, Gonerby, Great Ponton, Harlaxton, Harrowby, Londonthorpe, North Stoke, Old Somerby, Sapperton, Skillington, South Stoke and Welby. William also owned the grand manor of Kirton-in-Lindsey, and an even larger number of villages under its jurisdiction. Naturally, the king also rewarded his family, too – so his uncle, Count Alan, inherited large swathes of land in the Parts of Holland, while his half-brother, Odo, Bishop of Bayeaux, was granted over 80 Lincolnshire villages, plus the town of Grimsby.

Quirk Alert: *The King's Champion*

One of William the Conqueror's knights, Robert Marmion, was granted the manor of Scrivelsby, 2 miles south of Horncastle. Robert was also the King's Champion, a hereditary title that has passed ever since to the lord of Scrivelsby manor. It eventually passed from the Marmions to the Dymokes in 1350 and, remarkably, has remained with the latter family ever since. The role of the King's Champion at each coronation was to ride armed and clad in full armour into the coronation banquet at Westminster Hall and challenge to single combat anyone who should dare question the new monarch's right to the throne. The Champion then threw down his gauntlet, indicating that he would fight any challenger to the death. This ritual was observed three times and if no challenge had been made, the king, presented with a gold cup of wine, drank to the Champion, who in turn took the cup, finished the drink, and shouted "Long live your Majesties!" The Champion also took the cup as his fee, and many of these have been preserved at Scrivelsby.

Remarkably, history doesn't record any challengers to the King's Champion. Even more remarkable, is the fact that this custom was observed all the way up to the coronation of George IV in 1821. At more recent coronations, members of the Dymoke family have carried one of the Standards – a somewhat less risky duty!

For the first four years of William's rule, the new balance of power was subject to critical periods of uncertainty, particularly in the north of England. The first of these periods was in the summer of 1068, when William put down a rebellion in Yorkshire. On his march northwards from London, William and his troops travelled via Ermine Street. They also returned to London via the same route, and it was at this point that William commissioned the building of a series of Norman castles to which he could deploy garrisons that would be handily placed to quell any further uprisings.

This included castles at Lincoln, to control the north of the county, and at Stamford to control the south. Other castles were also built throughout the Midlands and the North such as those at Warwick, Nottingham and York, and the reason they all get a mention is because this means that Stamford was the only non-county town of this early batch of Norman castle sites.

Despite the castles, though, unrest and revolt persisted in the north of England, and this included the old Anglo-Saxon territory of Lindsey. For in late 1066, Edgar the Ætheling had been proclaimed King of England following Harold Godwinson's death at the Battle of Hastings, but had never been crowned. Having taken flight to Scotland, Edgar returned to York in 1069, while he was joined in York by the troops of a Danish fleet of 240 ships which had sailed up the River Humber. Using York as his base, Edgar and his supporters began to plunder old Lindsey territory, although they were forced to retreat to the Isle of Axholme when the Norman garrison from Lincoln struck back. As Yorkshire had been prepared to support this latest rebellion, William I returned to the north and began his infamous "Harrying of the North", where vast areas were ravaged; the aim being to lay waste to the northern shires in order to eliminate further rebellion. As well as fortified buildings, William's army also destroyed the homes, stock and crops of ordinary people, as well as the means of food production and many starved to death as a result. In Lincolnshire, William also held hostage at Lincoln Castle some of the county's most important people to ensure co-operation of the locals.

However, having secured the co-operation of northern Lincolnshire, the next rebellion occurred in the south of the county, led by the legendary Saxon thegn, Hereward the Wake (c.1035-1072), who hailed from Bourne and whose family had held extensive lands in south Lincolnshire prior to the Conquest. Based at the Isle of Ely, Hereward's rebellion was conducted throughout Fenland, which included northern Cambridgeshire, western Norfolk and southern Lincolnshire. Originally exiled in 1054 to Flanders by his father for "disruptive behaviour" and declared an outlaw by Edward the Confessor, Hereward returned to England sometime between 1069 and 1070 to find that his family's lands were owned by Normans who had killed his brother and put his head on a spike at the gate to his house. Hereward responded by killing the Normans responsible for his brother's death before going on an anti-Norman rampage throughout Fenland. He was joined by a small army sent by the Danish king, Sweyn Estrithson, and together they stormed and sacked Peterborough Abbey. In 1071, Hereward was joined by Morcar, the former Earl of Northumbria who had been disinherited by William I. Eventually pinned down in their stronghold on the Isle of Ely by the Normans, history has it that Morcar was captured but Hereward escaped. Accounts of what happened next, though, are varied and unclear.

The most symbolic representation of Norman power was their castles. Their first in Lincolnshire, at Lincoln, was of a Norman motte-and-bailey design, as you might expect, but actually had two mottes, one of only two of this design in the country. Unsurprisingly, and for its obvious strategic advantage, the Norman castle was built on the remains of the old Roman walled fortress located 200ft (61m) above the surrounding countryside. Also largely thanks to the Romans, Lincoln represented a vital strategic crossroads of many different routes, including the Roman Ermine Street and Fosse Way, plus the nearby valley of the River Trent to which Lincoln was still linked by the Fosse Dyke. Collectively, this infrastructure gave Lincoln convenient access to the coast and all other parts of the country. At the time that the castle was built, Lincoln had also become one of the largest and most prosperous towns in the country again, largely thanks to the Danes, and was home to a thriving commercial economy supporting a population of between 6,000 to 8,000 people and around 1,000 houses – 166 of which were demolished to make way for the 13-acre castle site! Given the strategic importance of the castle, it also had to go up pretty quickly which is why the first Lincoln Castle was largely wooden. A motte was constructed on the ridge overlooking the Witham valley, and a 46ft (14m) wooden keep constructed on top of it. The Normans then made use of the upper enclosure of the Roman town as a bailey, with ramparts and ditches dug within to form the inner bailey; the ramparts were then topped off with wooden fences. To complete the security, there were probably two wooden gateways with wooden bridges built on the sites of the present gates. The castle thereafter guarded several of the main strategic routes of what had been Danish Mercia, thus helping to consolidate control over much of today's East Midlands, plus serving as a base from which troops could be sent to repel Scandinavian landings anywhere on the mid-eastern English coast.

It is thought that the replacement of the wooden Lincoln Castle with an improved stone one commenced in around 1115 probably starting with the outer walls. The castle was enclosed by a stone curtain wall, with ditches, on three sides, while the southern fourth side encompassed the former Roman wall which stands on the edge of a steep slope. The Roman wall was therefore retained, partially as a curtain wall and partially as a revetment for the two mottes which interrupt the wall to the south-east and to the south-west. To the west, where the ground is more even, the Roman wall was actually buried within an earthen rampart, and then extended upward to form the Norman castle wall.

Much of 12th century Lincoln Castle survives today. However, very little of William the Conqueror's other Lincolnshire castle survives at Stamford. Also begun in 1068 as part of the plan to quell the natives, Stamford Castle was also initially wooden and of a motte-and-bailey design. It was built in the south-west corner of the walled town on the same spot that the Danes had built their *burh*. However, the castle was demolished in 1484, and the remains were eventually built over in the late 20th century – although a small part of the curtain wall survives at the junction of Castle Dyke and Bath Row, as do three pointed arches and a 13th century gateway that were part of the Great Hall.

In the wake of the strategic Lincoln and Stamford castles that were erected on the command of William I, numerous others followed, constructed by resident Norman gentry. Some were also of strategic use, such as that at Gainsborough, but by the 1080s, when the nation had been suitably subdued, castles started to become the centre of local administration; Stewart Bennett in *A History of Lincolnshire*, states that there were 32 such castles built in Lincolnshire in the century after the Conquest. Therefore by 1086, Lincoln Castle was home to the sheriff, the man responsible for implementing royal laws and collecting taxes for the entire county. And whereas Lincoln Castle administered the county, many of the other Lincolnshire castles administered their local estates. Probably the first of these estate castles was built in 1086 at Castle Bytham. The manor had initially been given by William I to his half-brother Odo, Bishop of Bayeaux and Earl of Albemarle, but by 1086, it belonged to Drew de Beurere, the lord of

The gatehouse to Lincoln Castle which was built in the 12th century, replacing an earlier late 11th century castle built shortly after the Conquest – although the pointed arch and turrets are later 14th century work.

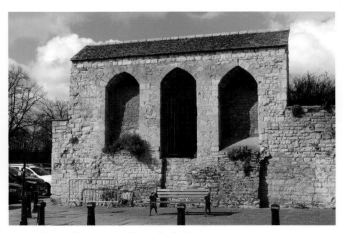

A surviving fragment of Stamford Castle.

Holderness. The castle went on to form the administrative centre of his estates, while it also lent its name to what had formerly been called West Bytham, thus still distinguishing it from its sister village to the east, Little Bytham. Although nothing of the castle remains today other than some impressive earthworks, back in the day it possessed an internal barbican, one of very few examples in this country. The castle was eventually destroyed in 1221, following a siege at which its owner, William de Fortibus, was holding out against Henry III. Henry ordered its destruction and returned the manor to its previous incumbents, the Colviles, who rebuilt and re-occupied the castle until the late 14th century. It then fell into decline and was in ruins by 1544. It was finally dismantled for building stone and by 1906 no remaining stonework was visible above ground.

Sleaford Castle was built a little later between 1123 and 1139 by Alexander de Blois, Bishop of Lincoln from 1123-1147. The castle was built to a quadrilateral format, with square towers and a large keep, but unlike most other castles, this one was located on flat fenland rather than on elevated ground. Nevertheless, the castle only came close to being besieged on two occasions, both due to kings doubting the incumbents' loyalty, and both of which were averted by effectively handing over the keys – the kings in question being Stephen in the 1140s and Edward II in the 1320s. And talking of kings, King John spent a night at Sleaford Castle shortly before losing his jewels in the Wash in October 1216, while Henry VIII spent at least two nights at the castle, one occasion being in 1541 with Catherine Howard. Back in Norman times, though, the castle was once again used as an administrative hub, this time for the incumbent Bishop's episcopal estates in south Lincolnshire. The castle eventually went into decline in the late 16th century, and nothing remains of it today other than some earthworks, the moat, and one lump of masonry which is all that remains of the north-eastern corner of the inner bailey. Also distinguishable in the southern half of the plot is the outline of a 49ft by 131ft (15m by 40m) tithe barn, and which is thought to have been the largest in Lincolnshire.

As well as the overhaul of gentry, the other overhaul imposed following the Conquest was of religious institutions. The Diocese of Lincoln at that time dated back to its founding as the Diocese of Lindsey (*Lindine*) in 678. The see of Lindsey was eventually united with the bishopric of Dorchester in the early 11th century and their combined territory stretched from the River Humber all the way down to the River Thames, while at the time of the Conquest, the bishop's seat was in the far south of the united territory at Dorchester-on-Thames in Oxfordshire. This might have had something to do with former Danish influence, as Lindsey had looked more to Danish York in the previous century than to Saxon Canterbury, and York certainly asserted that Lindsey was in its sphere of authority.

Indeed, Pope Nicholas II had waded into the debate in 1061 and issued a Papal Bull awarding the disputed

The surviving motte of Castle Bytham Castle, built in the late 11th century by Odo, half-brother of William I.

The only surviving masonry of Sleaford Castle, built by Bishop Alexander in around 1130 and demolished during the late Elizabethan era.

Some of the surviving walls and the moat of Bolingbroke Castle, built in 1220 by Ranulf de Blondeville, 6th Earl of Chester. The castle eventually passed to John of Gaunt in 1361, father of Henry Bolingbroke who went on to become King Henry IV in 1399.

Lindsey territory to the Diocese of Dorchester. However, in 1072, Remigius de Fécamp, Lincoln's new bishop under William I, moved the see to Lincoln, but also ensured that the Bishops of Lincoln retained significant landholdings within Oxfordshire. Matters were finally settled in 1092, when Lindsey was formally apportioned to the Diocese of Lincoln and just in time for the consecration of the new cathedral there built by the aforementioned Bishop Remigius. Her territory covered much the same as the previous united territory, again stretching from the Humber to the Thames and thus became the largest diocese in the country. As for Remigius's new Lincoln Cathedral, that nearly didn't happen, as he had originally started the new build at Dorchester in 1072. However, the Council of Windsor decreed that that episcopal sees should be located in large towns, so that ruled out Dorchester, while Lincoln was probably selected over the more central Leicester in order to cement the see's claim over Lindsey. The concentration of military and religious power at Lincoln, courtesy of castle and cathedral, also provided a potent nearby threat to any further thoughts of rebellion from Yorkshire, while it is also thought that the new cathedral was deliberately designed as something of a stronghold, too.

It was also at this time that the Diocese of Lincoln was divided into seven archdeaconries and which each roughly approximated to the county that the diocese covered, although a little later, Lincolnshire was divided into two: the archdeaconry of Stow, with its already impressive pre-Conquest church, and which covered the northern half of the county, and the archdeaconry of Lincoln which covered the rest of Lincolnshire. Incredibly, those two jurisdictions remained intact until 2013, when a third archdeaconry was created in the south of the county and was named the Archdeaconry of Boston.

Six years before the completion of the new Lincoln Cathedral, Domesday Book was compiled. The survey of 1086 recorded around 2,300 entries for Lincolnshire relating to 790 settlements. The grand majority of those 790 settlements still survive today, with the exception of those that had fallen victim to the various plagues of the 14th to the 17th century – particularly the Black Death of the mid-14th century which decimated England, possibly killing half of the population. The other thing that can loosely be derived from Domesday Book is population, although the survey was never intended as a census; the information collected was gathered mainly for the purpose of taxation. However, it would appear that Lincolnshire at that time was the second most populous county in England and had a working population of 25,301, second to Norfolk's 27,087. Lincolnshire, East Anglia and East Kent were also the most densely populated areas with more than 10 people per square mile. Also high was the number of free sokemen registered in Lincolnshire (10,851), while at the other end of the diocese, only one per cent of Oxfordshire's population were classified as sokemen – clearly indicative of former Danish dominance, as most sokemen were descendants of 9th and 10th century Scandinavians.

The most iconic building in Lincolnshire during the Norman period was undoubtedly Lincoln Cathedral, which was consecrated on 11th May 1092 two days after the death of its builder, Bishop Remigius de Fécamp.

However, the cathedral soon went through three unplanned incarnations. The 1092 build was largely destroyed by fire in 1141, after which it was rebuilt and expanded by Bishop Alexander. Alas, his build was then also mostly destroyed, this time by a freak earthquake in 1185 which has been estimated to have registered over 5 on the Richter scale and was therefore one of the largest ever felt in the UK. Certainly, the earthquake caused the nave to collapse, and the only remains today from the 1141 cathedral are the lower part of the west end along with its two attached towers. The builder of the fourth incarnation of Lincoln Cathedral in the late 12th century was Bishop Hugh de Burgundy of Avalon, France, and who later became known as St Hugh of Lincoln. He is known to have commenced with the rebuilding of the choir and the eastern transepts between 1192 and 1210, followed by the central nave, built in the Early English Gothic style, while the north transept was completed in 1235. The build of the north transept included the rose window known as the Dean's Eye while the build of the south transept included the Bishop's Eye, although the latter was reconstructed again, much later, in 1330. This wasn't the end of the cathedral's medieval structural woes, though, as the main tower collapsed in 1237. The build of the new central tower didn't commence until eighteen years later in 1255, when the bishop requested of Henry III that they be allowed to take down part of the town wall in order to enlarge and expand the cathedral. The central tower was then raised to its present height of 271ft (83m) between 1307 and 1311, and was topped by a spire made of oak and lead which rose to around 525ft (160m). The western towers and the front of the cathedral were also improved and heightened at this time.

This is what is known as Julian's Bower, a turf maze at Alkborough. The maze is 44ft across and sits to the west of Alkborough with stunning views across the mouth of the River Trent where it flows into the Humber. The maze is thought to have been made by medieval monks of a small cell established here which was affiliated to Spalding Priory, and was used for penitential purposes. However, others claim the Romans first cut the maze as part of a game. The same pattern has been cut into the porch floor of Alkborough church.

MAGNIFICENT LINCOLN CATHEDRAL

 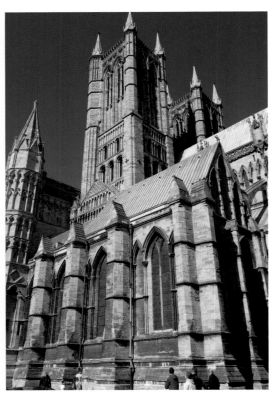

The build of the first Lincoln Cathedral by Bishop Remigius de Fécamp commenced in 1088 and was completed in 1092. This and the next two incarnations suffered terribly from fire (1141), earthquake (1185) and a structurally unsound tower (1237), respectively. Much of what we see today dates from the medieval period, and the build commenced by St Hugh of Lincoln in 1192; only the western frontage is still largely Norman (from the 1141 build). **Top left:** *View from the west with the front two towers of St Mary (left) and St Hugh (right) and the central tower set further back, all rearing above the mid-14th century Exchequer Gate and surrounding medieval buildings.*
Top right: *View of the central tower of Lincoln Cathedral from the north-east and which was raised to its current height of 271ft (83m) between 1307 and 1311.* **Bottom left:** *Close-up view from the south-west of the central tower, the 13th century south transept and the 13th century Galilee Porch.* **Bottom right:** *Close-up view of the rear of the twin 206ft towers of St Hugh and St Mary.*

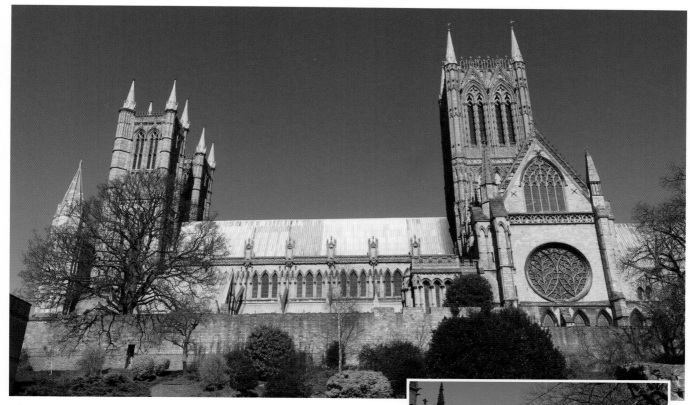

Above: *View from the Bishop's Palace (from the south), but which still doesn't come anywhere near to conveying the sheer size of Lincoln Cathedral, as almost half of the building is missing to the right (east) including the north and south choir aisles, the north-east and south-east transepts, the Sanctuary and the Angel Choir.* Below: *Most of the previously listed sections to the east of the central tower.* Right: *The 13th century Chapter House to the north-east of the building and which was built between 1220 and 1225.*

View of the west frontage of Lincoln Cathedral, including the three central Norman arches and the Norman doorways beneath, all of which date from the 1141 build.

NORMAN FEATURES IN LINCOLNSHIRE

Far left: The Norman font at Barholm St Martin's church. Centre: The centre door of the west frontage of Lincoln Cathedral.
Right: The west doorway at Barholm St Martin's complete with tympanum.

Above left: Fascinating carvings on the western frontage of Lincoln Cathedral above a typically Norman doorway arch.
Centre: Long-shot of the surviving Norman architecture on the western frontage of Lincoln Cathedral, including the three arches and the three doorways. Right: A dozen or so Kings of England, carved above the central doorway on the western frontage of Lincoln Cathedral.

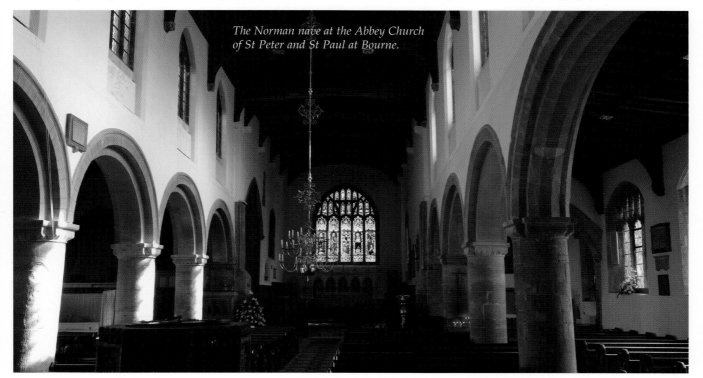

The Norman nave at the Abbey Church of St Peter and St Paul at Bourne.

The Norman nave at Barholm St Martin's church.

The Norman nave at Whaplode St Mary's church looking towards the Norman chancel arch.

The west doorway of Stow St Mary's church.

The magnificent late Norman chancel at Stow St Mary's

Quirk Alert: *Lincoln's Top Giza*

When Lincoln Cathedral was rebuilt in the late 13th and early 14th century, the 271ft tower was topped by an oak and lead spire that rose to a height of 525ft, making it the tallest structure in the world at that time. The building it surpassed was the Great Pyramid of Giza – and which had held the previous record for almost 4,000 years!

A number of monasteries had existed in Lincolnshire prior to the Norman Conquest, but all had been destroyed by the rampaging Vikings in the late 9th century. However, one monastery that was re-founded in the 10th century some time prior to the Conquest was Crowland Abbey in the south of the county. The original abbey had been formed in 716 after a monk called Guthlac had lived the life of a hermit on the same spot between 699 and 714. This particular abbey had been dedicated to St Mary the Virgin, St Bartholomew and St Guthlac but was destroyed by the Danes in 866. It was then re-founded during the reign of King Edred (946-955), only to be destroyed again in 1091, this time by fire. It was then re-built a second time in the early 12th century only to be largely destroyed by fire once again in 1170. The third rebuild was then conducted by Abbot Edward in the late 12th century, and this fourth incarnation of the abbey largely prospered until its Dissolution in 1539, its prosperity much due to the endowments of royal and noble visitors to the shrine of St Guthlac. During its lifetime, Crowland Abbey adopted the Benedictine rule (probably late 10th century), knew Hereward the Wake (who was a tenant of the abbey) and was witness to the "Miracle of Guthlac" when during the original hanging of the bells, a titanic beam broke loose and crashed to the ground where around twenty men were working in the confined space below – and yet not one of them was even injured, let alone killed. However, in 1537, a "gift of fish" to Thomas Cromwell only deferred the inevitable for two years, after which many of the monastic buildings were demolished, including the chancel, transepts and crossing of the church. Thankfully, the nave and aisles survived, and have been used as the parish church ever since.

A similar storyline panned out for Bardney Abbey in central Lincolnshire: founded in 697 (by King Æthelred of Mercia), sacked by the Danes in 869, but then re-founded as a priory, this time a little later in 1087 by Gilbert de Gant, 1st Earl of Lincoln, before eventually succumbing to the Dissolution in 1537. Very little remains today other than the abbey's earthworks and a surviving pillar base. That isn't the case where nearby Tupholme Abbey is concerned, though, as a two-storey single wall survives along with small square headed windows built into the lower storey which was a vaulted undercroft. The upper floor was the abbey refectory and is punctuated by fine lancet windows, while an impressive reader's pulpit survives, too. Tupholme Abbey was a Premonstratensian house founded a century after the re-founding of Bardney in between 1155 and 1165 by Gilbert and Alan de Neville. It initially comprised an abbot and twelve canons from Newsham Abbey and survived up until its dissolution in 1536.

Both Crowland and Bardney followed the Benedictine order, and it was this denomination that

The remains of St Leonard's Priory at Stamford, founded by William I and the Bishop of Durham in c.1082, allegedly on the site of a monastery founded by St Wilfrid in 658, and which was inevitably destroyed by the Danes!

The remains of Tupholme Abbey, a Premonstratensian abbey founded between 1155 and 1165 by Gilbert and Alan de Neville.

Quirk Alert: *Key Monk Business*

In 1347, Tupholme Abbey was heavily in debt. Cue some interesting enterprise by the resident abbot. Apparently, he stood accused of "forgery and counterfeiting of coin of the realm", which he then promptly used to buy corn and wine that was then sold for a profit! Later records in 1497 highlight a monk banished to Croxton Abbey in Leicestershire for having fathered a child with a local woman, and of rules in 1482 being imposed upon the monks forbidding them to leave the precincts of the abbey without prior permission, or to sit up drinking after Compline!

The gatehouse of Thornton Abbey, founded in 1139 by William le Gros, the (presumably large) Earl of Yorkshire.

The remains of Thornholme Priory, built between 1135 and 1154.

accounted for most of Lincolnshire's late 11th and early 12th century religious houses, while the next wave in the mid-to-late 12th century tended to belong to the Augustinians. In terms of location, the Witham Valley is notable for its high concentration of former medieval monasteries; six on the eastern bank, and three on the western bank. In fact, the Witham Valley between Boston and Lincoln had the highest concentration of abbeys and monastic foundations in the country, each in the perfect position to take advantage of the river for transportation of the wool that they produced in copious quantities; certainly, the monasteries at Kirkstead, Revesby, and also further south at Spalding, were major exporters of wool to Flanders and as far afield as Italy. By the end of the 12th century, 43 religious houses existed in Lincolnshire, with 23 of them founded during the period of The Anarchy, from 1135 to 1154, while another 67 were added over the next two centuries, with their numbers including abbeys, colleges, friaries, hospitals, monasteries, nunneries and priories; indeed, the only monastic order not represented in Lincolnshire was the Cluniac order. The map

on page 38 pinpoints the majority of Lincolnshire's medieval religious houses.

The map on page 38 also includes a number of Gilbertine houses, and this is the only denomination that originated in England – in Lincolnshire, as it happens. The order was established by Gilbert of Sempringham in 1131, and 26 Gilbertine houses were founded nationally with 11 of those in Lincolnshire. Gilbert was canonised in 1202 by Pope Innocent III, twelve years after his death at the ripe old age of 106. As for the remains of these former awe-inspiring edifices, we only have a few ruins to look at today, thanks to the destruction wreaked during the Reformation of the 16th century. And for those sites bereft of even ruins, archaeology provides the only viewpoint into the past. For example, research has indicated that in its prime, Louth Park Abbey was the largest Cistercian monastery in the country, with its church 256ft (78m) long, while Barlings Abbey's church was nearly 300ft (91m) long. However, in the 14th century, fortunes began to change for religious houses, triggered by a number of key events. An outbreak of sheep murrain in the early part of the century meant that by the 1320s, the resulting decline in the wool trade led to monastic hardship. Then when the Black Death struck in 1349, the communal living of monks and their caring for the sick and the dying meant that they were hit particularly hard. The prosperity of these houses never returned to their former heights, and many were already a pale shadow of their former selves when Henry VIII and Thomas Cromwell wielded their respective scythes.

A surviving part of the cloister of Thornton Abbey.

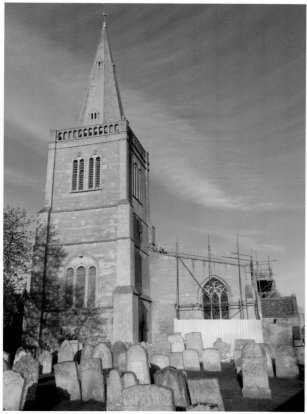

The Priory Church of Deeping St James includes surviving parts (i.e. the nave) of the priory founded here in 1139 by Baldwin FitzGilbert.

The western frontage of Crowland Abbey, with the lower part dating to the 12th century and the upper part to the 14th.

The only surviving remains of Barlings Abbey, founded in 1154. The shape always reminds me of the Trojan Horse!

The remains of the south transept of Kirkstead Abbey, originally founded in 1139 by Hugh Brito, but moved to this site in 1187.

Monastic Lincolnshire

Key

A	Augustinian
B	Benedictine
C	Carthusian
C	Cistercian
C	Colleges
F	Friars
G	Gilbertine
H	Hospitals
K	Knights Hospitaller
P	Premonstratensian
T	Knights Templar

(1215–1217). This was a civil war between the forces of first King John and then his infant son, Henry III, against a group of rebellious barons who were supported by the future Louis VIII of France. The dispute had resulted from King John's refusal to accept and abide by the Magna Carta, although following John's death on 19th October 1216, a number of barons were willing to change sides and support John's nine year-old son who had just been crowned Henry III. However, the war had now become a dynastic struggle, and Louis pressed ahead with his quest to become King of England. At the time of the battle, the city of Lincoln had been taken by Louis' forces led by the Comte de la Perche, but the castle remained under the control of its garrison which was loyal to King Henry III. However, Louis' forces were attacked by a relief force under the command of William Marshal, 1st Earl of Pembroke. The resulting battle took around six hours and would have been chaotic. Marshal's forces were approaching from the northwest, from Stow, and unsure of the size of the force, Louis' men adopted a defensive strategy, attempting to delay Marshal at the city gates while pressing on with their siege of the castle, the aim being to capture the castle and occupy this much stronger position. This left them effectively caught in a sandwich. Marshal's forces then took the north gate and rained crossbow bolts down on Perche's forces from the rooftops of captured houses, before charging the

During the period of English history known as The Anarchy (1135-1154), Lincoln played an important role in the outcome, especially during the First Battle of Lincoln in 1141. The Anarchy involved the dispute of the English throne between the nephew of Henry I, Stephen of Blois, and his daughter, the Empress Matilda, and which descended into civil war and a breakdown in law and order. In 1141, the forces of King Stephen had been besieging Lincoln Castle when they were attacked by a relief force commanded by Matilda's half-brother, Robert, the 1st Earl of Gloucester, and supported by Ranulf, 4th Earl of Chester and a large force of Welsh troops. During the battle, Stephen's earls fled and, after fierce fighting in the streets of Lincoln, the king was eventually captured. He was then imprisoned and effectively deposed, allowing Matilda to rule for a short time. As for Lincoln Castle, its stone tower was substantially damaged during the battle, and a new one was built in its place and became known as the Lucy Tower, named after Lucy of Bolingbroke, the former Countess of Chester.

Lincoln Castle was the subject of another siege followed by the Second Battle of Lincoln, on 20th May 1217, this time during the First Barons' War

This is the frontage of St Leonard's chapel at Kirkstead, and what is renowned as one of the best surviving examples of 13th century architecture in Britain.

Quirk Alert: *The Battle of Lincoln - Literally*

The Battle of Lincoln, 1141, is featured accurately, and in detail, in Ken Follett's best-selling historical novel The Pillars of the Earth. *A TV mini-series of the same name was aired in 2010 by Channel 4, starring Ian McShane, Rufus Sewell, Matthew Macfadyen and Eddie Redmayne.*

The Battle of Lincoln is also featured in When Christ and his Saints Slept *by Sharon Penman, while it also plays an important plot role in* Dead Man's Ransom, *by Ellis Peters, one of the novels in the Brother Cadfael series.*

---

besiegers. Perche refused to surrender and was killed, the siege collapsed, and the remnants of Louis' army who were not captured fled Lincoln by the south gate – many of whom were ambushed and killed on their flight southwards back to France. The whole event later became known as "Lincoln Fair" after the looting and sacking that took place afterwards – dubiously justified by Henry's forces claiming that the citizens of Lincoln had been loyal to Louis. Nevertheless, Lincoln had once again proven pivotal in a civil war, with many leading Louis supporters captured during and after the battle. The war went downhill from there for Louis until he eventually signed the Treaty of Lambeth in September 1217, relinquishing his claim to the English throne.

In between the two Battles of Lincoln, the city had become one of the wealthiest in England, boosted by the export of cloth and wool, much of it dyed in scarlet and the famous Lincoln Green. As well as cloth and clothing production, medieval Lincoln industries included construction, haberdashery, leather-making,

MAGNIFICENT MEDIEVAL (AND NORMAN) LINCOLN

At the foot of the hill leading to the magnificent pairing of Lincoln Castle and Lincoln Cathedral is High Bridge. The bridge itself straddles the River Witham and dates from 1160. A bridge chapel was built here in 1235 and was dedicated to Thomas Becket. It was eventually demolished in 1762.

A narrow passage and narrow steps lead up on either side into High Street, and this is the building from the other side. However, these buildings were built much later in around 1550.

Moving up High Street, you soon arrive at the Guildhall and Stonebow, built in around 1520, and the meeting place for council meetings since medieval times. It was built on the spot where the Romans had built the south gate of their extended city.

At the top of High Street before you head off up the narrow road called The Strait, is The Cardinal's Hat (nearside), which dates from the 15th century and is probably named after Cardinal Wolsey who was Bishop of Lincoln from 1514-15. Dernstall House (far side), contains masonry dating from the 12th century.

The Strait opens out into a little square here, where it meets Danes Terrace to the right and Steep Hill which takes you up to the cathedral.

From The Strait, we move onto Steep Hill.

Steep Hill opens up at the top into Castle Square, where Steep Hill is crossed by Drury Lane and Exchequer Gate. Here you will find Leigh-Pemberton House, a timber-framed merchant's house built in 1543.

Facing the cathedral (looking west) is Exchequer Gate, which dates from the 14th century and which separates Castle Square from the Minster Yard. It takes its name from a black and white chequered cloth which was used to help the counting of the rent monies.

Where The Strait and Steep Hill meet is the Jews House (left) which dates from the 12th century and the Jews Court (right), also late 12th century. It is said that Belaset of Wallingford, a Jewess, lived at Jews House in the 13th century, but who was hanged in 1290 for "clipping the king's coin". Jews Court may have been a synagogue at that time or perhaps a Jewish school.

Halfway up Steep Hill where it is crossed by Christ's Hospital Terrace and Michaelgate is Norman House, an exceptionally important example of domestic Norman architecture and which dates from between 1170 and 1180.

View of Lincoln Cathedral from Castle Square. The building in red brick to the right of the cathedral is the inn known as The Magna Carta.

Adjoining Exchequer Gate to the south is the Deanery, built in stages between the 13th and 15th centuries, and which was built on top of a Roman hypocaust.

Behind the Deanery and to the south of the cathedral is the ruined Bishop's Palace. Begun in the 12th century, and progressively improved by medieval bishops, it was severely damaged during the English Civil War.

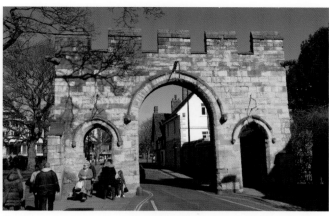

To the east of the cathedral is the Priory Gate, originally built in 1285. However, this one is an imposter in our medieval montage, for the original was destroyed in 1815 and the Priory Gate above reconstructed in its place a year later.

A few metres further down Pottergate from Priory Gate is this row of historic buildings, including the Chancery (in red brick) built by Anthony Bek in around 1316. Adjoining to the left is the Choristers' House, rebuilt in 1616.

And finally, at the bottom of Pottergate is the 14th century Pottergate Arch.

shipping and victualling. By the 13th century, Lincoln had become the third largest city in England behind London and Norwich, and was a favourite of more than one king, while sheep farming and the wool trade continued to bring great wealth to the surrounding area. In fact, Lincolnshire as a whole thrived economically in the two and a half centuries after the Norman Conquest, along with much of the rest of eastern England which took good advantage of a coast facing mainland Europe. As a result, the county became home to some of the most populated places in Britain. Throughout the Fens and towards the coast, populations were also booming, with estimates in 1332 putting the population of Sutton in Holland at over 5,000, followed closely by Pinchbeck (4,000-4,500), while each of Fleet, Moulton, Spalding and Weston were also estimated as having populations of around 3,000. The economies of these places were dominated by agriculture, salt-making, fishing and fowling and, as such, none of them were classified as a town – unlike Stamford, which was, courtesy of only six per cent of its population being agricultural workers, while 60 per cent of its population were involved in commerce as shopkeepers, leather-workers, merchants or dealers; many others were victuallers, publicans or skilled artisans.

As for the rest of Lincolnshire, this remained completely dependent upon agriculture, and which type depended upon the local topographical and geological characteristics. Wheat and barley were the main crops of the thinner, well-drained lands of the chalk Wolds and the limestone ridge that passed south to north through western Lincolnshire, while oats favoured the wetter conditions of the Fens, and were grown in particularly large quantities at Donington. In terms of livestock, cattle were more common on the clays, the marshlands and the fen edge, swine were more common in the woodlands of Kesteven and south Lindsey, and sheep were found all over, but particularly on the Wolds and the uplands north and south of Lincoln.

It was also during the medieval period that a growing population saw parishes extended to include the cultivation of marginal land, particularly in the

Fens, around the Wash and up and down coastal Lindsey areas. The increased wealth from agriculture thus stimulated a golden age of church building, with fine examples including those built at Algarkirk, Gedney and, of course, St Botolph's at Boston. It was wool that fired Boston's prosperity, plus its location on the River Witham. Foreign merchants opened trading houses here, buying English goods and selling their own, with Lincolnshire wool destined in particular for Flanders, the Rhineland and even Italy. Arthur Mee states that in the 13th century, Boston's trade was second only to London's, and that by the end of the century, was second to none. In addition, Stewart Bennett's *A History of Lincolnshire* states that Boston was "the premier port in the kingdom" at the beginning of the 12th century, "surpassing London and Southampton". He also qualifies those statements by saying that 43 per cent of the total amount of wool exported from England

MEDIEVAL GRANTHAM

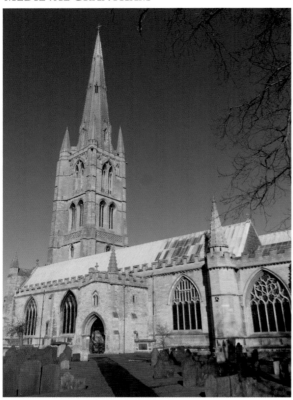

The Norman incarnation of Grantham St Wulfram's church was largely destroyed by fire when it was struck by lightning in 1222, with the exception of most of the north aisle arcades. The rest is mainly 14th and 15th century.

The original King's School building, part of Grantham Grammar School. It was endowed by Richard Fox, Bishop of Winchester in 1528 although the Old School and the Master's House beside it were dated by Pevsner in Buildings of England, *at 1497. A blue plaque on the front announces that Isaac Newton was taught here, for this was the school that he attended between 1655 and 1660.*

The Grade I-listed Grantham House is located on Castlegate in Grantham, and was built in 1380. Parts of this build survive, including the central hall.

The Angel and Royal on High Street, Grantham dates from the 13th century. It is one of the rare remaining medieval hostels originally established by the Knights Templars – this one in 1203 on Ermine Street. The hostelry was run by the Knights until their dissolution in 1312. King John was the first monarch to stop here in 1213.

was sent via Boston – presumably during the 12th century. Of course, although some of that 43 per cent was produced in Lincolnshire, particularly by the county's religious houses (for example, we know that by 1313, Thornton Abbey owned 7,453 sheep), a large proportion was transported to Boston from other counties, particularly from Derbyshire and Nottinghamshire. One of the main enablers for this trade was the Fosse Dyke which had been made navigable again in 1121, thus linking the River Trent with the River Witham at Lincoln, and thus further on to Boston and the North Sea. This development also brought Torksey on the Trent into play as a medieval port, too. Other goods coming via this route included Derbyshire lead.

Sticking with medieval Boston, St Botolph's church is commonly known as Boston Stump. Unfortunately that name does little to convey the church's magnificence. Built during the 14th and 15th centuries, its tower stands at a height of 272ft (83m) and can be seen for many miles around; indeed, Arthur Mee describes it as

aisle, while the stone groining within the tower is said to be the highest in England at 137ft, with the exception of Liverpool's 20th century cathedral. The sheer size and intricacy of St Botolph's speaks much of the medieval wealth of the town.

In terms of medieval industry, salt production remained important throughout the period and was produced on a large scale along the east coast. The industry also began to shape the east Lincolnshire coast along the lines that we see today, as the process of salt production gave rise to land reclamation. This came about because as the brine was separated from the sand, the waste was piled up into mounds which eventually forced the salt-makers to move nearer to the sea, thus reclaiming large tracts of land. Meanwhile, the land between Tetney and North Somercotes still bears the marks of this medieval industry, having left a patchwork of irregular mounds over 11sq miles (18sq km).

A little further up the coast, Grimsby was developing into a major port, too, mainly importing and

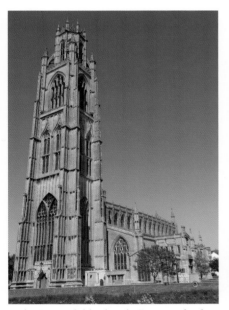  

Left: St Botolph's church, Boston, also known as Boston Stump. Built during the 14th and 15th centuries, and suitably indicative of Boston's medieval wealth, its beautiful lantern-crested tower rises to a spectacular height of 272ft. Centre: What is today known as the Kyme Tower in South Kyme was once part of a medieval castle built between 1339 and 1381 by Gilbert de Umfraville, 3rd Earl of Angus and Lord of Kyme. Most of the rest of the building was demolished in the 1720s. Right: The Great Tower of Tattershall Castle. Originally built in 1231 by Roger de Tattershall, this tower comes from the brick rebuild by Ralph, 3rd Lord Cromwell (and Treasurer of England) between 1430 and 1450.

"the highest and loveliest medieval lantern tower in the land". The build of the current church commenced in 1309 with the chancel, followed by the south aisle, and then the nave which was completed in around 1390, and which is a huge 242ft (74m) long and 104ft (32m) wide. The build of the tower did not commence until 1450, and was completed between 1510 and 1520. The tower was topped with a highly decorated octagonal lantern ringed with pinnacles. Aside from the tower, the chancel is adorned with rich parapets, as are the aisles and the clerestoried nave, with the latter boasting fourteen windows on each side. Also worthy of note is the pinnacle that adorns the eastern end of the north

exporting to Scandinavia, and was joined by other developing ports at Skegness, Saltfleethaven and Wainfleet. Exports were typically cloth, grain and wool, while imports from Scandinavia, Flanders and other countries who became members of the Hanseatic League from the turn of the 15th century, included cloth, stockfish, timber and wine. Meanwhile, other minor ports developed along the River Welland, at Spalding, and along the River Ancholme which was navigable as far as Bishopbridge, a few miles west of Market Rasen.

Internally, much Lincolnshire trade was conducted at markets and fairs, and by the middle of the 14th century, there were 120 official market charters held by

Left: This market cross in the centre of Grantham dates from c.1280. It was actually replaced in 1886 by a granite obelisk and by 1911 was languishing in a builder's yard – at which point, a successful local campaign was launched to reinstate it! Centre: This market cross in the centre of North Kyme dates from the 14th century and is both Grade II listed and a scheduled monument. Right: The market cross at Tattershall dates from the 15th century, although King John first granted a market here in 1201.

towns and villages throughout the county, with many more conducted unofficially. The largest concentration of these was in the Fens and around the Fen edge, with ten of them having two markets a week, and Lincoln three (Monday, Wednesday and Friday). For many of these markets, agricultural produce dominated. However, those markets held at the aforementioned ports had a wider variety of produce, with Boston's market also including luxuries like furs, hawks, silks, spices and wines as well as bulk items like timber. In addition to the weekly markets, other places held annual fairs that lasted for several days at a time, with these also tending to be concentrated around Holland and Kesteven. They also tended to occur along the coast or navigable waterways, such as those fairs that were held twice-annually at Barton, Boston, Grimsby, Horncastle, Lincoln, Pinchbeck, Skidbrooke, Spalding, Spilsby, Tattershall, Torksey and Wainfleet.

Alas, all of this prosperity and progress came to a shuddering halt, country-wide, during the 14th century. A series of natural disasters were largely to blame, particularly during the crisis years of 1315 to 1322 when it is estimated that the national population declined by at least 15 per cent. This period was marked by widespread outbreaks of sheep murrain and poor, wet summers, with the latter resulting in poor harvests and subsequent famine. The flooding – particularly in the lands reclaimed from the sea for cultivation over the previous century – was disastrous, but other areas were badly hit by flooding too – including the Lindsey coastal marshes, the Ancholme Valley and the Trent Valley. In addition to this, climate change had also brought about the silting of key trade-based rivers, particularly along the Fosse Dyke and between Boston and the sea. At a national level, Edward II's wars with the Scots, Welsh and particularly the French was very

bad for trade, but on a more local level, Lincoln was made one of England's eight staple ports in 1326. This meant that merchant barges or ships exporting produce such as wool, hide, skins and tin, had to unload their goods at Lincoln, and display them for sale for a certain period, usually three days. Thereafter, the trader was allowed to reload his cargo and travel onwards with the remaining unsold produce. This worked perfectly well for Lincoln's trade and prosperity, but at the expense of other Lincolnshire ports – as Lincoln found out to its cost when the staple port right was transferred to Boston in 1341, and most of Lincoln's c.200 wool weavers were unable to remain viable.

However, all of these setbacks were nothing compared with the Black Death which first arrived in England in 1349 and is estimated to have taken anything from a third to half of England's population, essentially returning it to its Domesday Book level of just over two million. It is thought that Lincolnshire's population was reduced from 385,000 in the first half of the 14th century, to about 212,000 in 1350. Some villages were totally wiped out, and became abandoned, which

St Mary's Guildhall in Lincoln was built in around 1167.

This building is the Tobie Norris Inn at Stamford, but it has only been a pub since 2007. Parts of the building date back to 1280, while in 1617 a certain Tobie Norris (1586-1626), who owned the house, set up a bell foundry behind it.

is why we see certain places designated as deserted or shrunken medieval villages on modern maps. These include villages such as Biscathorpe, Brackenborough, Brauncewell, Casewick, Maidenwell, North Cadeby, Walmsgate and West Wykeham. By the 1350s, thousands of Lincolnshire fields lay uncultivated.

The combination of these disasters meant that Lincolnshire's economy didn't recover again for another four hundred years. Also indicative of this decline was that by the 16th century, a large number of weekly markets and annual fairs had disappeared, with the survivors tending to align to what had become market towns, such as Boston, Bourne, Horncastle, Louth, Sleaford and Spilsby. Meanwhile, lurking just around the corner in the 1530s was the Dissolution of the Monasteries. The majority of religious houses were already struggling by this time, anyway, but thus disappeared yet another consistent source of county wealth over the previous five hundred years. In fact, when Lincoln Cathedral's great medieval spire rotted and collapsed in 1549 and was not replaced, it was a rather significant symbol of Lincoln and Lincolnshire's economic and political decline.

Finally for this chapter, we must cover Lincolnshire's brief involvement in the Wars of the Roses of the late 15th century. A number of Lincolnshire men were involved in the Battle of Losecoat Field, just over the border into Rutland in 1470, but the only other incident of note took place nine years earlier in January 1461, when Queen Margaret (of Anjou) led the Lancastrian army through the south-western corner of the county. According to a monk from Crowland Abbey, this was "over a breadth of thirty miles, like a swarm of locusts, as they pillaged and even dug in their insatiable quest for plunder". Apparently on their hasty return from London, pursued by the troops of Edward IV, the monk simply records their passage as "a stampede" and states that "they were compelled to abandon their booty".

LATE MEDIEVAL LINCOLNSHIRE

Ayscoughfee Hall in Spalding was built in around 1451, probably for Richard Ailwyn, a local wool merchant.

Boston Guildhall was built in the 1390s by the Guild of St Mary at a time when Boston's wealth was second only to Lincoln's in Lincolnshire.

Magdalen College School at Wainfleet All Saints, founded by the Bishop of Winchester, William Waynflete, in 1484. Waynflete had also been Lord Chancellor from 1456 to 1460 and had obtained the town's charter in 1457.

Gainsborough Old Hall was built for the Burgh family in around 1460. It is one of the best preserved medieval manor houses in England.

The hospital founded in 1485 in Stamford by Sir William Browne (1410-1489), a rich, local wool merchant, who was also Lord Mayor and Merchant of the Staple of Calais.

Stamford All Saints' church has a small amount of 12th century work, but much of it dates from the 13th century. It was extensively expanded in the 15th century by the father of Sir William Browne, John Browne, while Sir William funded the build of the steeple in 1465.

Stamford School was founded in 1532 as a chantry school by William Radcliffe, a local merchant and alderman. Remarkably, it survived the Abolition of Chantries Acts of 1545 and 1547 thanks to the personal intervention of Sir William Cecil (later Lord Burghley).

It was the same William Cecil who bought these Stamford bedehouses in 1549. Formerly part of a medieval hospital, which had fallen into disuse by the 15th century apart from its chapel, which itself was dissolved in the late 1530s. Cecil endowed the bedehouses for 13 old men of Stamford.

From the Dissolution to the Eve of the Industrial Revolution

At the beginning of the 16th century, there was a close relationship between the Catholic Church and the people of Lincolnshire. However, alongside this backdrop of Lincolnshire loyalties, Henry VIII was battling with Pope Clement VII and the Catholic Church over his divorce from Catherine of Aragon, a battle which culminated in the Act of Supremacy 1534, which recognised Henry as head of the Church in England…at which point the Pope excommunicated both Henry and the Archbishop of Canterbury, Thomas Cranmer.

Thus began the English Reformation, with dissenters such as the Carthusian Martyrs executed for their views as, in 1535, was Sir Thomas More, Henry's former Lord High Chancellor, for not recognising Henry as the Supreme Head of the Church of England. Thereafter, Henry's opposition to the Church became extreme, resulting in the Dissolution of the Monasteries between 1536 and 1541. Authorised to do so by the Act of Supremacy, Henry disbanded Catholic monasteries, priories, convents and friaries in England, Wales and Ireland, confiscated their income for himself, disposed of their assets and dismissed (and in some cases executed) the previous incumbents. Thus followed the Suppression of Religious Houses Act 1535 (the First Suppression Act) which was designed to expropriate the lesser religious houses to Henry, and which was followed by the Suppression of Religious Houses Act 1539 (the Second Suppression Act) which took out the remaining 552 larger religious houses.

Faced with this brutal treatment of their religion, and fearful of the uncertainty caused by change, the Roman Catholics of Lincolnshire rebelled, in what became known as the Lincolnshire Rising. During 1536, the first 20 of Lincolnshire's smaller religious houses had been closed following the First Suppression Act 1535. The people of Lincolnshire witnessed this, as roofs were removed in order to sell the lead, stairs and battlements were demolished, and anything of value from inside the religious house was taken for sale; in fact, the damage incurred was probably comparable to that of the Vikings, 700 years earlier!

Shortly after the closure of nearby Louth Park Abbey, the rising began on Monday 2nd October 1536 at St James's church in Louth. The previous night, the Reverend Thomas Kendall had delivered an impassioned sermon in anticipation of the King's Commissioners arriving the following day to assess the wealth of the church. At that point, the Commissioners were at Caistor, about to begin their assessment, and their numbers included Thomas Moigne from North Willingham, Sir Edward Maddison from Fonarby, and Lord Burgh from Gainsborough. Fearing that the church treasury would be appropriated, and which they considered community property, some of the Louth congregation decided to keep vigil overnight. The following morning, they rang the church bells – an

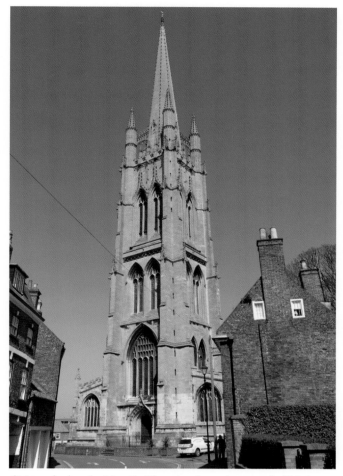

St James's church at Louth. The spire shown here was built between 1501 and 1515, making it the tallest parish church spire in the county and reputedly the tallest Anglican church in the UK, discounting cathedral spires. The £305 that it cost in the 16th century would have been significantly comprised of funds bequeathed by locals, most of whom were Catholic – and many of whom may well have taken part in the Lincolnshire Rising of 1536. The rising was triggered in St James's church on 1st October following an impassioned speech by the vicar of Louth against the Dissolution and the appropriation of church possessions.

ancient call to rebellion – and sure enough, a large crowd gathered. The objective of their uprising was largely to protest at the suppression of Catholic religious houses, and was careful not to oppose the personal rule of Henry VIII. The rising gained rapid support in the nearby towns of Caistor, Horncastle and Market Rasen, as well as other villages in the Lincolnshire Wolds such as Alford and Spilsby.

It seems as if at this point, the Commissioners were taken by the mob to Louth where they were forced to swear an oath to "Almighty God, to Christ's Catholic Church, to our Sovereign Lord the King, and unto the Commons of this realm, so help you God and Holydon and by this book". Having sworn this in fear of their lives, it would appear that no harm came to the officials, other than the pride of one who was apparently clapped into the town's stocks. This wasn't the case at Horncastle, though, where two officials, including the King's Commissioner, Dr Raynes were killed by the

The gatehouse to Stamford Greyfriars still survives today, despite the dissolution of the friary in October 1538. It was founded prior to 1230, as this was the year that Henry III donated a grant of fuel to the friary.

This building is located adjacent to the Central Library in Lincoln and was once the infirmary of the friary known as Lincoln Greyfriars. Dating from the mid-13th century, Lincoln Greyfriars was also dissolved in 1538.

mob which was allegedly led by a priest. Dr Raynes, who was also the chancellor of the Bishop of Lincoln, was staying at nearby Bolingbroke, after having held a Commissioner's session there. According to accounts, he was dragged from his bed and taken to Horncastle. Once there, according to Francis Aidan Gasquet, the 19th century Benedictine monk and historical scholar, he was set upon by the mob. Gasquet describes what happened next in his book *Henry VIII and the English Monasteries*, as "one of the two acts of violence, which alone in this or the subsequent Yorkshire rising, disgraced the movement!" He also writes that the mob, who included amongst them many parsons and vicars, were chanting "Kill him, kill him," at which point poor Dr Raynes was pulled violently from his horse and "with their staves they slew him" with the priests still allegedly crying "Kill him, kill him". The rebels then sought out a certain Thomas Wolsey, one of Thomas Cromwell's servants, and killed him, too.

Despite this disastrous turn of events, the previously chaotic movement began to gain some organisation by the fourth day of the rising, thanks to leading members of the Lincolnshire gentry, such as Sir Robert Dymoke, Sir William Maddison, Sir Robert Tyrwhit and Robert and Sir John Sutton. By the sixth day, around 12,000 rebels had mustered at Grange de Lings in the parish of Riseholme, around 3 miles north of Lincoln. Unfortunately for them, news of the uprising had found its way to Henry VIII two days earlier at which point he sent note to the rebels to disperse or face the forces of Charles Brandon, 1st Duke of Suffolk, which had been mobilised, although Suffolk didn't reach Lincolnshire until 12th October. Suffolk's force was also due to meet up with a smaller force led by Lord John Hussey of Sleaford before marching on Lincoln, but Hussey decided to flee to Nottingham instead – an action which cost him his life in the summer of 1537 when he was beheaded in Lincoln for treason.

As for the rebels, their force had steadily grown since the muster just north of Lincoln on the sixth day, and varying reports mention an army of anywhere

between 22,000 and 50,000 who eventually marched on Lincoln and took the cathedral. Their demands included an end to the Dissolution, an end to Thomas Cranmer's Ten Articles (the first guidelines of the Church of England after its break from Rome), the freedom to continue worshipping as Catholics, and protection for the treasures of Lincolnshire churches, as well as an end to all taxes in times of peace. Unsurprisingly, Henry completely dismissed these demands, and responded by calling Lincolnshire "one of the most brute and beastly shires in the realm". Suffolk's force then went in to Lincoln on the 14th October and dispersed the rebels, effectively ending the Lincolnshire Rising after just 13 days. Of course, that wasn't the end of the matter, as most of the ringleaders were executed over the following twelve days, including Thomas Kendall, the vicar of Louth whose impassioned speech had ignited the whole affair. He was hanged, drawn and quartered at Tyburn. The Lincolnshire Rising did, however, help to inspire the more widespread Pilgrimage of Grace, a further rising in Yorkshire shortly afterwards and which has been described as "the most serious of all Tudor rebellions".

> **Quirk Alert:** *Cobbled Together*
> *A number of reports state that the leader of the rebels who marched into Lincoln during the Lincolnshire Rising of October 1536, was a monk and a shoemaker…who also went by the nickname of Captain Cobbler!*

In the aftermath of the Lincolnshire Rising, the religious houses at Barlings and Kirkstead were seen as supporters of the rebellion and were immediately dissolved, with Bardney following shortly afterwards. As for the parishioners of Louth, their worst fears were confirmed when the treasures of St James's church were sequestered, while the Dissolution of the Monasteries played out over the next three years. Towards the end

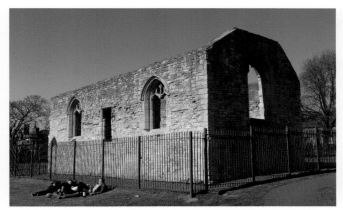

Monks Abbey in Lincoln and which once belonged to the Priory of St Mary Magdalen in Lincoln. The priory was founded in c.1135 and dissolved in 1539.

Shodfriars Hall in Boston incorporates remains of the former friary known as Boston Blackfriars, founded in the mid-13th century and dissolved in 1538.

of September 1538, religious houses were dissolved at Alvingham, Bullington, Catley, Haverholme, Newstead, Nunormsby, Sempringham and Sixhills, with these closures alone appropriating nearly £24,000 for the king's coffers. By the end of 1539, all of Lincolnshire's religious houses had gone.

Quirk Alert: *A Whip-Round for Raventhorpe*

In the church of St Peter and St Paul at Caistor, there is an old relic known as a gad whip – possibly originally used for driving oxen. In 1536, this gad whip was used for the first time as part of a bizarre annual ritual on Palm Sunday by which land at Raventhorpe was held. For more than three centuries, a man from Raventhorpe would arrive at the church during the Palm Sunday service, and would crack the whip while the first lesson was read. During the second lesson, while kneeling down, he would wave the whip three times over the minister's head, after which the whip – to which was attached a purse containing 30 silver pennies and three pieces of wych elm – would be placed in the seat of the Hundon manor pew. The Victorians eventually dispensed with the ritual in 1846, when the land-holding expired, but the whip still survives in the church today.

What happened next was that the nobility and gentry – who had once been the patrons of these great religious institutions – suddenly partook in a mad scramble to acquire the then-redundant buildings from the Crown. Of course, properties only went to the nobility and gentry who had remained loyal to the king, so somewhat unsurprisingly, it was Charles Brandon, the Duke of Suffolk who came off best, thanks to his Lincolnshire Rising dispersion – not to mention being related to Henry VIII through marriage! He actually acquired 16 religious houses, making him the leading landowner in Lincolnshire by some distance. A list of who profited and what remains of each religious

house can be found on the author's website (andy-beardmore.com).

Those who inherited these religious institutions and their land, increased their social standing, thus strengthening their position which enabled many of them to dominate local society for centuries to come. The largest inheritors were Lord Edward Clinton, the Tyrwhit and Heneage families, and of course the aforementioned Charles Brandon. As for the common people, nothing changed for them too much, although the shift towards Protestantism within their parish churches was obviously a big thing; churches became simpler and anything related to superstition was removed, while rood screens were pulled down and iconic statues and paintings destroyed. The English Bible was introduced into all churches, too.

When the tables were briefly turned during the reign of Mary I (1553-1558), no Lincolnshire folk were put to death – which is saying something! Having said that, the archdeacons of both Stow and Lincoln fled to the continent to avoid Mary's justice, and 70 priests

The surviving tower of Temple Bruer Preceptory, an extremely rare medieval relic, as the majority of England's preceptories, formerly run by the Knights Templar, were completely demolished. The preceptory was founded in the 12th century by William of Ashby, but was transferred to the Knights Hospitaller in around 1312 following the suppression of the Knights Templar in England. The institution was dissolved in 1540 and became one of many former religious houses granted to Charles Brandon, Duke of Suffolk.

were removed from their roles for having married. When the tables were reversed again for the beginning of Elizabeth I's long reign in 1558, there was even less of a stir in the reversion to Protestantism, the only blip being the Bishop of Lincoln's refusal to comply and accept the end of papal authority in England. This was also the age where the pulpit and the pews were introduced, while a goodbye to the old guard was typified at Walesby when the holy water vat was turned into a horse trough!

One of Lincolnshire's lasting legacies of the period from the 16th century to the 18th century is the number of iconic stately homes that were built, usually by the resident member of the aristocracy. A fine example is the late 16th century Elizabethan mansion and Grade I-listed Doddington Hall at Doddington, a few miles west of Lincoln. It was built between 1593 and 1600 by Robert Smythson for Thomas Tailor, registrar to the Bishops of Lincoln, and is an intriguing build, for although the façade is wide, the house is only a single room deep at the centre. The hall was inherited by Tailor's son, and then his granddaughter Elizabeth Anton who married Sir Edward Hussey of Honington. A few generations further on, Sir John Hussey-Delaval made improvements to the Hall in 1761. It was also Sir John who in 1762 covered every inch of the Holly Room with early 17th century Flemish tapestries depicting country scenes.

Another mansion largely dating from the 16th century is Grimsthorpe Castle, which is located around four miles north-west of Bourne. First built in the mid-12th century, much of the current building dates from the mid-16th century, although the huge, embattled southeast tower known as King John's Tower is a survivor of the early 13th century and has walls that are 7 feet thick. The 16th century build belonged to our old friend, Charles Brandon the Duke of Suffolk, using stone from the nearby demolished Vaudey Abbey, one of many religious houses granted to Brandon after the Dissolution of the Monasteries. By the time of the build, Brandon was on his fourth wife, Catherine, who as well as becoming Duchess of Suffolk via the marriage, was already the 12th Baroness Willoughby de Eresby, a family who had been granted the manor of Grimsthorpe by Henry VIII in 1516 and who are still in-situ today. Interestingly, at the time of their marriage in 1533, Charles Brandon was aged 49 and Catherine only 14.

Built slightly later in 1605, the Grade I-listed Scawby Hall was built by Richard Nelthorpe and is another Lincolnshire home still in the possession of the family who first built it several hundred years ago. Meanwhile, dating from a century earlier is Ellys Manor House at Great Ponton, a wool-merchant's house built in the late 15th and early 16th century, and which contains a scheme of early 16th century wall paintings that are said to be the most complete, extensive and important domestic decoration of this period in the country.

Next, Belton House was built just north of Grantham between 1685 and 1688, probably by William

Winde, and definitely for Sir John Brownlow whose family had acquired the manor in 1609. The house, built with fine Ancaster stone in the classic late Elizabethan H-shape, has not only been hailed as the most complete example of a typical English country house, but it is also claimed to be the model upon which British signposts direct traffic to stately homes! It was also the same Sir John Brownlow who had the gardens laid out in 1690 with avenues, and which included 21,400 ash trees, 9,500 oaks and 614 fruit trees. The building is Grade I listed as are its stables and south gateway, all of which are now owned by the National Trust.

> ## Quirk Alert: *Autumn Thieves*
> Legends say that Doddington Hall is haunted every autumn by the screams of a girl who threw herself from the roof whilst being pursued by a lustful squire! What a pity that thieves chose the summer of 2011 to steal lead from the very same roof of Doddington Hall, causing £2,500 of damage. A couple of months later and they might have met with some suitable ghostly justice!

> ## Quirk Alert: *Creeton Mythology*
> St Peter's church at Creeton is home to two curiosities. The first is a wooden model of the church, while the second is a Bible dating from 1611. For in the 36th verse of the 26th chapter of St Matthew, during the story of Jesus and the disciples in Gethsemane, the printer mistakenly names Jesus as Judas!

Other stately homes include Brocklesby Hall, built in the 16th century for the Pelham family, Irnham Hall built for the Thimbleby family in around 1600, and the L-shaped Denton Manor, built in the 17th century by Marshall Sisson for Sir Bruno Welby. Meanwhile, the seat of the Heneage family, who gained so much property from the Dissolution, was at Hainton Hall, and has been since the reign of Henry III (1216-1272). However, the current Hainton Hall was built in 1638 while its gardens were landscaped by Capability Brown in around 1763. The Heneage family were eventually raised to the peerage in 1896, but the title expired in 1967 on the death of the Reverend Thomas Robert Heneage, 3rd Baron Heneage.

Aslackby Manor House still contains parts which date from the medieval period, with the east wing added in the mid-17th century, while Norton Place (near Bishop Norton) was designed by John Carr for John Harrison in 1776. Next, Hackthorn Hall was built in the 1790s for the Cracroft family, who still live there today, having been associated with the estate for over 400 years, while North Carlton Hall, built in the late 16th century by Sir Robert Monson has remained with the Monson family for over 400 years.

One final house of this period worth covering is the

The Grade I-listed Doddington Hall, built between 1593 and 1600 by Robert Smythson for Thomas Tailor who was a lawyer and the Recorder to the Bishop of Lincoln.

Grimsthorpe Castle was first built in the mid-12th century, but much of the current building dates from the mid-16th century, built by Charles Brandon Duke of Suffolk, using stone from the nearby demolished Vaudey Abbey.

Ellys Manor House is a former wool merchant's house in Great Ponton that was built in the late 15th to early 16th century.

Harrington Hall, built in the late 17th century by Vincent Amcotts to replace the previous mansion built in c.1575 by the Copledyke family.

Willoughby Memorial Library, founded as a school in 1669.

Scawby Hall at Scawby near Brigg, was built in around 1605 for the Nelthorpe family who have owned it ever since. PHOTOGRAPH © RICHARD CROFT.

Fydell House, Boston, was built in 1720 by Samuel Jackson and bought and altered by Joseph Fydell in 1726, a local cloth merchant.

Gunby Hall, built in 1700 for Sir William Massingberd.

early 17th century Woolsthorpe Manor House at Woolsthorpe-by-Colsterworth, for this was the birthplace of Sir Isaac Newton on 25th December 1642. It was also here in 1666 that Newton is said to have developed his law of universal gravitation, and is therefore the location of the famous apple tree that inspired his theory. Of course, he went on to become one of the most influential scientists of all time. His book *Philosophiæ Naturalis Principia Mathematica*, first published in 1687, formulated the laws of motion and universal gravitation, and thus developed the concept of the physical universe which dominated scientific thinking for the next three centuries and came to be known as Newtonian Mechanics. Theories developed in the book included a derivation of Kepler's laws of planetary motion from Newton's mathematical description of gravity, while he used the same principles to account for the tides, the seasons and even the trajectories of comets. Newton also built the first practical reflecting telescope and developed a theory of colour based on the observation that a prism decomposes white light into the many colours of the visible spectrum, plus he also studied the speed of sound. In the field of mathematics, Newton shares the credit with Gottfried Wilhelm Leibniz for the development of calculus, while he also contributed to the study of power series, generalised the binomial theorem to non-integer exponents, developed a method for approximating the roots of a function, and classified most of the cubic plane curves. Finally, a devout but unorthodox Christian, Newton also dedicated much of his time to the study of biblical chronology and alchemy. In his later life, Newton became president of the Royal Society while he also served the British government as Warden and Master of the Royal Mint.

Quirk Alert: *Pawn of Prophecy*

When the English Civil War broke out in August 1642, Robert Pierrepont, Earl of Kingston, stated that if he ever took up arms for either side, a cannon ball would divide him between them. However, he then found himself holding Gainsborough for the king, and shortly afterwards, the town was taken by the Parliamentarians. Taken prisoner and en-route down the River Trent to incarceration at Hull, the Earl of Kingston was killed by a shot from the bank – which turned out to be a cannon ball, and sadly did indeed cut him in two!

Before launching into Lincolnshire's role in the English Civil War, it is worth summarising this hugely important historical event. England had been ruled by monarchs for centuries and, having ascended the throne in 1625 King Charles I, like so many of his predecessors, believed in the Divine Right of Kings. However, this was a time when Parliament was beginning to assert greater control and to limit the royal prerogative. Nevertheless, Charles ploughed on with his unpopular religious poli-

cies, leading to costly intervention in Europe in 1627, a move which was opposed by Parliament, and eventually led to Charles dissolving Parliament.

Despite his desperate need for money, Charles refused to recall Parliament for another decade. Unable to raise funds through Parliament, Charles therefore resorted to a series of deeply unpopular taxes that gradually turned large parts of the country against him – particularly the imposition of Ship Money on landlocked areas. Furthermore, Charles' drive to impose High Anglicanism antagonised many in England, but when he attempted to enforce this on the Scots in 1637, rebellion broke out leading to what became known as the Bishops Wars of 1639-1640. Again without sufficient funds, Charles' forays into Scotland were another disaster and ultimately led to the Scots taking Newcastle and Charles having to pay Scotland war expenses.

Desperate for cash, Charles finally recalled Parliament in England in 1640 – an opportunity for Parliament to discuss grievances against the Crown and to oppose an English invasion of Scotland. True to form, Charles took offence to this slight on his Divine Rule, promptly dissolved Parliament again and forged ahead with his attack on Scotland. This time, not only did he lose again, but the Scots promptly occupied Northumberland and Durham and Charles had to pay £850 a day to stop them from advancing further! So in November 1640, Charles had no choice but to recall Parliament again. Naturally, by now, Parliament was openly hostile to Charles, and with control slipping away, Charles withdrew to the Royalist stronghold of northern England.

The resulting English Civil War was fought in three distinct phases between the Parliamentarians (the Roundheads) and the Royalists (the Cavaliers). The first phase ran from 1642 to February 1646 when the King surrendered to Scottish forces in Nottinghamshire. Alas, Charles refused to accept Parliament's demand for a constitutional monarchy, and temporarily escaped captivity in November 1647, and hence the second phase of the war (1648-1649), but which again resulted in his capture, this time by Oliver Cromwell's now established New Model Army. This time, he was tried, convicted and executed for high treason on 30th January 1649. The monarchy was subsequently abolished and the Commonwealth of England established in its place. However, the third phase of the war took place between 1649 and 1651, when supporters of Charles II battled with Parliamentarians, and which ultimately resulted in Royalist defeat at the Battle of Worcester on 3rd September 1651.

So, when the English Civil War first broke out on 22nd August 1642, Parliament probably had the greater element of support in Lincolnshire, backed by the majority of the county's 12 MPs. Elsewhere, general antipathy to the Royalist cause in Lincolnshire had been brought about by three particularly unpopular policies of Charles I, relating to religion, tax and drainage.

Fatal Policy #1: Religion: From a religious perspective, the reign of Charles I had seen a leaning towards Catholicism at a time when Puritanism was an important force – particularly in areas such as Boston. During the reign of Charles' father, James I, a number of Bostonians, unhappy with the return to old religious doctrines, left England for Holland in 1609. These people ultimately ended up on *Mayflower* in 1620, sailing for the New World and setting up the new town of Boston Massachusetts, named after the Lincolnshire home of many of its settlers. This feeling of growing unease with the Crown and the encroaching return to more superstitious religious practices continued into Charles I's reign. In 1633, John Cotton, the vicar of St Botolph's at Boston since 1612, also left for Boston Massachusetts where he joined around 250 of his former congregation, and Cotton himself went on to become the pre-eminent minister and theologian of the Massachusetts Bay Colony. As for his departure from Boston, Lincolnshire, this had much to do with the campaign of William Laud, Bishop of London, to suppress Puritan practices. Cotton spent much of his final year in England in hiding following his summons to appear before Laud, and finally took ship on *Griffin* in the summer of 1633, having resigned his pastorate at St Botolph's on 7th May, thanking the Bishop of Lincoln, John Williams, for his "flexibility and mildness". Meanwhile, William Laud was ordained as Archbishop of Canterbury during that same year (1633), appointed by Charles I – a clear indication of future direction. Then in 1637, Laud imprisoned the aforementioned John Williams, Bishop of Lincoln, on a trumped-up charge. However, Williams refused to resign as Bishop of Lincoln, and Charles was forced to release him under pressure from the recalled Parliament in 1640. By the time of the English Civil War, the fortunes of Williams and Laud had switched around, with Williams made Archbishop of York in 1641 and Laud imprisoned in the Tower himself for treason; Laud was eventually executed in January 1645.

Fatal Policy #2: Taxes: We've already mentioned the deeply unpopular Ship Money, a tax levied on all towns, whether they be a port with ships or not. It was also levied primarily to fund a similarly unpopular war with Scotland that the disbanded English Parliament opposed, as did the people of Lincolnshire – so to have to pay for it as well was a double hammer blow. Despite the opposition, though, Lincolnshire met its target of £8,000 during the first two years of imposition (1635 and 1636). However, as the tax became progressively more unpopular over the next three years, the county began to default on its payments.

Fatal Policy #3: Drainage: The final reason for Charles's unpopularity was a huge one in Lincolnshire. That said, it is one for which we could have a certain amount of sympathy with Charles, for drainage of the Fens and the Isle of Axholme in order to reclaim land for agriculture was certainly a progressive development. However, this wasn't the opinion of the farmers

St Peter's church at Markby was built in 1611 and is one of very few thatched churches surviving in Britain. It was probably built of the remains of Markby Priory, which had been founded here in 1160. The first thatched roof was introduced in 1672 by church warden, Richard White.

and landowners of the undrained lands which, for centuries, had supported a thriving local economy of fowling and fishing. The commencement of drainage resulted in riots at Pinchbeck and Donington, while one riot near Boston lasted for three days. Meanwhile, at Bolingbroke, dykes were filled in, houses were destroyed and crops worth £1,000 were deliberately ruined. In the Isle of Axholme, though, opposition was softened by a series of bribes, and drainage actually went ahead, while some areas in the Fens remained loyal to Charles such as Crowland. Indeed, the remains of Crowland Abbey were fortified by the Royalists early on, although it was besieged and taken by Cromwell in May 1643.

At the commencement of the English Civil War in 1642, the Parliamentarians appointed the Earl of Lincoln and Lord Willoughby of Parham as lord lieutenants of Lincolnshire, while the Royalists appointed the Earl of Lindsey. With one of the most important Royalist strongholds in the north just over the River Trent at Newark, and therefore a hugely strategic point guarding the Trent, this made Gainsborough, a little further north and the next major crossing, of great strategic importance. At the start of the war, Lord Willoughby managed to secure Gainsborough for Parliament, effectively cutting off Royalist access to north Lincolnshire, plus disrupting an important communication route between Newark and heavily Royalist York. Unsurprisingly, therefore, Gainsborough became a target for the Royalists and was besieged by forces led by Charles Cavendish, godson of Charles I, and cousin to the Duke of Newcastle, William Cavendish, who controlled the Royalist forces in Yorkshire. However, Oliver Cromwell sent in reinforcements which resulted in Parliamentarian success at a battle just south of Gainsborough at Lea in which Charles Cavendish was killed (see *Quirky Lincolnshire [Lea]* for more). Back came the Royalists, though, led by the Duke of Newcastle, who then took Gainsborough and forced Cromwell's forces to beat a rapid retreat all the way to Boston, Spalding and then out of Lincolnshire to Peterborough, while Newcastle secured Lincoln and Tattershall Castle for the Royalists during their pursuit.

This proved to be a critical point in the war, because had Newcastle pressed home his advantage, he could have secured the entire county for Charles. However, instead, he decided to concentrate on attempting to oust the Parliamentarians from their stubborn enclave at Hull. This gave the Parliamentary forces of the Eastern Association time to reorganise under the leadership of the Earl of Manchester, who led an army back into Lincolnshire via Boston and Bolingbroke. At the same time, on 18th September, Cromwell ferried part of his besieged Parliamentarian cavalry from Hull back into Lincolnshire at Barton-upon-Humber and the rest under Sir Thomas Fairfax went by sea to Saltfleet a few days later. In return, he despatched infantry and ammunition reinforcements to Hull to enable them to continue to hold the crucial arsenal there. Both of the Parliamentarian cavalry factions then joined Manchester's forces at Spilsby. A small Royalist force was defeated at Wainfleet and then, on 9th October, Manchester's forces laid siege to Bolingbroke Castle. This action lured the Royalists out of Newark, led by Sir John Henderson, Governor of Newark, with his force comprising 1,500 men, predominantly cavalry with some dragoons and infantry. Henderson's force took Horncastle on 10th October, forcing Manchester to turn westwards, albeit leaving enough men to maintain the siege of Bolingbroke and prevent the Royalist garrison there from launching an attack from the rear. The scene was set for the biggest battle of the English Civil War in Lincolnshire.

The two sizeable forces met on 11th October 1643 at Winceby, around 4 miles east of Horncastle, with the Parliamentarians led by Oliver Cromwell himself along with the Earl of Manchester and Sir Thomas Fairfax, while the Royalists were led by Sir John Henderson and Sir William Widdrington of Blankney, who had been left in charge of the Lincolnshire Royalists by the Duke of Newcastle. Sometime between 12:00 and 14:00, Manchester ordered a general advance towards Horncastle. The Parliamentary cavalry, which obviously moved faster than the infantry, met the Royalist cavalry advancing in the opposite direction at Winceby, with both forces being of roughly the same size and composition. The battle only lasted for around half an hour. Cromwell feigned a retreat and lured the Royalists from a good defensive position onto flat ground. A small group of Parliamentarians advanced on the Royalists who discharged their weapons at them, at which point Cromwell led his main body of cavalry in a charge hoping to press home his attack before the Royalists had time to reload. The ploy didn't quite come off as some dismounted Royalist dragoons managed to fire a second volley, one of which shot Cromwell's horse from under him and he was only able to re-join the battle after he had secured another mount. In the following melee, the Royalists lost cohesion when a command to about face was taken to be an order to retreat. A flanking attack by Cromwell's cavalry was then enough to cause the Royalists to flee the field. A number of them were hunted back to Horncastle to a place now known as "slash hollow" – for it was here that some Royalists became trapped against a parish boundary gate that their ensuing panic had forced to jam shut. For the remainder of the day the Parliamentarians hunted down Royalist stragglers, only stopping at dusk when they were recalled by Manchester. At the final toll, the battle and subsequent pursuit accounted for around 300 Royalists, while only around 20 Parliamentarians were killed with a further 60 wounded. And just to rub salt in Royalist wounds, on the same day, the Duke of Newcastle's army at Hull was attacked by the Parliamentarian garrison with such ferocity that the siege of Hull was given up the next day.

With Parliament now in the ascendancy, it didn't take long for them to re-occupy Lincoln, without conflict, and garrison the town with troops from the Eastern Association. Gainsborough followed shortly afterwards, thus liberating all of Lincolnshire from Royalist occupation other than a small enclave on the

This bridge over the River Welland between Deeping St James and Deeping Gate was constructed at the end of the English Civil War in 1651.

Belton House was built for Sir John Brownlow in the 1680s.

Isle of Axholme. By the end of February 1644, the Parliamentarians had turned their attention to besieging Newark. However, this topsy-turvy conflict then saw another twist as Prince Rupert brought an army to the rescue of Newark and, with the Parliamentarians in disarray, pushed home the Royalist advantage by marching on to Lincoln and re-taking the castle there. Shortly after Prince Rupert had returned to Oxford, though, the same trio of Cromwell, Manchester and Fairfax returned to claim back Lincoln – although not until a fierce defence by the Royalists left the upper part of the city incurring substantial damage. Nevertheless, this was the last time that Lincoln would change hands, although Royalists did still win skirmishes elsewhere, such as that a mile north of Riby in June 1645. However, the first phase of the English Civil War ended in May 1646 when the King surrendered.

Quirk Alert: *The Arch Rebel*

During the Battle of Winceby, 1643, Oliver Cromwell had his horse shot from under him, apparently by Sir Ingram Hopton, who was himself killed later in the battle and is commemorated by a memorial canvas in St Mary's church, Horncastle (shown below). The canvas's inscription describes Cromwell as the "Arch Rebel" and bears the incorrect date of October 6, 1643 for the Battle of Winceby (instead of the 11th).

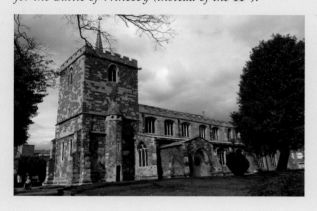

During the second phase of the war (1648-1649), Lincolnshire only suffered a few minor incursions. The most significant was when Royalist forces led by Sir Philip Monckton, marched into Lincolnshire via the Isle of Axholme and on to Lincoln where they briefly occupied and widely plundered the city. They were soon expelled though, and that was largely that for Lincolnshire's English Civil War. The cost, however, had been substantial. Like most other English counties, common folk had fallen victim to both sides commandeering "free quarter" and using that as an excuse to take whatever they wished. But there were other costs, too. Like the cost to age-old churches, vandalised by Parliamentarians in the name of Puritanism, with statues and screens smashed and altar rails removed because they didn't fit with the new ideology, while the biggest

crime of all was reserved for the smashed monuments and medieval stained glass windows of Lincoln Cathedral. Individuals suffered too, like Sir Edward Hussey who had wool to the value of £2,500 taken by the Parliamentarians from his Honington store, or at Osgodby where animals to the value of £2,000 were taken.

There was one final consequence of the English Civil War, though, as Charles II, following the Restoration in 1660 was in no mood to forgive and forget those who had conspired to execute his father. Many were executed, whereas Viscount Monson, a prominent Parliamentarian during the war, was imprisoned for life. However, every year, on the anniversary of Charles I's death, Monson was drawn on a sledge from the Tower to Tyburn and back, via a rope tied around his neck.

As well as the English Civil War, Lincolnshire's 17th century was also defined by the question of drainage and a number of advancements in dealing with it. Areas prone to flooding included the Isle of Axholme in the north-west, the Vale of Trent to the west of the Lincolnshire escarpment and the Ancholme Valley in the central northern part of the county. However, it was in the south of the county in Fenland where the problem was most acute due to inundation from the sea and drainage from the land. We've already mentioned the opposition in Lincolnshire to drainage during the English Civil War, and this delayed implementation along with severe technical difficulties, too. Nevertheless, industrial-scale drainage did pre-date the English Civil War in Lincolnshire, as the Dutch engineer, Cornelius Vermuyden, had been hired to drain Hatfield Chase in the Isle of Axholme in 1626, using proven Dutch land reclamation techniques. Vermuyden was hired by Charles I, primarily because the King owned the four principal manors in the area, namely Crowle, Epworth, Hatfield and Misterton, as well as 13 of the adjacent manors, and he wanted to increase his cultivable acreage in the area. As a reward, Vermuyden was to receive one third of the drained land – although somewhat controversially, much of that one third had previously been commons (land accessible to all locals). Furthermore, Charles – as Lord of the Manor – intended to enclose another one third of the remaining common fen in his "right of improvement" – leaving just one-third for those local residents who had common rights of pasturage in the fens.

Needless to say, the locals were outraged. The enclosure clearly threatened their commons rights and livelihoods, as they depended on the fens for pasturage and for peat for burning as fuel. Unsurprisingly, these announcements led to riots by large groups of commoners while the wealthier folk challenged the project in court via lawsuits – but which actually dragged on into the 18th century which was of little immediate help in the late 1620s! Despite being knighted in 1629 for his work, Vermuyden's Hatfield Chase project was only a partial success. His work involved the re-routing of the Rivers Don, Idle and Torne and the construction of drainage

The River Torne on part of its eastbound course towards the River Trent. Prior to Cornelius Vermuyden's drainage work in the Isle of Axholme in the late 1620s, the Torne had met the northbound River Idle to the north-east of Wroot, and hence terminated 9 miles further west.

The pumping station at Candy Farm on the River Torne to the south-west of Wroot.

channels, but it actually led to flooding in Yorkshire, and further legal proceedings. As for the Lincolnshire part of his project, the alteration of the course of the River Idle (largely in Nottinghamshire), left the River Torne with no outfall – as its two channels to the west of Wroot had originally joined the Idle here, but Vermuyden had dammed the Idle to the south of Wroot at Idle Stop and then routed the river eastwards to join the Trent at Stockwith. A completely new channel was therefore constructed for the River Torne in Lincolnshire's Isle of Axholme, which was embanked on both sides. It ran in a largely north-easterly direction from Wroot for 6 miles (9.7km) then turned eastwards for its final 3 miles (4.8km) before emptying into the River Trent near Althorpe. At the same time, a drain was constructed which ran northwards in a straight line across the Isle of Axholme for 8 miles (13km) from Idle Stop to Dirtness, passing under the new channel of the River Torne at Tunnel Pits. At Dirtness, the drain was joined by another flowing in from the west, and the combined flow was carried to the east for a further 5 miles (8km), to enter the Trent at another sluice also at Althorpe.

The draining of the Isle of Axholme in the 1630s wasn't the only drainage scheme that left Lincolnshire

folk disenchanted with Charles I, as he also had a direct and unpopular hand in the Earl of Lindsey's plan to cut the South Forty Foot Drain, the main channel for the land-drainage of the Black Sluice Level in the Fens to the south-west of Boston. The £45,000 plan was to make 26,000 acres of land available for agricultural use, and included the construction of the Skirbeck Sluice near Boston, along with the construction of the first 8 miles (13km) of the watercourse from Boston to Great Hale, the construction of two drains (the Double Twelves) from there to Guthram, and the construction of the Clay Dyke Drain. Once again, though, this threatened the vested interests of the locals who made a living from fishing and fowling, and the commoners, who had rights to graze animals on the common land when not flooded – and so they promptly destroyed the drains, the crops, the buildings erected by Lindsey's workers, and burnt Skirbeck Sluice. Meanwhile, the North Forty Foot Drain was constructed in 1720 by Earl Fitzwilliam, and ran from Chapel Hill, through Holland Fen parallel to the River Witham and terminated at Lodewick's Gowt in Boston, where the River Witham empties into The Haven.

The first large-scale attempt at Fen drainage, though, occurred in 1631, led by Sir Anthony Thomas. The scheme was aimed at draining the East and West Fens between the River Witham and the coast, reclaiming 1,600 acres of land in the process, of which 400 acres was to be given to the poor. New drains were cut in the West and Wildmore Fens leading to natural outlets to the sea at Friskney and Wainfleet, and to the River Witham at Anton's Gowt and New Gote. Thomas also enlarged the Maud Foster drain, which had actually been cut as early as 1568 from Cowbridge to The Haven – although it is likely that the Maud Foster sluice was destroyed by commoners in 1642 when they went on a rampage protesting at their loss of common land. Other contemporary schemes with Thomas's included an attempt by the Earl of Lindsey to drain a large area between Kyme Eau and the River Glen, and another scheme by Sir Philibert Vernatti to drain the Crowland and Deeping Fens in south Lincolnshire for the Earl of Bedford.

Quirk Alert: *Gowts and Reens*

One of the most unusual place-names in Lincolnshire, Anton's Gowt is a hamlet located approximately 2 miles north-west of Boston. It is situated on the junction where the River Witham meets the Frith Bank Drain, and Anton's Gowt Lock provides access between these two waterways. It is believed that the lock got its name from Sir Anthony Thomas who led the drainage of the Witham Fens in the early 1630s. The word "Gowt" is an old term meaning "a water-pipe under the ground, a sewer, or a flood-gate, through which the marsh-water runs from the reens into the sea," while a "reen" is a drainage ditch, or canal, used to turn areas of wetland at around sea level into useful pasture.

The South Forty Foot Drain from Donington High Bridge. Initially cut by the Earl of Lindsey in the 1630s to drain the Black Sluice District, it runs from Boston Haven to Guthram Gowt.

The North Forty Foot Drain seen from Benton's Bridge with Boston Stump in the distance. The drain was first constructed in 1720 by Earl Fitzwilliam, and ran from Chapel Hill, through Holland Fen to a sluice at Boston on The Haven.

Quirk Alert: *For the Essex Calves*

The unpopularity of the drainage engineers of the 17th century amongst the "commoners" is nicely captured by this poem printed in W. Dugdale's book called Imbanking and Drayning

They'll sow both beans and oats, where never man yet thought it,
Where men did row a boat, ere undertakers bought it:
But, Ceres, thou, behold us now, let wild oats be their venture,
Oh let the frogs and miry bogs destroy where they do enter.

Behold the great design, which they do now determine,
Will make our bodies pine, a prey to crows and vermine:
For they do mean all Fens to drain, and waters overmaster
All must dry, and we must die, 'cause Essex calves want pasture.

Several decades later, in 1762, the Witham Drainage Act was passed by Parliament, and which covered the drainage of the area including Asgarby, Ewerby, Great Hale, Heckington, Holland Fen, Howell, Little Hale and South Kyme. The Act was given added impetus when much of the area to the south and west of Boston was inundated by the Great Flood of 1763. The Black Sluice Drainage and Navigation Act 1765 then created the Black Sluice Commissioners, giving them power to raise taxes and authority to carry out drainage works in the area to the south of Boston. This scheme largely revived the Earl of Lindsey's plans of the 1630s, and was carried out by Langley Edwards, on loan from the Witham Commissioners. A new sluice, called the Black Sluice, was built at Boston as a direct replacement for the previously destroyed Skirbeck Sluice, comprising three openings with a total width of 40ft (12m). The 8 miles (13km) of the drain were scoured from Boston to Great Hale, beyond which the Main Drain was upgraded by cutting a new 14-mile (23km) channel, effectively extending the South Forty Foot Drain to Guthram, on the banks of the River Glen.

In October 1766, the Grand Sluice was constructed on the River Witham, close to Earl Fitzwilliam's Lodowick's Gowt, in order to prevent tidal water from entering the river and flooding Holland Fen. The same year, the Boston Harbour Commissioners were created by the Boston Port Act 1766, and they carried out improvement works to The Haven, which resulted in more efficient draining from the South Forty-Foot Drain with water pumped into the drain by a series of windmills driving scoop wheels. Maps of the area from 1783 show 46 such mills, which provided drainage for 32,000 acres of agricultural land. With the improvements to the River Witham, the final section of Earl Fitzwilliam's drain to Lodewick's Gowt was filled in, and the channel was diverted to join the South Forty-Foot Drain. Fitzwilliam's former watercourse was re-named as the North Forty-Foot Drain, and it now supplies Cook's Lock and Holland Fen pumping stations.

There were further attempts to improve drainage in Lincolnshire throughout the remainder of the 17th century, but it wasn't really until the 18th century that radical changes were introduced. In the meantime, a problem had been introduced by the earlier drainage schemes, because as the land dried out, it began to shrink, leaving large stretches at or below sea level. Furthermore, this development impeded the natural flow of water between the higher main drainage channels such as the South Forty Foot Drain and the smaller channels and drains because they were now lower. The solution was to deploy pumping engines, to pump

The packhorse bridge at Northbeck, Scredington. Some suggest it dates back to 1250, but it is more likely to have been constructed in the 17th century.

Georgian Stamford.

water from the lower drains to the upper drains, and which are commonplace in the Fens and the Isle of Axholme today. The first engine in the Fens was deployed in the mid-17th century, albeit powered by horses, but by 1685, the first windmills were deployed to pump the water using wind power; later, of course, the pumps became powered by steam, then diesel and finally by electricity. By the end of the 18th century, there were 63 windmills along the banks of the South Forty Foot Drain alone, while there were 50 windmills working in Deeping Fen by 1763.

Alas, all of these drainage schemes were insufficient during times of flooding due to extreme weather. During the winter and spring of 1762-63, for example, 22,000 acres of Holland Fen were flooded – partly remedied by the previously-mentioned Black Sluice drainage system. Then in 1800, it was reported that the Fens to the east of the River Witham had been flooded during "four of the last six seasons" and that "many hundreds of acres of harvest of 1799 were reaped by men in boats". As a result, significant drainage improvements were made in both East Fen and West Fen to such an extent that after 1812, new townships began to appear, such as those at Carrington, Eastville, Frithville, Midville, Thornton-le-Fen and Westville.

Finally for drainage, as well as land reclamation during the 17th and 18th centuries, measures were also taken along the coast to limit periodic inundations from the sea. Clay banks had been constructed during medieval times, but in the 17th century, over 17,000 acres were safeguarded, largely marshland to the south of the River Welland. At the end of the 18th century and beginning of the 19th, another 4,595 acres of marshland was embanked and safeguarded in the areas around Gedney, Holbeach, Moulton, Spalding and Whaplode, along with a further 700 acres between Freiston and Friskney. The coastline of Lincolnshire was gradually becoming more in keeping with the one that we know today.

Between the mid-18th and mid-19th centuries, Lincolnshire became subject to the Agricultural Revolution. These agricultural changes were fundamental and long-lasting, and rubber-stamped Lincolnshire's standing as one of Britain's leading agricultural economies, one which has lasted all the way into the 21st century. Parts of Lincolnshire did, of course, undergo the Industrial Revolution – and we'll come to that in due course – but it was on nothing like the scale that was experienced elsewhere.

One of the most important enablers to the Agricultural Revolution in Lincolnshire was land enclosure, as this allowed farmers to invest in land that they owned. The grand majority of enclosures occurred between 1760 and 1836, but some parishes had already been either fully or partly enclosed during the 16th and 17th centuries. Typically, this would have involved the enclosure of common and arable pasture for personal use, perhaps turning it over for grazing sheep. This obviously removed such common land from the communal system and often provoked violent opposition from evicted tenants. It also had social consequences, leading to the depopulation of some parishes and an increase in vagrancy.

By the middle of the 18th century, though, a tighter regime was in place and enclosure could only take place via private agreement or by an Act of Parliament. Around forty per cent of Lincolnshire's parishes were privately owned at this time; indeed, of the 45 parishes owned by a single proprietor, only six were not privately enclosed. In the Parts of Kesteven, 52 per cent of parishes were privately enclosed, while the number was higher in Lindsey (63 per cent) and lower in Holland (31 per cent). Before 1760, only 15 Acts of Parliament for land enclosure had been passed; between 1760 and 1836, there were another 310 Enclosure Acts. Enclosing land didn't come cheap though, which says something about the return these landowners were getting from what was then a buoyant market. For example, at Kirton Lindsey between 1793 and 1801, the cost of enclosure was £5,267.80 – a huge sum of money back then – while the enclosure of Hibaldstow between 1796 and 1803 cost £8,243.11. In terms of cost breakdown, the enclosure of Wrawby between 1800 and 1805, cost the following:

Commissioners' fees	£806
Fencing	£1,207
Legal and Parliamentary fees	£968
Road making, drainage and bridge construction	£1,202
Surveyor's fees	£566
Sundries	£201
Total:	£4,950

As was common during such enclosures, the bulk of that cost was borne by the landowner – in the case of Wrawby by Robert Carey Elwes, who received 1,372 acres and paid just £3,061 of the total cost. At the other end of the scale, a certain Christopher Richardson – who received a mere sixth of an acre – paid just 5s! As for Squire Elwes, he would probably have recovered costs by charging higher rents thanks to the increased production generated by the enclosure. What is surprising, though, is that although these arrangements seemed to be heavily weighted in the favour of the traditional landowners and lords of the manor, there wasn't a noticeable decrease in the number of smaller proprietors like Christopher Richardson, who presumably made his sixth of an acre pay dividends! This latter fact also ensured that rural depopulation didn't occur, as there was much work to be had in the original enclosure process and then via the increased production that it brought.

Despite this revolution of land enclosure, at the turn of the 19th century, only 21 per cent of the total land in Lincolnshire was given over to arable farming, with the most productive area in the Wolds only designating 25.6 per cent to arable land. Much of the rest of the land was still used for pasture which had, of course, dominated through medieval times – although we mustn't forget that the remaining 79 per cent also included areas taken up by towns, villages, woodland, commons, fallow land and what was termed "waste". Of the 21 per cent of arable land, each area had different conditions that suited the growth of different crops. So wheat was the most important crop in the Isle of Axholme, the lower Trent Vale and along the low-lying coastal marshes of the north-east. However, in the Fens, oats were still the most popular crop, although barley dominated around Deeping St James. As for the Wolds, this area favoured turnips and oilseed rape, while the lighter and well-drained lands of the Heath concentrated on barley, wheat, turnips and oilseed rape in equal measures. There were even differences within parishes, with those straddling the Lincoln Cliff favouring barley on the lighter soils of the limestone Heath to the east, but favouring pasture due to the heavy clays which retain water to the west. Overall, though, barley was the most commonly cultivated crop in Lincolnshire in the early 19th century, followed by wheat and oats, and then relatively small acreages of rye grass and potatoes. Elsewhere, of course, sheep still dominated and were sold at major fairs at Boston, Caistor and Lincoln, although by the 1830s, wool was beginning to be eclipsed by imported cotton.

> **Quirk Alert:** *Solomon's Lines*
> The Angel and Royal inn at Grantham is one of the oldest inns in Britain. An even greater rarity is that it is one of few medieval hostel survivors founded by the Knights Templars for travellers. However, it is probably the only inn for which a deceased landlord (Michael Solomon, d.1796) left forty shillings in his will for a sermon to be preached in the parish church, every year, warning of the perils of drunkenness!

> **Quirk Alert:**
> *Dr Seuss Would Be Proud!*
> In the 18th century, Sir Cecil Wray built Fillingham Castle and enclosed both house and park with a wall – which somewhat controversially blocked a public right of way, and which was a particular favourite route of Squire Whichcot, MP, who lived at nearby Harpswell. Seriously irked at the loss of his favourite route, the squire made a point of visiting the new wall once a year in his coach-and-four, bringing with him his labourers who would proceed to pull down part of the wall. He would then drive through the breach, across the park and back again, before disappearing off home – at which point, Sir Cecil Wray would repair the damaged wall…and again the following year, and the year after that…and so on until Squire Whichcot eventually passed away. Thereafter, the wall suffered no further breaches and the right of way lapsed.

Throughout the Agricultural Revolution, the agricultural industry became progressively more business-like. As a result the first bank was founded in 1754 by William Garfit, and was followed by others at Lincoln and Stamford; indeed, Boston alone had four banks by 1790, and six by 1815. Many banks were founded between the agricultural boom years of 1795 to 1815 (during the Napoleonic Wars), including those at Gainsborough, Grantham, Holbeach, Sleaford and Spilsby. Wheat prices achieved a ceiling of 120s per quarter during this period, but the end of the war brought a dramatic collapse to below 80s. Tenants struggled to pay rents agreed at a time when the price of wheat was much higher, although many landowners were sympathetic and duly lowered the rent accordingly. Fortunately, the industry was due to recover in the mid-19th century, by taking advantage of improved methods of farming.

Prior to the 18th century, the responsibility for maintaining roads had rested with local parishes. This was both unfair and inefficient, and so the Lincolnshire road network was in a poor state of health by the 18th century. Road travel was particularly difficult in the Fens, especially in winter when flooding was common, often making road travel impossible. The solution was the introduction of turnpike trusts – bodies set up by Acts of Parliament with powers to collect tolls in order to main-

The George Inn at Stamford was a popular coaching in on the turn-piked section of the Great North Road during the 18th century.

This is also a George Inn, this time at Grantham but on the same coaching route as the same-named coaching inn at Stamford. The inn is mentioned as "one of the best inns in England" in Charles Dickens' Nicholas Nickleby.

The Grade II-listed Greyhound Inn at Folkingham was on the London to Lincoln coaching route and was built between 1788 and 1789. The right-hand bay was once used as an Assize Court and Assembly Room, thus hinting at Folkingham's former importance.

The London Inn at Stamford was yet another 18th century coaching inn on the Great North Road.

tain principal highways, and which were generally run by groups of local trustees. The first turnpike road in Lincolnshire arrived in 1726 when the Great North Road was turnpiked from Grantham to Newark. The stretch southwards from Grantham to Stamford was improved courtesy of an Act of Parliament of 1739, while in the same year the first Act was passed which covered a route totally inside Lincolnshire when the route between Lincoln and Baumber was turnpiked. Thereafter, turnpike trusts came thick and fast, with the majority set up during the 1750s and 1760s, and by 1765, all of Lincolnshire's key market towns were connected.

This new turnpike network meant that coaching routes became more prevalent, although they were largely only for the wealthy as the fares were pretty high. Fares on the first coaches from Lincoln to London in 1784 were £1.11s. 6d. for an inside seat, of which there were usually four; an outside berth, of which there would typically be up to ten, was 15s. 9d. The Stamford to London leg usually took around one day to complete. By 1830, there were 70 mail and stage coaches that passed through Stamford each day, with the mail route having commenced in 1801 and which ran into the county from the south, up to Sleaford, then Lincoln,

and later to Hull via the Barton-upon-Humber ferry; a later mail coach also ran from Boston to Louth. By 1830, a fairly complex network of coaching routes existed across Lincolnshire, with the county also linked to cross-country routes such as those that went to Lincoln via Nottingham and Manchester. Quite naturally, the main coaching routes saw a number of impressive coaching inns built during the period from 1750 to the 1830s, while existing inns were significantly improved.

It was also common for these turnpike routes to have what were known as carriers: companies who operated regular delivery of goods from a particular town to another location. One town that was still running five carriers in the 1850s was Caistor, these being to Market Rasen on a Tuesday and Thursday, to Louth on a Wednesday, to Brigg on a Thursday and to Grimsby on a Friday. However, by this stage, turnpikes and coaching routes were already playing second fiddle to the railways, which first appeared in the 1830s and expanded rapidly from the 1840s onwards – although initially, the carriers cashed in by carrying goods to railway stations for onward distribution to further afield. However, most turnpikes were redundant by the late 19th century, which was when their routes tended to be taken over by the newly-created County Councils.

Before completing this chapter and launching into Lincolnshire's Industrial Revolution, we will return to the subject of religion, this time in the 18th and 19th centuries. Lincolnshire was the birthplace of one of the most influential religious characters in British history, this being John Wesley who was born in Epworth in June 1703, and who is credited with the foundation of Methodism along with his brother, Charles, and fellow cleric George Whitefield, while his work and writings also played a leading role in the development of the Holiness movement and Pentecostalism. John Wesley was educated at Charterhouse School and Oxford University, and was ordained as a priest on 22nd September 1728, after which he served in his father's parish at the tiny village of Wroot in the Isle of Axholme (see *Quirky Lincolnshire [Wroot]* for more on this period of his life). However, it was after joining a religious society led by Moravian Christians in London that John Wesley experienced what has been termed his "evangelical conversion" – on 24th May 1738 to be precise – after which he left the Moravian Society and began his own ministry, travelling and preaching outdoors throughout Great Britain and Ireland as well as North America. He always insisted that his movement lay well within C of E tradition, but in the small Christian groups that he formed, he appointed unordained evangelists to travel and preach as he did. These "Methodists", as they became known, became leading campaigners in the big social issues of the 18th century, including prison reform and the abolition of slavery. One of Wesley's key beliefs was that Christians could outwardly exude holiness by achieving a state where the love of God "reigned supreme in their hearts", while he also encouraged people to experience Jesus Christ personally. By the end of his life, he was a hugely respected figure and had even been described as "the best loved man in England". Meanwhile, his brother, Charles, who was also born at Epworth, wrote almost 7,000 hymns, including some of the best known such as Jesus, Lover of My Soul, Hark the Herald Angels Sing, and Love Divine, All Loves Excelling.

The popularity of Methodism kept on growing beyond John Wesley's death in 1791. Various factions also began to appear, including the Free Methodists and the Primitive Methodists in the early 19th century, with Primitive Methodism arriving in Gainsborough and Grantham in 1809. By the time of the Religious Census of 1851, there were 462 Wesleyan Methodist chapels in Lincolnshire and another 221 Primitive Methodist chapels, too. Indeed, *White's Directory* of 1856 listed the presence of six non-conformist institutions in Gainsborough, these being churches or chapels aligning to Roman Catholics, Wesleyan Methodists (built 1804), Primitive Methodists (built 1838) and Unitarians, while there was also an Independent chapel (built 1821) and a Friends' Meeting House (built late 18th century). Similarly, Market Rasen was home to a Roman Catholic chapel (built 1823) and a Free Methodist chapel (built 1852), while the former Wesleyan chapel (built 1800) was

taken over by the Primitive Methodists in 1838 when the Wesleyan's moved to a larger, newly-built chapel. And in South Willingham, almost the entire population were Wesleyan Methodists, while the rector of Donington bemoaned that there was "not a single person whom I can designate a member of the Church of England".

In general terms, though, Methodism tended to be more popular in the north of the county and Anglicanism in the south, but as the 19th century wore on, both denominations not only co-existed peaceably, but even began to co-operate. It wasn't all plain sailing for Methodists, though, particularly in the early days, as a number of preachers were targeted by mobs in the early 19th century, with incidents reported at Lincoln, Holbeach, Waddington and Welbourn. The latter place was also owned by the Countess of Buckinghamshire who threatened one of her tenants with the loss of his farm if he didn't stop using his barn for preaching. By contrast, though, Lord Yarborough positively encouraged Methodists on his land, because he saw them as sober and industrious, and by 1841, he had 12 Wesleyan chapels on his estate and one Primitive Methodist chapel.

> ## Quirk Alert: *Preacher's Practice*
> *In the last 52 years of his life, John Wesley preached roughly 15 sermons per week. Largely travelling on horseback, he therefore notched up around 250,000 miles and preached c.40,000 sermons. He visited every part of England and Wales, visited Scotland 22 times, and Ireland 42 times. In fact, he actually preached up until nine days before his death on 2nd March 1791, aged 87.*

> ## Quirk Alert: *Preacher's Pulpit*
> *When John Wesley preached in his home town of Epworth, he would typically stand on the steps of the town's market cross. However, Thomas King had a more unique method of elevating himself above his congregation, for he delivered his sermons whilst standing inside a wheelbarrow!*

As for the Roman Catholics, their lot improved greatly following the Catholic Emancipation Act of 1829. However, Catholics never really re-established a foothold in Lincolnshire, with the Religious Census of 1851 revealing that Catholicism was limited to pockets of the county like Stamford, where they accounted for 7.5 per cent of worshippers. Elsewhere, there was a minor spat in the late 1830s between the Bishop of Lincoln and the rector of Leadenham, Bernard Smith, over the latter's reintroduction of "Popish ceremony" into the parish church. And later, in 1885, it was the incumbent Bishop of Lincoln himself, Edward King, who courted controversy and accusation of "promoting Priestcraft", by wearing a mitre and other vestments!

LINCOLNSHIRE GREATS: NEWTON, TENNYSON AND WESLEY

Woolsthorpe Manor House, built in the early 17th century and the birthplace of Sir Isaac Newton on 25th December 1642.

The famous apple tree in the grounds of Woolsthorpe Manor, where Isaac Newton first came up with his theory of gravity.

The dining room of Woolsthorpe Manor. The house and grounds are now owned by the National Trust.

Nearside is Somersby Grange, built in 1722 for the Burton family, while alongside is the Rectory (now called Somersby House), birthplace of Alfred, Lord Tennyson in 1809.

Statue of Sir Isaac Newton (1642-1726) in Grantham market square, the town where Newton went to school and which set him on his way to become one of England's most celebrated and influential scientists of all time. He specialised in physics and mathematics, and was also known as a "natural philosopher". Part of the metal for this statue, created in 1858, came from melted cannon!

Statue of Alfred, Lord Tennyson (1809-1892) in the grounds of Lincoln Cathedral. Tennyson is one of Britain's greatest ever poets, and was Poet Laureate of Great Britain and Ireland for much of Queen Victoria's reign. The statue was sculpted by his friend, G. F. Watts in 1905, and shows Tennyson looking at a flower with his beloved wolfhound, Karenina, by his side.

St Margaret's church at Somersby where Tennyson's father, George Clayton Tennyson, was rector from 1806 to 1831. The church largely dates to the 15ᵗʰ century and contains the bells that Tennyson regularly tolled and the plain font in which he was baptised.

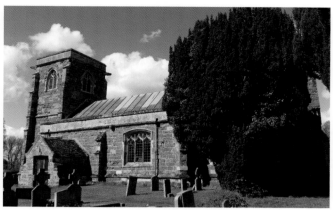

Also known as St Margaret's, this church at neighbouring Bag Enderby was built in 1407, and was also under the rectorship of Tennyson's father from 1806 to 1831.

The Grade I-listed Old Rectory at Epworth, home to rector Samuel Wesley in the 18ᵗʰ century and to his more famous children, John and Charles Wesley

Statue of John Wesley in Epworth.

Lincolnshire's Industrial Revolution

As one of England's foremost agricultural counties, the impact of the *Industrial* Revolution on Lincolnshire was felt somewhat less than it was by fellow counties of the Midlands. However, as mentioned earlier, the agricultural industry went into crisis after the end of the Napoleonic Wars in 1815, typified by a dramatic collapse in wheat prices. National tension gradually increased, with the Pentrich Revolution in Derbyshire in 1817 and the infamous Peterloo Massacre in Manchester in 1819, while periods of famine and chronic unemployment were also exacerbated by the introduction of the first of the Corn Laws. Meetings were held throughout Lincolnshire on issues such as extending the franchise and free trade in corn. However, it was the winter of 1830 before widespread rural violence broke out in Lincolnshire as part of what became known as the Swing Riots. The tension in the countryside had never really abated, so when new working practices were introduced to reduce the amount of work available during the winter months, some of the disenchanted rural community began to express their anger by setting fire to barns and hayricks and, in particular, destroying the threshing machines that were directly responsible for taking away traditional winter manual work. The Swing Riots were named after Captain Swing, a fictitious hero of the rural poor who committed these acts of sabotage, and the first Swing-related arson in Lincolnshire occurred at Moulton near Holbeach in November 1830. Thereafter, a number of anonymous threatening letters were sent to farmers, with one sent to a farmer in Great Hale concluding with the line: "Bread or blood my boys, or fire and smoke".

> **Quirk Alert:** *The Odd of Edenham*
> *Edenham is home to two curiosities. The first is the 16ᵗʰ century roof of the nave of St Michael and All Angels church, for it is 3 feet higher at the west end than at the east, and eighteen inches higher on the north side than the south. Meanwhile, nearby Grimsthorpe Castle is home to a clock which allegedly stopped ticking the minute that King George III breathed his last on 29ᵗʰ January 1820.*

Despite this widespread discontent, and the general migration of rural folk to urban areas elsewhere in the county, Lincolnshire's rural population actually increased in the first half of the 19th century, and to such an extent that it put a severe strain on parish and village authorities. The greatest increases occurred in what were termed "Open" parishes, those owned by a number of landowners, as opposed to "Closed" parishes which had few or just one landowner. Open parishes included those in the Fens, the Isle of Axholme and the coastal strip around Grimsby, with the increase in population in the Fens between 1800 and 1850 (excluding Boston and Spalding) amounting to 101 per cent. By contrast, the 44 most Closed parishes were in the Lindsey uplands, and in those with one landowner, the average population increase during this period was only 55 per cent – albeit still a large increase, and contrary to what was going on in most other English counties. Of course, the Closed parishes had less excess labour and therefore less demand for new housing; in fact these landowners positively discouraged house building and some even demolished housing to prevent unwanted labourers moving in. At around the same time, the Laws of Settlement were being imposed and which determined which parish had responsibility for individuals and hence enabled landowners to turf out unwanted "foreign" labourers.

This combination of a growing rural population and less work available, put a tremendous strain on the, by-

Lincolnshire Poor Law Union	Date of Formation	Workhouse Location
Boston Union	22/09/1836	Boston
Bourne Union	25/11/1835	Bourne
Caistor Union	18/12/1836	Caistor
Gainsborough Union[1]	18/01/1837	Gainsborough
Glanford-Brigg Union	18/01/1837	Wrawby
Grantham Union[2]	14/01/1836	Grantham
Holbeach Union	07/12/1835	Holbeach
Horncastle Union	16/01/1837	Horncastle
Lincoln Union	28/11/1836	Lincoln
Louth Union	12/04/1837	Louth
Sleaford Union	20/09/1836	Sleaford
Spalding Union	30/11/1835	Spalding
Spilsby Union	18/04/1837	Hundleby
Stamford Union[3]	17/11/1835	Stamford

Non-Lincolnshire Poor Law Union	Date of Formation	Workhouse Location
Goole Union[4]	24/10/1837	Goole
Newark Union[5]	24/03/1836	Claypole
Peterborough Union[6]	03/12/1835	Peterborough
Thorne Union[7]	24/07/1837	Thorne

[1] Also included some Nottinghamshire parishes
[2] Also included some Leicestershire parishes
[3] Also included parishes in Northants, Hunts and Rutland
[4] Included some north-west Lincolnshire parishes
[5] Inclusive of many East Notts and West Lincs parishes
[6] Included Crowland
[7] Included some Isle of Axholme parishes

The former Holbeach Union Workhouse, built between 1836 and 1837 by architect Robert Ellis Junior, for a cost of £4,830. It was home to 386 inmates, including poor Thomas Bingham (see Quirk Alert).

now, outdated poor-law system. Since the 16th century, the parish was responsible for providing for its own poor, and many parishes provided their own work-house where the destitute were housed. Alas, these workhouses were meagre and overcrowded. Some

Quirk Alert: *A Hideous Happening in Holbeach (only read if you have a strong stomach)...*

In April 1882 the master of Holbeach Workhouse, Walter Brydges Waterer, was accused of the manslaughter of a work-house inmate, 22-year-old Thomas Bingham. Poor Thomas suffered from a skin disease, and therefore to treat him, Waterer had left the man in a sulphur-burning cabinet, which was used as a treatment for what was known as "the itch", or scabies. The patient stood naked inside the cabinet with his head poking out of the top. The sulphur was then placed on an iron tray at the bottom of the cabinet, beneath a grating, and ignited by a piece of hot iron. On this fateful day, though, Waterer had left Bingham encased in the cabinet and disappeared to attend to a matter elsewhere, but then completely forgot about his patient. Others were eventually alerted by Bingham's cries for help, and he was released...but on stepping out of the cabinet, he had been so hideously burned that skin and flesh appeared to just slide away from his body. Thomas Bingham died a few hours later. At the trial, Waterer was eventually found not guilty of manslaughter.

dated back to the 18th century, including those at Boston (1730), Bourne (1735) and St Swithin's parish in Lincoln (1737). In most parishes, around 20% of parishioners were being relieved in one way or another, and hence a large part of each parish budget was being spent on looking after them; for example, at Billinghay, one year's expenditure on the poor came to £448, while only £39 was spent on the highways. It was against this desperate need for reform that the Poor Law Amendment Act of 1834 was passed. By the middle of 1837, Lincolnshire had been divided into 14 Poor Law Unions, each with their own workhouse, as shown in the table, *opposite*.

Quirk Alert: *Doubled-up Cross*
Deeping St James is home to a 19th century stone lock-up (shown below) which was used for housing local ne'er-do-wells found guilty of petty crime; they would be incarcerated in the lock-up overnight until appearing before the local magistrates the next morning. The lock-up first started functioning as such in 1819. However, before that it was actually the town's market cross, created during the reign of Edward III (1327-1377).

As we have already established, Lincolnshire's waterways had been pretty important dating all the way back to the 1st century when the Romans connected the Rivers Witham and Nene via the Carr Dyke, and also built the Fosse Dyke to connect Lincoln to Torksey on the River Trent – effectively Britain's first canal. By the mid-18th century, the growing demand for agricultural produce coupled with the birth of finance, meant that the need for major waterway development could be met. However, the first project of note in the pre-Industrial Revolution period occurred when an Act was passed in 1570 to make the River Welland navigable from Stamford to The Wash – although the work wasn't completed until between 1664 and 1673, at which point it became the longest locked waterway in the country. It was then another one hundred years or so before the waterway improvement revolution commenced in around 1760, and which lasted for around 70 years until the 1830s when the railways took over. The late 18th century saw a number of Acts of

Parliament passed, including Acts for the Witham Navigation (1762), the Louth Canal (1763), the Ancholme Navigation (1767), the Bourne Eau Navigation (1781), the Glen Navigation (1781), the Horncastle Navigation (1792), the Slea Navigation (1792), the Grantham Canal (1793), and the Stainforth and Keadby Canal (1793).

One of the earliest projects was the Louth Canal, which ran for 11 miles from the town of Louth in a north-easterly direction to Tetney at the mouth of the River Humber. The feasibility study was carried out as early as 1756, but the Act wasn't passed until 1763; building commenced in 1767 and the canal was completed and opened in 1770. The justification for the Act and subsequent construction was the prior cost of shipping goods over land to Saltfleetby, around 9 miles east of Louth. The Louth Canal was constructed under the supervision of first John Grundy Jr, and then James Hogard, and included a system of eight locks down the eastern slope of the Wolds, as well as a tidal lock at Tetney. Interestingly, six of the eight locks in the Wolds were constructed with sides consisting of four elliptical bays, a design that wasn't to be used on any other canal in Britain.

The Bourne Eau at Bourne, a 3.5 mile waterway that linked Bourne with the River Glen following an Act of Parliament in 1781.

The remains of a lock at Alvingham on the Louth Canal, built between 1767 and 1770 by John Grundy Jr and James Hogard.

A number of these Acts of Parliament were as much to improve drainage as they were to provide navigable waterways, and this was certainly the case with the River Ancholme. Great improvements had been made by Sir John Monson in the late 1630s when the river was straightened from Bishopbridge to Ferriby, but the watercourse soon fell into disrepair due to silting, sand-banks and weeds. The Act of 1767 was passed to improve both drainage and navigation, and work between 1767 and 1769 included the provision of a tidal lock at the mouth of the Ancholme at Ferriby.

Also implemented for both drainage and navigation reasons were the improvements made to the Bourne Eau and the River Glen. The Bourne Eau Act was passed in 1781, stating that both watercourses were to be made 30ft wide (9m) and 5ft deep (1.5m). Although not widely used commercially, Bourne certainly saw the construction of a wharf at Eastgate on the Bourne Eau in the early 19th century. In terms of construction, the Bourne Eau was a mere 3.5 miles long, running eastwards from the centre of Bourne to the River Glen. The Act of 1781 also appointed trustees, who were to scour and cleanse the River Glen, and could charge tolls to fund the operation. Once in use, the main inbound cargo was coal and groceries while the Bourne traders initially exported mainly corn and wool, destined for Boston, but by the 1790s had added timber bound for Spalding.

Two further Acts resulted in navigable waterways known as the Sleaford Navigation and the Horncastle Navigation. The Sleaford Navigation was a 12.5 mile (20.1 km) canalisation of the River Slea, and which ran in a south-westerly direction from its confluence with the River Witham, near Chapel Hill, to Sleaford via seven locks. The waterway came about as a result of an Act passed on 11th June 1792, and which resulted in the creation of The Company of Proprietors of the Sleaford Navigation. The waterway was opened in 1794. Meanwhile, the Horncastle Navigation was authorised by another Act of 1792, and ran for 11 miles, also from the River Witham near Dogdyke, but this time heading off in a roughly north-easterly direction to Horncastle via 12 locks and largely following the course of the River Bain. As the confluence of both watercourses with the River Witham lay only a mile or so apart, albeit heading off in totally opposite directions, the two companies negotiated to find an engineer who would

oversee both projects, and that man was William Cawley of Cheshire. However, although Cawley started work on the Horncastle Navigation in April 1793, workmanship was poor; for example, the lock at Tattershall collapsed when first filled with water. As a result, Cawley was dismissed in October 1793, to be followed by a series of other engineers, none of whom lasted for very long. Eventually, the engineer John Rennie was consulted and he advised against following the winding course of the River Bain, but instead, to construct a new and straighter cut from Dalderby to Horncastle. This meant that a new Act of Parliament was passed on 9th July 1800, and the Horncastle Navigation was finally completed and opened in 1802, having cost nearly four times the original estimate.

Of these twin waterways, the Sleaford Navigation was moderately prosperous, and saw dividends paid to shareholders in 1795, 1817, 1818 and 1824, while from 1826 onwards it became an annual event; indeed from 1836 to 1856, dividends ranged from five per cent to eight per cent. There were even plans to extend the waterway westwards to Wilsford, and also via a 16 mile (26km) route south-westwards to Grantham, although neither plan came to fruition. Eventually, the popularity of the waterway declined when the railways arrived

The tidal sluice at South Ferriby on the Ancholme Navigation. The first tidal lock here was built in the late 1760s following an Act of Parliament in 1767 to improve both the drainage and the navigation on the River Ancholme.

Further up the Ancholme Navigation at Brandy Wharf.

– in this case, the Grantham to Sleaford line which was opened in 1857. By contrast, the over-budget Horncastle Navigation didn't pay its first dividend until 1813, although profits gradually increased thereafter. In fact, by the early 1850s, the canal was carrying around 9,710 tons of coal to Horncastle, and around 5,420 tons of goods, including corn and wool, in the reverse direction. Alas, its success gradually took a nosedive after the mid-1850s due to the railways – although initially, when the Great Northern Railway opened a line from Lincoln to Boston in 1848, the canal actually saw an increase in use thanks to the GNR building a coal wharf at Dogdyke. However, the railway company then opened a branch line from Kirkstead to Horncastle via Woodhall Spa in 1854, in direct competition to the Horncastle Navigation, and the latter's fortunes declined dramatically thereafter. The final dividend was paid out in 1873.

Quirk Alert: *Ding-Dong!*

In the 18th century, James Rheson of Benington lived in one of the local almshouses. Just before he died, he claimed he had "nowt to leave", but did make a will leaving all of his worldly possessions to start a fund for a clock in the church tower. However, on his death, 1100 half-crowns were found in an old chest of Rheson's – and hence the church got its clock!

Both the Sleaford and Horncastle Navigations linked up with the Witham Navigation, by far the most important waterway in Lincolnshire, as when it was functioning properly, it linked the port of Boston on the east coast with the port of Torksey on the River Trent and, very importantly, doing so via Lincoln. From the medieval period to the 18th century, though, the waterway was affected by silting which restricted trade, despite the construction of a number of sluices, and by the 17th century, navigation on the Fosse Dyke section, in particular, was very difficult. However, the passing

of the 1762 Act resulted in significant improvements to both navigation and drainage. Construction began in April 1763, and the drainage element of the project was completed in 1768, having cost £42,000. This included the construction at Boston of what became known as the Grand Sluice and which was completed in 1766, its purpose to prevent flooding by the sea, maintaining river levels around Boston, and also scouring the channel below it. The Grand Sluice was a major construction project and consisted of three channels each 17ft (5.2m) wide, fitted with pointed gates on both sides, and a lock adjacent to the north bank, which could be used as an additional flood relief channel if required. When complete, the Grand Sluice maintained the height of water above Boston to approximately high tide level and its huge flood gates were built to cope with any tides above that level. As for the navigation work, this was completed by 1771 to a cost of £6,000, and included the deepening of the Brayford Pool alongside Lincoln which meant that river traffic could flow from The Haven to the Trent again. Also part of the navigation improvements was the creation of three locks at Barlings, Kirkstead and Stamp End.

The 1762 Act for the Witham Navigation also created the Witham Navigation Commissioners and the Witham Drainage General Commissioners, and it was the latter organisation that created the drainage network discussed in the previous chapter and which was known as the Witham Navigable Drains. This work transformed much of the surrounding countryside from fen to farming land.

Despite all of these improvements, there remained a sticking point in the navigation from Boston to Torksey, this being a narrow channel in Lincoln over which a medieval bridge known as the Glory Hole had been built and where tolls were still being charged – both by road and by boat. Rather than re-route the navigation, the channel was deepened underneath the bridge and the foundations reinforced, while the collection of tolls were also dropped – and which was more than recompensed by the tolls paid at the locks by the increase in traffic that the channel deepening brought. Within forty

One of the four locks at Boston known as The Grand Sluice, and which marks the start of the Witham Navigation.

The Brayford Pool at Lincoln, effectively Lincoln's port on the Witham Navigation.

Quirk Alert: *Pillars of the Earth*

In 1787, the lords of Yarborough started planting trees on their Brocklesby estate, and they have continued to plant trees there in their thousands ever since. Their first enterprise saw the planting of 40,000 trees, and by 1797, the annual number of planted trees reached 668,801. A record 680,451 were then planted in 1816, all of which meant that the first Earl of Yarborough, Charles Anderson-Pelham, planted 12,552,700 trees between 1787 and 1823. For this reason his son and later grandson erected a monument to record this feat and which became known as Pelham's Pillar. Built as a viewing tower to enable the earls to view their entire estate, the monument stands at 128ft high (39m). Much later when the 4th Earl of Yarborough died in 1936, he had planted nearly half of the total (back then) of over 30 million trees during his 60-year stewardship.

Meanwhile, the 92ft (30m) high Dunston Pillar was erected by Sir Francis Dashwood of Nocton Hall in 1751 as a beacon to guide travellers on crossing the heath to the south of Lincoln where highwaymen, including Dick Turpin, were known to operate. However, the large octagonal lantern at the top of the structure was struck by lightning and destroyed in 1808, so it was removed and replaced in 1810 by a statue of King George III to celebrate the King's Golden Jubilee. Sadly, the mason, John Wilson, fell to his death whilst erecting it. Then in 1940, the statue was also removed as it had become a danger to low flying aircraft from nearby RAF Coleby Grange and RAF Waddington. The statue can be found today in the grounds of Lincoln Castle.

Left: *The Grade II-listed Pelham's Pillar commemorates the 12.5 million trees planted on the Brocklesby estate by the 1st Earl of Yarborough.* PHOTOGRAPH: © DAVID WRIGHT.
Right: *Also Grade II listed is Dunston Pillar. Six miles south of Lincoln, it was erected by Sir Francis Dashwood in 1751 as a beacon to aid travellers crossing the heath.* PHOTOGRAPH: SHAYNE WARD.

years, though, the Witham Navigation was again in need of improvement. A new Act of Parliament was passed in 1808, covering £70,000 for navigation improvements and £30,000 for drainage improvements. As a result, two new locks were built at Stamp End and Bardney, and a new channel was also cut near to Fiskerton. In terms of profits, tolls on the Witham Navigation had gradually increased along with the improvements, and the £263 raised in 1763-4 had increased to £898 by 1790. By 1819, income exceeded £4,100 for the six months from March to September, and a five per cent dividend was paid in the following year. By this stage, the river was hosting the first steam packet boat, named *Witham*, and built by Shuttleworth and Robinson, whose yard was on Sincil Dyke to the south of Lincoln, while in 1829, William Pool of Lincoln had introduced a new and faster type of paddle steamer.

Of course, by this stage the heydays of the canal were numbered, although it was 1846 before the railways reached Lincolnshire, when the Midland Railway line from Nottingham to Lincoln was opened. However, it was the Great Northern Railway (GNR) who bought out the Witham Navigation in 1848, at which point the GNR leased the waterway back to the proprietors for 999 years for a payment of £10,545 per year – a figure which represented the average profits for the previous three years, plus five per cent. The GNR then opened their railway from Lincoln to Boston on 17th October 1848, and which ran along the eastern bank of the river. Of course, the two public travel services couldn't co-exist profitably, particularly since most of the railway stations were located near to Witham Navigation landing stages used by the steamboats; indeed the GNR even offered fourth-class carriages in

1850, with fares set at a halfpenny per mile. The navigation stood no chance, and by 1863, all passenger steamboats had ceased operation. Freight traffic did continue, but the difference in tonnage passing through the Grand Sluice between 1847 and 1857 – from 19,535 tons down to 3,780 tons – tells its own story. Nevertheless, the railway company still had to maintain the river, and in 1871, at the request of the drainage commissioners, the GNR spent £5,000 on making the lock at Bardney 5ft (1.5m) deeper. A century later, the waterways were nationalised following the Transport Act 1962, initially becoming the responsibility of British Waterways, while since 2012, they have been managed by the Canal & River Trust.

Three other canals created following Acts of Parliament in 1793 were the Grantham Canal (built between 1793 and 1797), the Caistor Canal (built between 1793 and 1798), and the Stainforth and Keadby Canal (built between 1793 and 1802). The Grantham Canal ran for 33 miles from Grantham to West Bridgford where it joined the River Trent; prior to its build, goods were barged up the Trent to Newark and then taken by packhorse and cart down the Great North Road to Grantham. The Grantham Canal was also another waterway which was bought by a railway company, this time the Ambergate Railway Company in 1854, and which subsequently fell into disrepair before eventually closing in 1936. Since the 1970s, the Grantham Canal has been partly restored with two stretches now navigable to small vessels. As for the Caistor Canal, this waterway ran for 4 miles (6.4km) from the River Ancholme near South Kelsey to Moortown, via six locks – and therefore ended up 3.5 miles (5.6km) short of Caistor, its original chosen destination, due to financial reasons. The canal had fallen into disuse by the 1850s, and today, it is no longer navigable, but is maintained by the Environments Agency as an important drainage channel. Finally, the Stainforth and Keadby Canal ran from Bramwith on the River Don Navigation in South Yorkshire to Keadby on the River Trent, via Stainforth, Thorne and Ealand. It was yet another canal bought by a railway company in the late 1840s, but later in 1895, it became part of the Sheffield and South Yorkshire Navigation, a company whose aim was to wrest several canals from railway control. However, the operation of this particular waterway was always impeded by the relatively small size of Keadby Lock, although vessels longer than the lock could pass through when the river was level with the canal and *both* sets of gates could be opened!

The Grantham Canal around 4 miles to the west of Grantham. The canal was built between 1793 and 1797.

> ## Quirk Alert: *The Staunchkeeper*
> *Water levels in the Horncastle Navigation were controlled by a sluice or staunch near the point at which the River Bain joined the River Waring. Adjustment of the sluice was controlled manually by the Staunchkeeper who manned a cottage which had been built next to the sluice specifically for this purpose, as adjustment of the sluice was vital in times of drought or flood.*

Goodnow Swing Bridge on the Stainforth and Keadby Canal.

Despite all of these waterways improving transportation in Lincolnshire, they didn't especially link the county to the rest of England. However, Lincolnshire's relative isolation most certainly came to an end with the arrival of the railways in the late 1840s. Within a decade, main lines were joined by branch lines and for the first time in history, Lincolnshire folk could be elsewhere within the country in hours, a truly revolutionary phenomenon. Furthermore, the railways brought prosperity to Lincolnshire's ports which expanded rapidly, and the county began to develop a substantial tourism industry, too; for the first time in centuries, Lincolnshire was important again both nationally and internationally.

As mentioned earlier, the first railway to reach Lincolnshire was the Midland Railway's line from Nottingham to Lincoln, completed in 1846, while they followed that up two years later by linking

Peterborough to Stamford. However, during those two years, the real battle was being fought to claim the first London to York railway, and whichever company won would probably take a different route through Lincolnshire. First of the main players was the London & York Railway (L&YR), and which became known as the Great Northern Railway (GNR) following the London & York Railway Act of 1846. But on 17th April 1844, and whilst still known as the L&YR, their first proposal was for a line from London to York, via Hitchin, Biggleswade, Huntingdon, Stamford, Grantham, Newark, Gainsborough and Doncaster; joining the Leeds and Selby, and York and North Midland Railways near South Milford, with branch lines to Bedford and Lincoln, and a junction with the

> ## Quirk Alert: *Quotes of the Day*
> *The emerging importance of Lincolnshire thanks to the railway revolution is nicely encapsulated by a statement issued by a committee established in Lincoln in 1835, which was part of the race to lay the first London to York railway line: "Railway transport appears destined to restore to the Eastern side of the island some of the advantages which it lost, when the discovery of America and other causes turned the current of commerce to the Western shores of Great Britain."*
>
> *Contrast that with Colonel Charles de Laet Waldo Sibthorpe, Tory MP for Lincoln from 1826 to 1855, whose country seat at Canwick overlooked the Witham Gap at Lincoln through which prospective railways were looking to be routed. Regarding the railways, he said: "they are public frauds and private robbers whose nefarious schemes will collapse, and the old and happy mode of travelling the turnpike roads, in chaises, carriages and stage, will be restored".*

Manchester and Sheffield Railway. So this was a proposal that would only benefit the far west of Lincolnshire.

The second of the main players was the Direct Northern Railway, and their proposal was slightly further east, running up through Peterborough and passing through Doddington around 5 miles west of Lincoln before exiting the county at Gainsborough and travelling on to Doncaster and then York. Meanwhile the third route proposed by the Eastern Counties Railway would have been further east again, entering the county from Wisbech in the south-east heading in a north-westerly direction to cut through the Witham gap at Lincoln and again exiting at Gainsborough.

One drawback of the railway revolution was that the cost of finance was high, so the majority of major railway decisions were not made by Lincolnshire folk, as they had largely been with the canals, but by companies run from other parts of the country. That wasn't the case with the third of the three candidates, though, as the Eastern Counties Railway was supported by Charles Chaplin of Blankney, Henry Handley of Culverthorpe, and George Hussey Packe of Caythorpe. Of course, there were still others who propounded a London-to-York route much further west, like George Hudson, the "Railway King", who had interests in the Midlands and therefore proposed a route via Leicester and Derby.

In the meantime, the L&YR had included a modification to their proposal in late 1844, which happily for Lincolnshire included a loop line from Peterborough to Bawtry, via Spalding, Boston and Lincoln. When put to Parliament, this proposal passed its second reading in the Commons despite fierce opposition from the London and Birmingham Railway, the Midland Railway and the Direct Northern Railway, who at that time had a monopoly of the London to Leeds and York traffic. Nevertheless, 1845 saw further deliberations in Parliament, with plenty of opposition, largely led by George Hudson with the support of Robert Stephenson, both of whom were now supporting the Eastern Counties Railway proposal. The result was that the London and York bill, although not defeated, failed by running out of time. Eventually in 1846, though, an amalgamation contract was signed by the L&YR with the Direct Northern Railway where it was agreed their funds would be combined to complete the London and York line. The London and York bill finally received Royal assent on 26th June 1846 as The Great Northern Railway Act, 1846, and the Great Northern Railway was born. The Act granted the powers to construct the main line and loop lines, but also to various allied companies to make lines from Boston to Grimsby and Stamford to Spalding – although the latter was never built.

The new railway lines and branch lines then came thick and fast. The GNR's loop line through Lincolnshire was actually built first in 1846, as the ease of construction over the flat fens promised an earlier return on investment, while the GNR route through Grantham, Newark and Retford wasn't completed until 1852. In between those dates, the East Lincolnshire Railway connected Boston to Louth and Grimsby and on to New Holland, in 1848, and Lincoln was connected to Gainsborough in 1849. Further branch lines were laid in the south of the county, mainly by the GNR, while north Lincolnshire was mostly developed by the Manchester, Sheffield and Lincolnshire Railway (MSLR) which later became the Great Central Railway in 1897. Indeed, by 1849, the latter company had connected Retford on the GNR with Gainsborough, Lincoln, Market Rasen and Brigg in a large loop, with another branch heading off to Grimsby and Cleethorpes where it met the East Lincolnshire Railway's line coming up from Louth.

Quirk Alert: *Bell's End*

Before 1834, Lincoln Cathedral was the only church in the country with two separate bell peals – one from the 13 bells in St Hugh's, the south-west tower, and the other from the 6 bells of the central tower. However, the single bell in the third tower – St Mary's, the north-west tower – and which sounded the curfew at 8 o'clock had cracked. Known as Great Tom, it had been sounding the curfew for 300 years, but in 1834, it was taken down and along with the six bells of the central tower, known as the Lady Bells, was re-cast into a new Great Tom that was six feet high and weighed over 5 tons and which has hung in the central tower ever since.

The Lincolnshire place that perhaps benefited the most from the railways was Grimsby. Back in May 1796, an Act of Parliament known as the Grimsby Haven Act had seen the creation of the Grimsby Haven Company. Its purpose was to widen and deepen what was known as The Haven and to generally improve the port of Grimsby. As a result, the fortunes of the port had already revived during the early 19th century, with the port importing iron, timber, wheat, hemp and flax. By the 1840s, this increase in trade required an expansion of the docks, and this was facilitated by The Grimsby Docks Act of 1845. Three years later, the railways arrived and that was when Grimsby's expansion began to accelerate, as it now had a fast and convenient transport network on tap to oil the logistical wheels of the port's ever-increasing trade. Coal mined in South Yorkshire and Derbyshire was brought by rail and exported through Grimsby, while the GNR link direct to London and the Billingsgate Fish Market allowed for fresh Grimsby fish to gain national acclaim. The town's iconic Dock Tower was completed in 1851, followed by the Royal Dock in 1852. But when No.1 Fish Dock was completed in 1856, the town was set up to become a centre for the development of the commercial fishing industry; No.2 Fish Dock followed in 1877, while Alexandra Dock and Union Dock were completed in 1879.

The Dock Tower at Grimsby was built in 1851 a couple of years after the railways arrived in the town. Thereafter, the number of vessels using Grimsby Docks increased from around 20 to 605 by 1894. The tower is 309ft high, a height that is somewhat emphasised when focusing on the smaller six-storey tower to the left, which under normal circumstances, would appear quite high!

During this period, the fishing fleet was greatly expanded. Prior to the railways arriving, Grimsby only had a local fishing industry, but the number of vessels began to increase in the late 1850s, rising from just 22 in 1857 to 112 by 1863, 396 by 1881 and 605 by 1894. The first two legitimate steam trawlers ever built in Great Britain were also based in Grimsby in the second half of the 19th century. By 1880, the annual haul of fish was 45,000 tons, while by 1912 it had risen to 193,000 tons. Large numbers of fishermen joined Grimsby's fleet from the South East and Devon, with another 40% of

newcomers arriving from Barking in East London, and other Thames-side towns, while by 1900, a staggering one tenth of all fish consumed in the United Kingdom had been transported via Grimsby's docks.

The other Lincolnshire town that expanded rapidly following the arrival of the railways was Scunthorpe, mainly off the back of its ironstone and later steel industry. The ironstone processed at Scunthorpe in the mid-19th century was most needed in Yorkshire as part of the smelting process, and a railway was custom-built on both sides of the Trent to transfer the stone from the Scunthorpe quarries. On the eastern side, the mining companies laid down a track to meet another on the west side of the Trent built by the South Yorkshire Railway Company. A bridge was then built over the river in 1866 to link the two.

However, when the Trent Iron Works opened at Scunthorpe in 1864, followed by a furnace at Fordingham (now also part of Scunthorpe), the town began processing its own iron, and it was the finished product rather than the raw material that was shipped out after that point. Indeed, by 1880, there were 21 furnaces in the Scunthorpe area. Such expansion inevitably meant a rapid increase in population, as houses were built to accommodate the increasing number of workers, and between the censuses of 1851 and 1901, Frodingham's population rose from 113 to 1,396, while Scunthorpe's rose from 303 to 6,750.

There were also quarries at the opposite end of the county, mainly to the south-west of Grantham and which were able to tap into the main London to York line via a number of short, industry-funded branch lines. In fact, the Great Northern Railway even built their own line from Honington to Lincoln in 1867, which served a number of quarries between Leadenham and Grantham, and thus also provided Lincoln with its first direct line to London.

The tourism industry also blossomed in the second half of the 19th century, again thanks to the railways. Prior to the 1850s, there were a few hotels and inns on the Lincolnshire coast at Cleethorpes, Ingoldmells, Mablethorpe, Saltfleetby, Skegness and Sutton on Sea,

The Bass Maltings at Sleaford were built between 1901 and 1907 alongside the railway, and remained in use until the 1960s. They are the largest group of malt houses in England, and are Grade II listed.

Almshouses were originally built at Sleaford in 1636 by Robert Carre, but the above are actually a rebuild of the originals by Charles Kirk, in 1857.

The Italian Garden and Orangery at Belton House were designed by Jeffry Wyatville in the early 19th century.

Stamford Railway Station was opened on 20th March 1848 when it was on the Midland Railway's Syston and Peterborough Railway.

but they weren't what could be termed holiday resorts. These places were also only frequented on a recreational basis by the relatively wealthy, plus those seeking to take advantage of the restorative nature of sea-bathing and the fresh east-coast air. Of course, the railways changed all that. Branch lines were soon constructed from the GNR and MSLR main lines, with one added to Cleethorpes in 1863, and which was followed by Skegness (1873), Mablethorpe (1877) and Sutton on Sea (1886). Working class people from the Midlands and South Yorkshire flocked to these resorts at a time when Bank Holiday's first appeared, and which were complemented by reduced working hours and, for many, an annual week's holiday. Indeed, in the year that the branch line to Cleethorpes opened, the town of just 1,400 inhabitants was swamped by 30,000 visitors! Naturally, over time, these resorts also saw their populations climb dramatically. Skegness went from a quiet rural backwater of 134 people in 1801, to 2,140 by 1901. The seaside resort was considerably helped in the 1870s by its landowner, the Earl of Scarbrough. He made major improvements to the town during this decade, building new streets and hundreds of new houses, while he was also largely responsible for the build of the pier which cost £20,840, as well as the Steamboat Company, the baths, the cricket ground and the Pleasure Gardens. As for the pier, when it was built in 1881, it was the fourth largest in England at that time, at 614 yards (562m) long. Three years later on August Bank Holiday, it is recorded that the town had over 20,000 day-trippers, so many that the last train didn't leave until 02:00 a.m. the following morning.

Quite naturally, industrial sites began to spring up alongside Lincolnshire railways. At Boston, the GNR even had its engineering offices and workshops here until they were moved to Doncaster in 1853, while at Lincoln, there were considerable railway sidings to the south of the city. Even a small station like the one at Spilsby, linked by a 5 mile branch line from the Boston to Cleethorpes line, had sidings with coal depots, livestock pens and warehouses. As for the waterways, they

didn't suffer as much in Lincolnshire as they did in other counties where many became completely redundant; Lincolnshire's waterways survived longer because many of them still had a role to play in terms of drainage. That didn't stop railway companies from buying up canal companies, though – primarily to then remove them as a competitor to their own companies! It is no surprise to learn, therefore, that in 1848, the Witham Navigation and the Fosse Dyke saw 278,154 tons carried on the combined waterways, but by 1868, this had fallen to 85,134 tons.

Probably the most significant impact of industrialisation throughout the 19th century was the impact upon population in Lincolnshire's largest towns. Between 1801 and 1901, the population of the county increased from 208,624 to 407,222, an increase of 95.19%. However, the county increase was nothing compared to some of the population percentage increases experienced in the towns, as is highlighted by the tables shown opposite.

The statistics are worth some studying – starting with Scunthorpe. The final table reveals that Scunthorpe is Lincolnshire's third largest settlement today, but back in 1801 (first table), it was a small village of only 169 people. Of course, it was the iron and steel industries that brought people flocking to the town between 1851 and 1901 and which brought about that 2,128% increase between those dates (top right table), and a 3,894% increase from 1801 to 1901 (bottom right). And incidentally, if you compared the 1801 population with the 2011 population, you're talking an astronomical 38,458% increase! By the Second World War, Scunthorpe was producing 14 per cent of the country's pig iron and 10 per cent of its steel. The town received its Charter of Incorporation as the Borough of Scunthorpe in 1936 when its population was around 38,000.

The other place that is regularly "hot" is Grimsby. Only a small fishing town in 1801, it grew in similar proportions between 1801 and 1851 (by 481%) and between 1851 and 1901 (by 316%) as the town developed into Britain's premier deep sea fishing port. Not following the same pattern was Boston. The town saw a 155% population increase between 1801 and 1851, but only a 7% increase over the next fifty years. A mirror image of Grimsby, this once hugely important British port became something of a backwater, as the west and south coast ports took over along with London. Those two population increases also tell the tale of successful engineering in the first half of the 19th century. For example, William Howden built the first Lincolnshire steam engine at Boston in 1827, while William Webb Tuxford established the Boston and Skirbeck Iron Works building a wide range of agricultural machinery, such as threshing machines, as well as portable steam engines which were exported to the former Hanseatic comrades of Scandinavia and eastern Europe, as well as to distant markets in Australia. Alas, Boston's position, far from the raw materials of coal, iron and steel, brought an end to the town's expansion in the second half of the 19th century, symbolised by the closure of Tuxford's iron works in the 1880s.

Finally, it is also worth drawing attention to the "cold" cells in the top right table (i.e. the negative percentages). These places are "cold" because they either didn't increase their populations by a deal between 1851 and 1901 or, as in the case of Caistor, Horncastle, Louth and Stamford, they actually *decreased* in numbers – a factor which clearly emphasises those places where the Industrial Revolution *didn't* have a big impact. It is therefore no coincidence that these were more rural-oriented towns, while the rural population as a whole was symbolised by the fact that 79% of rural parishes had declining populations during this period. Another irony was that much of the new 19th century labour-saving farm machinery, which was instrumental in leading people from rural villages into the towns to look for work, was actually being manufactured in the towns, too.

Lincolnshire Towns –
Population Statistics – 1801-2011

#	Town	Pop 1801*
1	Lincoln	7,193
2	Boston	5,926
3	Gainsborough	4,506
4	Grantham	4,288
5	Louth	4,258
6	Stamford	4,022
7	Spalding	3,296
8	Horncastle	2,015
9	Bourne	1,664
10	Sleaford	1,596
11	Grimsby	1,524
12	Alford	1,040
13	Caistor	1,022
14	Scunthorpe	169

#	Town	Population 1801	1851*	% Diff
1	Lincoln	7,193	17,533	144%
2	Boston	5,926	15,132	155%
3	Grantham	4,288	10,870	153%
4	Louth	4,258	10,553	148%
5	Grimsby	1,524	8,860	481%
6	Spalding	3,296	8,829	168%
7	Stamford	4,022	7,332	82%
8	Gainsborough	4,506	7,261	61%
9	Horncastle	2,015	5,017	149%
10	Bourne	1,664	3,717	123%
11	Sleaford	1,596	3,539	122%
12	Caistor	1,022	2,407	136%
13	Alford	1,040	2,262	118%
14	Scunthorpe	169	303	79%

#	Town	Population 1851	1901*	% Diff
1	Lincoln	17,533	48,268	175%
2	Grimsby	8,860	36,857	316%
3	Gainsborough	7,261	17,740	144%
4	Grantham	10,870	16,467	51%
5	Boston	15,132	16,174	7%
6	Louth	10,553	9,619	-9%
7	Spalding	8,829	9,381	6%
8	Stamford	7,332	7,218	-2%
9	Scunthorpe	303	6,750	2128%
10	Bourne	3,717	4,361	17%
11	Horncastle	5,017	4,118	-18%
12	Sleaford	3,539	3,934	11%
13	Alford	2,262	2,478	10%
14	Caistor	2,407	1,767	-27%

#	Town	Population 1801	1901*	% Diff
1	Lincoln	7,193	48,268	571%
2	Grimsby	1,524	36,857	2318%
3	Gainsbor'gh	4,506	17,740	294%
4	Grantham	4,288	16,467	284%
5	Boston	5,926	16,174	173%
6	Louth	4,258	9,619	126%
7	Spalding	3,296	9,381	185%
8	Stamford	4,022	7,218	79%
9	Scunthorpe	169	6,750	3894%
10	Bourne	1,664	4,361	162%
11	Horncastle	2,015	4,118	104%
12	Sleaford	1,596	3,934	146%
13	Alford	1,040	2,478	138%
14	Caistor	1,022	1,767	73%

#	Town	Population 1901	2011*	% Diff
1	Lincoln	48,268	119,541	148%
2	Grimsby	36,857	88,243	139%
3	Scunthorpe	6,750	65,163	865%
4	Grantham	16,467	41,998	155%
5	Boston	16,174	41,430	156%
6	Spalding	9,381	28,722	206%
7	Gainsbor'gh	17,740	20,842	17%
8	Stamford	7,218	19,701	173%
9	Sleaford	3,934	17,671	349%
10	Louth	9,619	16,419	71%
11	Bourne	4,361	13,961	220%
12	Horncastle	4,118	6,815	65%
13	Alford	2,478	3,459	40%
14	Caistor	1,767	2,674	51%

#	Town	Pop 2011*
1	Lincoln	119,541
2	Grimsby	88,243
3	Scunthorpe	65,163
4	Grantham	41,998
5	Boston	41,430
6	Spalding	28,722
7	Gainsbor'gh	20,842
8	Stamford	19,701
9	Sleaford	17,671
10	Louth	16,419
11	Bourne	13,961
12	Horncastle	6,815
13	Alford	3,459
14	Caistor	2,674

* Denotes sort field

Moving over to western Lincolnshire, and Gainsborough, Lincoln and Grantham all grew their populations significantly during the 19th century, and were each centres for agricultural engineering which proved to be particularly lucrative during the boom in British farming between 1860 and 1875. A port of the River Trent, 19th century Gainsborough was also home to Smiths of Gainsborough, who were building vessels of up to 800 tons, while Marshall's Engineering was opened in 1848 and became a major employer in the town making steam engines and agricultural machinery. In 1856, Marshall's moved to a new 28 acre site alongside the railway, where raw materials were imported from Sheffield, and by 1900, they were employing 3,600 workers. Meanwhile, at Grantham, Richard Hornsby's dominated local employment in a similar way, manufacturing steam engines and agricultural machinery; indeed, Hornsby's steam engine won first prize at the Great Exhibition of 1851, with international prizes following. By 1854, Hornsby's were operating 34 furnaces, with their agricultural products including steam-powered threshing machines and a self-binding harvester. By the end of the 19th century, Hornsby's had diversified into machinery used in the South African gold mines, electric generators and, after 1891, the oil-powered internal combustion engine. By 1905, Hornsby's were employing 2,000 workmen, while in 1877, another large employer, the Phoenix Iron Works was also established in Grantham by the Hampstead family – again, producing steam engines and agricultural machinery.

However, the really big engineering hitters of the 19th century belonged to the county town. By 1856, *White's Directory* was listing six iron founders, including Robey and Scott, Proctor and Burton, and William Foster. Of these, Robert Robey had established his factory in 1854 and by 1864 employed 114 people, producing the ubiquitous portable steam engines and threshing machines, but later adding traction engines and steam ploughs that were exported as far afield as Australia and South America. Also producing steam engines and threshing machines, as well as traction engines and steam tractors, was William Foster whose business was founded in 1851 and which had a workforce of 44 by 1861.

The 1856 *White's Directory* also listed Clayton Shuttleworth & Co at their Stamp End Iron Works. The partnership between Nathaniel Clayton and his brother-in-law, Joseph Shuttleworth, was formed in 1842, merging Clayton's foundry with Shuttleworth's boat-building business, and which happened to be located next door to each other. In partnership, they initially produced iron bridges, pipes (for example, for the Boston Water Works), and undertook a lot of the railway work that was beginning to come Lincolnshire's way in the late 1840s. By 1848, though, they were also producing – yep, you've guessed it – steam engines and threshing machines – and already had a workforce of 100 people. Like Hornsby's of Grantham, they also exhibited at the Great Exhibition

Warehouses at Stamp End on the Witham Navigation through Lincoln. A few yards further east I was hoping to snap the premises of former 19th century engineering giant, Clayton & Shuttleworth – only to find it in the process of being dismantled with just the "AND SHUTTLEWORTH LTD" half surviving!

Grantham Town Hall was built between 1867 and 1869.

of 1851, a move that probably generated lots of business as their workforce had increased six-fold by 1854. Thereafter, the business expanded into Europe with branches opening in Krakow, Prague and Vienna, while their products were also sold to Australia and South America as well as to Canada and Egypt amongst others. By 1870, the Clayton Shuttleworth workforce had expanded to 1,200, and they were a real international player, producing 1,000 steam engines and 900 threshing machines per year.

Meanwhile, the earlier-mentioned firm belonging to James Toyne Proctor and John Burton were joined in partnership by Joseph Ruston in 1849, with the latter becoming the main owner by 1865. By 1870, Ruston was building locomotives for the Great Eastern Railway, along with steam excavators, steam shovels, road rollers and tractors, and by the end of the 19th century, his site occupied 52 acres.

Of course, the places that saw huge population increases required a massive demand for new housing and, rather handily, brick-making became a key industry throughout Lincolnshire – although brick works weren't limited to the towns; a number of villages had them, too. In fact during the mid-1820s, there were only 35 brick and tile works in Lincolnshire, but this number had risen to 187 by the 1880s. Examples of areas where 19th century housing proliferated included the Spittlegate area of Grantham, where rows of houses for the employees of Hornsby Engineering saw the population of Spittlegate rise from 500 in 1801 to 6,500 a century later. Inevitably, though, it was in Lincoln where the largest demand for houses occurred, mainly to the south of the city in the parishes of St Botolph, St Peter-at-Gowts and St Mary-le-Wigford, with populations increasing by 497, 529 and 401 per cent respectively, and with each area marked by many arrays of terraced housing. The industrial sites also expanded the city southwards, as well as eastwards along the north bank of the River Witham, and westwards to the north of the Brayford Pool, and would have been one of very few Lincolnshire sights that befits the stereotypical vision of 19th century industrial Britain, with rows of tall, belching chimneys.

One of the effects of the huge population changes was that people lived in squalor, and disease, and epidemics were rife – although to a lesser extent in Lincolnshire compared with the rest of the Midlands. Conditions at work were little better, where children often worked 72-hour weeks from as young as five. However, there were also huge advancements in town amenities. Sleaford's streets were paved and a drainage system was implemented between 1829 and 1831, with gas street lamps following in 1839 and other buildings appearing such as the new town hall. Louth's streets were paved and lit following an Act of Parliament in 1826, while a Corn Exchange was built there in 1853; indeed corn exchanges were built in a number of Lincolnshire towns including those at Spalding (1856) and Stamford (1857).

Of the other Lincolnshire towns that didn't see such dramatic population increases, there were still foundries, but obviously not on the scale of Gainsborough, Grantham and Lincoln. At Louth, for example, three smaller scale foundries existed in the second half of the 19th century: Aswell's Iron Works, the Newmarket Iron Works and Joseph Morton's iron foundry, all of which were producing a wide range of domestic and agricultural machines and implements.

NINETEENTH CENTURY LINCOLNSHIRE WINDMILLS

Above, left: *The Grade I-listed Maud Foster Windmill at Skirbeck in Boston is a seven-storey, five-sail windmill that was built in 1819. Standing at 80ft tall (24m), it is one of the largest operating windmills in Britain.*

Above, centre left: *The Grade I-listed Heckington Windmill was built in 1830 and is the only eight-sailed tower windmill in Britain with its sails still intact.*

Above, centre right: *This windmill at Moulton claims to be Britain's tallest windmill at 100ft. It was built in 1822.*

Above, right: *The Grade I-listed, seven-storeyed, five-sailed Alford Windmill at Alford is also still operational. It was originally built in 1837 by the well-known millwright, John Oxley.*

Far left: *Dobson's Windmill, another Grade I-listed windmill at Burgh-le-Marsh. This five-sailed windmill was built in 1813, again by the Oxley's of Alford, and is unusual owing to the fact that its sails rotate in a clockwise direction.*

Left: *Sibsey Trader Mill, another Grade I-listed windmill this time in Sibsey around 5 miles north of Boston. This six-storey six-sailed windmill was first built in 1877.*

The Market Place at Market Deeping. The town has held a market charter since at least 1220.

Market Deeping Town Hall, built in 1835.

Sleaford was also home to companies owned by William Henry Smith and John Henry Payne, with the former manufacturing steam ploughs and the latter running a brass and iron foundry. However, the majority of these Lincolnshire towns remained rural at heart.

Prior to the 19th century, many drainage schemes were powered by windmills. However, because of the effectiveness of the drainage schemes, the level of the Fens continued to drop, and wind power just wasn't powerful enough to deal with it – particularly when wet weather was followed by a calm spell without wind. Fortunately, by the mid-19th century a prolifera-

tion of steam-powered drainage engines had been successfully deployed. These new engines gradually began to replace the windmills and thus resulted in numerous red-brick drainage buildings with tall chimneys appearing around the county.

Finally, sea defences were also improved during the 19th century, with a sea wall built at Skegness in 1878 and another at Cleethorpes in 1902. Groynes were constructed along the coast commencing in the 1860s, their aim to halt the natural movement of the beaches southwards by interrupting water-flow and limiting the movement of sediment.

This Grade II-listed drinking fountain in Sleaford market place was erected in 1874 by Charles Kirk in memory of the 6th Earl and 2nd Marquis of Bristol.

Quirk Alert: *A Trifling Inconvenience*
In 1862, Nocton church was rebuilt in memory of Viscount Goderich, briefly English Prime Minister from 31st August 1827 until 21st January 1828, and also known as the Earl of Ripon. Incredibly, though, the previous church had been pulled down because the local landowner at Nocton Hall, George Hobart, and father-in-law of Viscount Goderich, had considered the church to be too near to his hall for his liking!

Quirk Alert: *R.E.C.T.O.R.*
Apart from the first two years of the 19th century, Barrowby was served by only two vicars – these being Jonathan Kendal (1802-1849) and George Earle Welby (1849-1900). However, these two gentlemen were surpassed by the successive rectors of Navenby a century earlier, with Simon Every holding the post from 1703 to 1753 and Dearing Jones from 1753 until his death in 1804. Hence the four of them were sequentially incumbent from 1703 to 1900! This quartet of rectors is also challenged by a trio from Saltfleetby St Peter (1744-1905), these being Joseph Smith (1744-1802), John Bond (1802-1856) and William Richard Watson (1856-1905). Given the title of this Quirk Alert and the second of these three rectors, they could hardly have been left out, could they?

From the Late Victorians to Present Day

The end of the 19th century saw the birth of modern local government, which was introduced following the Local Government Act 1888. This was the Act which introduced county councils and county boroughs in England and Wales, alongside administrative counties based on the boundaries of their historic county counterparts. However, in the case of Lincolnshire, matters were slightly different, and the county was divided into *three* administrative counties that became known as the Parts of Lindsey to the north of the county, the Parts of Kesteven to the south-west and the Parts of Holland to the south-east. Each of the Parts had their own county council, plus their own county town. So whereas Lincoln had traditionally been the county town of Lincolnshire up until 1889, between 1889 and 1974, it was now only the county town of Lindsey; Sleaford became the county town of Kesteven and Boston the county town of Holland. Just to be clear, though, the Local Government Act 1888 did *not* abolish or alter the historic counties and went to great lengths to distinguish between historic and administrative counties, making it clear that the two were distinct entities and that the former still existed. The name "Lincolnshire" also survived over the next 85 years (1889-1974), because the proper title for each of the Parts was prefixed by the historic county name. So the full title of Lindsey, for example, was "the administrative county of Lincolnshire, Parts of Lindsey". As for Lincoln, the town was created as a county borough in 1889, thus having control over its own local services and therefore having its independence from the county council. Grimsby followed in 1891, with the county borough named as Great Grimsby as it also covered outlying areas as well as the town.

Of course, the separate entities of Lindsey, Kesteven and Holland were certainly not a new concept in 1889, as they were something of a throwback to both the former 6th century Anglo-Saxon Kingdom of Lindsey, and the later 10th century subdivisions that had the same names as their late 19th century counterparts and largely the same areas, too. As for the three administrative counties (the Parts), they remained in place for 85 years until the 1st April 1974 when the Local Government Act 1972 was implemented – but more on that a little later.

The early 20th century saw the railway revolution of the 19th century joined by a revolution on the roads, and

This monument in the market square at Caistor celebrates the 60th year of the reign of Queen Victoria in 1897.

which started with motor buses. One of the first services offered in 1900 was in Mablethorpe. It was run by the Barton Bus Company, who later moved to Nottingham in 1908 offering services to the Lincolnshire coast, and did so until their eventual demise in 1989. By 1906, Grimsby was offering several services to surrounding villages, the first of which was a route to Caistor – a town that was unusual, as it wasn't connected to the railway network. This was followed by routes to Louth, North Somercotes and Woodhall Spa. Then in 1913, Appleby's began operations out of Louth, a company which is still going strong today, while the 1920s saw Lincoln-based The Silver Queen Company operating in central Lincolnshire and Scunthorpe-based Enterprise and Silver Dawn offering routes all over North Lincolnshire. The Silver Queen Company changed its name to the Lincolnshire Road Car Company in 1927 and went on to dominate the entire county.

This revolution on the roads made it possible for Billy Butlin to open his first holiday camp at Ingoldmells in 1936, with the thousands of holidaymakers arriving at Skegness Station able to hop on a bus for the short journey up the coast. The first significant foundation for his holiday camp occurred in 1927 when Butlin leased a stretch of land from the Earl of Scarbrough in Skegness. Here, he built up an amusement park which included attractions such as a hoopla, a tower slide, a haunted house and a scenic railway, while the following year, Butlin secured an exclusive licence to sell dodgem cars in Europe and promptly set up the first dodgems in Britain at his park at Skegness. By 1930, Butlin had added a zoo to the Skegness amusement park and opened another park in Mablethorpe. However, construction on his first proper holiday camp began in September 1935 at Ingoldmells. His plans were to accommodate around 1,000 people in 600 chalets with electricity, running water, 250 bathrooms, dining and recreational halls. When built, the camp cost £100,000, and also included a theatre, a boating lake, a swimming pool, tennis courts, cricket pitches, bowling greens, putting greens and a gymnasium. The Ingoldmells camp was formally opened by Amy Johnson on 11th April 1936. At around the same time, Butlin had put an advert in the *Daily Express*, inviting people to book for a week's holiday where they would get three meals a day and free entertainment, for anywhere between 35 shillings and £3, depending upon the time of year. Shortly afterwards, the concept of the Redcoats was born at Ingoldmells and the rest is history.

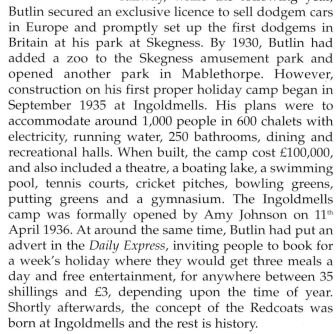

An age-old scene on the golden sands at Skegness. It was a couple of miles further up the coast at Ingoldmells that Billy Butlin opened his first holiday camp in 1936.

The clock tower at Skegness was built in 1898 to mark Queen Victoria's Diamond Jubilee of the previous year.

Quirk Alert:
Chalet Made (in Ingoldmells)
One of Billy Butlin's original 1936 chalet's still survives at his Ingoldmells holiday camp. It is also Grade II listed in recognition of its historical importance, it being one of around 600 that were built at the camp between 1935 and 1936 – and thus part of the first holiday camp built in Britain.

One place that grew rapidly in the early 20th century was Immingham. At the turn of the century, it was a relatively unpopulated and under-developed village, but the development of a deep sea port there, partly funded by the Great Central Railway, commenced in 1906 and was formally opened by King George V on 22nd July 1912. The dock covered 1,000 acres (405 ha), with 45 acres (18 ha) of water. The GCR had, naturally, extended their railway line from Grimsby to Immingham, while another railway line to the north-west, the Barton and Immingham Light Railway, was opened in 1912. The port opened just in time to serve as a submarine base for British D class submarines during World War I while there was also an anti-aircraft battery in the town, manned with a one-pounder and later a 12-pounder gun. By the 1920s the port had outgrown the village of Immingham, while today it has grown into a town, civil parish and ward of nearly 10,000 people.

The railways were still enjoying their halcyon days at the beginning of the 20th century, but the gradual increase in roads and motor vehicles inevitably resulted in a gradual decline in the importance of the railways. This decline continued following the nationalisation of railways in 1947, and many of Lincolnshire's lines suffered following the Beeching Report of 1963. The first line to close was the Woodhall to Boston line, followed by the Honington to Lincoln line in 1965. Then in 1970, several lines closed, including Boston to Spalding, Lincoln to Firsby, Firsby to Grimsby and Willoughby to Mablethorpe. Throughout these years,

though, the line out to Skegness survived, due to the town's reliance on the railways for its tourist trade.

Quirk Alert: *School's Out*
The village school at Huttoft was home to an interesting custom which was still going in the years after World War I. For every Clerk Thursday (the day after Ash Wednesday), the boys were allowed to lock the headmaster out of the school. If they managed to keep him out until midday, the boys were granted the afternoon off as holiday. According to reports, the boys often won this battle of guile.

As Lincolnshire moved into the 20th century, the county began to build up a close affiliation with the Royal Air Force – although when the first airfields were constructed during World War I, the RAF had yet to be born, and Lincolnshire was home to the air corps of the army and the navy, the Royal Flying Corp (RFC) and the Royal Naval Air Service (RNAS), respectively. Having said that, many of these airfields, such as the one at Leadenham, were little more than cleared fields! Nevertheless, they were needed to repel German air attacks, with one Zeppelin at Cleethorpes in 1916 causing considerable damage; aircraft were therefore used on a number of occasions from the RFC Home Defence Squadrons at Elsham, Gainsborough, Kirton, Leadenham, Scampton and Tydd St Mary, as well as RNAS defence from Cranwell and Killingholme. After the war, many of these airfields became unused, and those that remained tended to focus on training. Even in the early 1920s, both flying and apprentice training was centred on the Royal Air Force College at Cranwell, although the Apprentice School did move to Buckinghamshire in 1926. Bomber training took place over remoter coastal sites such as those at Donna Nook in the north-east of the county and Holbeach in the south-east, while pilots were also trained at Digby and Grantham and armaments training was conducted at North Coates and Sutton Bridge.

Given this huge presence, it was no surprise when Lincolnshire became one of England's key counties for offensive bombing campaigns during World War II. Its geographic advantage – proximity to Germany and occupied Europe – also worked in reverse, and so Luftwaffe attacks were a constant threat. As a result, fighter squadrons were stationed at Hibaldstow and Kirton-in-Lindsey to the north of Lincoln, and at Coleby Grange, Digby and Wellingore to the south. In terms of bomber stations, though, there were 11 in Lincolnshire by March 1943, and 29 by April 1945, each of them operating Avro Lancasters for bombing raids on Germany. The most famous of those raids was on 16th May 1943, when 18 Lancasters of 617 Squadron took off from RAF Scampton under the command of Wing Commander Guy Gibson. This was the famous Dambusters raid on the industrial heartland of Germany. Also known as Operation Chastise, the bombers took out strategic targets in the Ruhr Valley, attacking the dams at Eider, Mohne and Sorpe and causing devastating flooding of crucial German industrial sites. This was undoubtedly one of the key moments in the Allies' eventual victory over Germany.

In addition to the bomber and fighter bases, radar installations were built at Ingoldmells, Langtoft, Orby, Skendleby and Stenigot, while centres were developed at North Coates and Strubby for attacking enemy shipping in the North Sea. As well as Avro Lancasters, Vickers Armstrong Wellingtons, and later, DeHavilland Mosquitos, it is also worth noting that the first British jet-powered aircraft flew from RAF Cranwell in May 1941.

Despite the success of the RAF in Lincolnshire, the airman death toll was huge, with over 25,000 from Lincolnshire and nearby airfields killed in action; indeed, on the night of 30th March 1944, 44 aircraft out of 381 failed to return home. The vast majority of those killed were British airmen, but airmen of Australia, Canada and New Zealand also died, particularly those who flew out from RAF Wickenby. As for the Americans, they were largely based in East Anglia and the only key USAAF base in Lincolnshire was at Goxhill which was mainly used for training – although there were postings at Barkston, Folkingham, Fulbeck and North Witham, but mainly for troop-carrying in C47 Dakotas.

> **Quirk Alert:** *Painting by Bombers*
> *During World War II, a bomb fell near to the church at Pickworth and the explosion dislodged much plasterwork. However, when the plaster was cleared away, a number of medieval paintings were found which had been hidden behind the plaster for centuries. The paintings are of immense historical interest and have been dated to around 1380.*

The end of World War II inevitably resulted in the decommission of many RAF bases, and by 1946, there were only 12 airfields still active, at Binbrook, Kirton-in-Lindsey, Manby, Metheringham, North Coates, Scampton, Skellingthorpe, Spilsby, Sturgate, Sutton Bridge, Swinderby and Waddington. However, as Britain moved into the Cold War period, a new bomber – the Avro Vulcan – arrived at both Scampton and Waddington in 1956. By the early 1960s, though, defence emphasis had shifted from bombing to missile delivery, with American Thor ICBMs stationed at Bardney, Caistor, Coleby Grange, Folkingham, Hemswell and Ludford. However, by 1969, the nuclear deterrent role had been taken on by Britain's nuclear submarine fleet.

Throughout these post-war years, RAF training continued apace in Lincolnshire, primarily at Cranwell, but also at Manby, Strubby and Swinderby. However, the end of the Cold War in the late 1980s saw a number of RAF sites close down and by the turn of the 21st century, only Cranwell survived for officer and flying training; Digby remained as a signal centre, Coningsby as air defence, and Waddington as a radar station, while the bombing ranges at Donna Nook, Holbeach and Wainfleet also survived. The final flight of a Vulcan from Waddington took place in 1984.

Throughout the last century or so, therefore, local economies have fluctuated with the ebb and flow of RAF personnel – although in the early days, RAF bases tended to be pretty self-contained. Equally, by the 1960s, many current and ex-servicemen were also setting up homes and families in close proximity to their bases, leading to a demand for new housing. Places like Leasingham, Ruskington, Scopwick, Sleaford, Tattershall and Welton therefore expanded as a result.

These two aircraft can be found at the Lincolnshire Aviation Visitor Centre near to East Kirkby, one of several such attractions in Lincolnshire that celebrate the county's affiliation with the RAF, and the air forces of other countries based here, particularly during World War II. PHOTOGRAPHS: SHAYNE WARD.

The development of the aeroplane throughout the 20th century also helped Lincolnshire's engineering industries. During World War I, Lincoln's Ruston Proctor built over 2,000 aircraft and 3,000 engines, while other Lincolnshire aircraft builders included Clayton and Shuttleworth of Lincoln, Robey's, also of Lincoln, and Marshall's at Gainsborough. Lincolnshire was also the county where the first tanks were produced in 1915, at W. Fosters of Lincoln. At the end of the war in 1918, Ruston, Proctor & Co. Ltd. merged with Richard Hornsby & Son Ltd., to become Ruston & Hornsby Ltd. They diversified into producing cars, while Clayton and Shuttleworth Ltd. remained committed to the production of steam engines, which eventually brought about their demise in 1930, when steam engines were superseded by the internal combustion engine.

By World War II, Ruston and Hornsby were producing locomotives, plus they continued the production of the tanks begun by Fosters during World War I. Also building tanks as well as machine-gun carriers was Aveling-Barford at Grantham, and who had been formed in 1933. After the war, Ruston and Hornsby moved into the production of industrial gas turbines, but in 1961, they were taken over by English Electric Co. Ltd (part of General Electric Co. Ltd [GEC]), to form Ruston Gas Turbines. By the 1970s, they were the leading producer of gas turbines in Britain and a major exporter, and continue to do so today, albeit under the name of Alstom.

One other relative newcomer to Lincolnshire's industries is oil. The first workable deposits were found at Nocton in 1943, but it was during the 1980s when more sites became active at Nettleham, Scampton, Stainton and Welton. The latter site gathers around 4,000 barrels per day, and is linked by a railway line to a refinery on Humberside. For more on Lincolnshire's oil, see *Quirky Lincolnshire [Wressle]*. Meanwhile, the Viking North Sea Gas terminal was built at Theddlethorpe in 1972 and receives gas from more than 20 North Sea platforms.

By the end of the 19th century, much of the current drainage system was in place, and so the 20th century was more a case of carrying out maintenance and improving systems where possible. The steam drainage engines were eventually replaced by more powerful diesel ones and then electric engines, while the dredging of channels continued as did the strengthening of embankments. The 1940s also saw long lengths of unsightly, but essential concrete coastal defences erected, such as those at Chapel St Leonards, Ingoldmells, Sandilands, Sutton on Sea and Trusthorpe. Alas, they weren't strong enough to prevent the disastrous storm surge on 1st February 1953, which breached the Lincolnshire coast from north of Immingham down to Gibraltar Point. Forty one people were killed in Lincolnshire out of 307, country-wide, while 1,836 people were killed in the low-lying Netherlands. The storm surge was as a result of a high spring tide combining with a severe wind-storm over the North Sea. Unsurprisingly, sea defences were subsequently strengthened down the Lincolnshire coast, and have been strengthened further several times since – and with good reason, too, as around 50,000 people now live behind the sea defences that run from Mablethorpe to Skegness. One of the more recent sea defence improvements is to pump sand ashore from under the sea to raise the level of the beaches.

Quirk Alert: *Fatal Transaction*

The house known as Haverholme Priory was located around 4 miles north-east of Sleaford, and had initially been a medieval Cistercian monastery, founded in 1137 by Alexander, Bishop of Lincoln. It was then dissolved in 1538 and eventually passed to the Finch-Hatton family. The priory was then rebuilt in 1830 by George Finch-Hatton, and was used as a family home for almost a century before going up for sale in the early 1920s. It was eventually bought in 1926 by an American woman who had most of it dismantled, stone by stone, fully intending to rebuild it back in America. Alas, with the masonry ready and waiting at Liverpool docks, the buyer died in a train crash. The stones were therefore never shipped to America, and didn't travel much further in their life either, as they were used to build new docks in Liverpool!

Quirk Alert: *Always Look On The Bright Side*

Tupholme Abbey was founded in c.1155 by Albert and Gilbert de Neville. It was dissolved in 1536 and all that survives today is a two-storey wall. However, in 1972, the grounds of the former abbey hosted one of England's biggest ever pop festivals for four days in late May, with Rory Gallagher, Rod Stewart (then in The Faces), the Beach Boys and Joe Cocker headlining each of the four nights, and supported by huge names of rock and pop such as Status Quo, Lindisfarne, Slade, The Strawbs, The Groundhogs, Humble Pie, Roxy Music, Wishbone Ash, The Average White Band, Spencer Davis, Helen Reddy and Don McLean. And then, on the festival poster in smaller print, a number of up-and-coming artists are listed, including Nazareth, Focus, Billy Joel…and soon-to-be British Supergroup, Genesis! Furthermore, second bill-toppers on the Sunday were none other than Monty Python's Flying Circus! What a Bank Holiday weekend that must have been! Although having said that, forget your images of beautiful summer days in deepest rural Lincolnshire; reports talk of freezing wind and rain which "lashed the site relentlessly", and by Saturday (day two), "the site was a quagmire, knee-deep in mud"! But then again – and this will make you weep – the cost to attend all four days was only £5!

A sea of daffodils west of Spalding. Flowers have been produced in this part of Lincolnshire on an industrial scale for decades.

Conversely, these abandoned warehouses on Grimsby Dock are symbolic of the decline of the deep sea fishing industry there.

Throughout the 20th century, the population of rural parishes continued to decline, particularly in the central and southern Wolds and central and southern Kesteven. Conversely, the population of most fen parishes and those on the north-eastern coastal marshes has generally increased. As well as the main urban areas, other places that saw significant population increases in the 20th century were Coningsby, Cranwell, Waddington and Skegness, the first three thanks to the presence of the RAF and the latter thanks to the holiday industry. Meanwhile, in the south of the county, Bourne, Deeping St James, Langtoft and Market Deeping also saw significant increases as dormitory towns for nearby and rapidly expanding Peterborough. Nevertheless, despite these urban growth areas, Lincolnshire remains very much a rural county, although the means of producing crops, flowers and vegetables, has become increasingly sophisticated and industrialised. There is certainly very little natural landscape in the county with almost 90 per cent given over to farming (75 per cent under the plough and 12 per cent grassland and rough grazing). Productivity and quality is also substantially helped by the fact that 44 per cent of the county's soil is categorised as Grade 1 or 2 compared to a national average of 16 per cent.

The number of sheep in Lincolnshire declined from just over a million at the turn of the 20th century to around half that number by 1937. The war then saw the importance of the land increase dramatically, and increasing the amount of land under the plough at the expense of grassland became a priority. One business that benefitted from this, though, was the iron-founders Marshall, Son & Co. Ltd. of Gainsborough, who produced 2,000 threshing machines during this time – more than half the total produced during the war. After the war, industrialisation, mechanisation and advancements in the understanding of chemical fertilisers took the agricultural industry into a new era, but by the close of the 20th century, farming was suffering from the reduction of subsidies and the industry has since gone into decline again.

One other casualty of the late 20th century was deep sea fishing at Grimsby, but at the same time, the town saw diversification into food processing. Major employers such as Birdseye-Wallace, Blue Crest and Ross-Young, began producing frozen vegetables and fish; indeed at the turn of the 21st century, 20 per cent of fish was being processed at Grimsby, while the port was also producing more pizzas than anywhere else in England. Meanwhile, the south of the county is now a centre for the large-scale production and distribution of flowers and chilled foods.

The latest industrial victim in Lincolnshire is the steelworks at Scunthorpe. At the beginning of the 20th century, there were five different steel companies, but in the 1930s, three of them amalgamated into one giant company called the Appleby-Frodingham Steel Company. This company lasted until 1953 when the steel industry was nationalised. The British Steel company then survived until 1999 when it merged with the Dutch company Koninklikje Hoogovens to form Corus, who were then acquired by Tata Steel in 2007. Since then, there has been a gradual running down of steel production, with Tata announcing 900 job losses at their Scunthorpe site in 2015. What remained was sold for £1 in April 2016 to Greybull Capital.

In terms of road infrastructure, Lincolnshire is still relatively under-developed in the 21st century, with few dual carriageways and only one motorway, the M180, which runs across the top of the county linking Scunthorpe, Immingham and Grimsby with the M18 (and thence the M1). The M180 also now provides a direct link with Hull on the other side of the Humber via the A15 which has been taken across the river by the Humber Bridge since 1981. The bridge is a spectacular sight, stretches for 4,626ft (1,410m), and was built to politically consolidate the relatively new Humberside County Council – which brings us nicely onto the local government and county border changes implemented towards the end of the 20th century.

Historically, Lincolnshire was the second largest English county behind Yorkshire, as it still is today – although the largest *modern*-day ceremonial county is now *North* Yorkshire. However, in between 1974 and 1996, Lincolnshire looked somewhat different around its traditional northern areas, as is demonstrated by map 3 in the following sequence of maps. This result was brought about by the Local Government Act 1972, and which came into effect on the 1st April 1974. The Act introduced the most radical overhaul of English county boundaries in their one thousand year history, with six new metropolitan counties being formed along with four new non-metropolitan counties. One of the latter was Humberside, which swallowed up most of the area previously occupied by the East Riding of Yorkshire, plus it acquired part of the south-east portion of the former West Riding around Goole. However, south of the Humber, the new county also acquired large tracts of northern Lindsey, including the former municipal borough of Scunthorpe, and the former county borough of Grimsby. A number of new non-metropolitan districts were then created, as shown by the map on page 7, from which districts 6 to 9, plus the southern half of district number 5 were carved from the former

historic county of Lincolnshire (and administrative county of Lindsey [1889-1974]). As a result, Lincolnshire lost its "crown", and thus the county boundaries appeared as also shown in map number 3. At the same time, the "new" county of Lincolnshire had its county council headquarters restored to Lincoln.

As it turned out, though, Humberside was pretty much doomed from the start. To quote James Cran (MP for Beverley), "almost the day after the decision was announced, a campaign began to have Humberside abolished" , and by 1990, a Local Government Boundary Commission (LGBC) report revealed that 63% of respondents thought that the creation of Humberside was "bad", with only 14% stating "good". Indeed, despite the Humber Bridge connecting the two halves of Humberside in 1981, the LGBC were already looking at reform a year later. This continued throughout the 1980s, when the slogan: "Lincolnshire – From the Humber to the Wash", became popular. By November 1990, the LGBC had formed a proposal to transfer the four districts south of the Humber back to the non-metropolitan county of Lincolnshire. However, before this could be implemented, a general local government review for England was announced. The Commission eventually recommended that Humberside be abolished and replaced with four unitary authorities: East Riding of Yorkshire and Kingston upon Hull, north of the Humber, and North Lincolnshire and North East Lincolnshire south of the Humber. This all came into play on 1st April 1996, when Humberside was formally abolished, and Lincolnshire reacquired its former northern territory. The new unitary authority of North East Lincolnshire roughly took on the former Humberside non-metropolitan districts of Grimsby and Cleethorpes, and North

1. Surrounding Counties: 1889-1965

2. Surrounding Counties: Redcliffe-Maud Proposals, 1969

3. Surrounding Counties: 1974-1996

4. Surrounding Counties: 1996-2016

The Humber Bridge, as seen from the Lincolnshire side at Barton-upon-Humber. Built in 1981, as well as vastly reducing journey times around the Humber estuary, it was seen as solidifying the link between North and South Humberside. Alas, the non-metropolitan county of Humberside only survived for another 15 years!

The gardens of Ayscoughfee Hall at Spalding are popular with locals and tourists alike. The house was built in around 1451 for a local wool merchant, while some of the surviving gardens were laid out by William Sands in the early 18th century.

Lincolnshire roughly took on the former non-metropolitan districts of Scunthorpe, Glanford, and the southern part of Boothferry. The maps on page 7 break down both modern Lincolnshire and Humberside into their constituent districts.

It is worth noting, though, that this re-unification of Lincolnshire was only for ceremonial and Lieutenancy purposes – so the two returning unitary authorities remained independent of Lincolnshire County Council, but along with the other seven districts (shown on page 7), they still form the *ceremonial* county of Lincolnshire, with one Lord Lieutenant covering the entire area. As for the abolished non-metropolitan county of Humberside, one of its lasting legacies is that the region Yorkshire and Humberside (created in 1994) includes all of its former area. This means that Lincolnshire is actually split, regionally, with the two northern unitary authorities belonging to the Yorkshire and Humber region, and the rest of Lincolnshire belonging to the East Midlands.

There is one final element of boundary change to cover, though, and that is by referring to the second of the four maps opposite and which covers the highly controversial proposals for Lincolnshire issued by the Redcliffe-Maud Report of 1969. This report marked the culmination of the Royal Commission on Local Government in England, which had run from 1966 to 1969 under the chairmanship of Lord Redcliffe-Maud, and had been looking at restructuring local government in England. The Redcliffe-Maud report was also looking at changing local government in the Humberside area, but it didn't include a cross-Humber authority. The territory north of the Humber would have formed part of a new county/unitary area of "North Humberside", and the area to the south, a new county called South Humberside – and which largely approximated to today's two unitary authorities of North Lincolnshire and North East Lincolnshire. What is interesting about map 2, though, is that Lincolnshire

would also have lost much of its southern territory, too – this going to the proposed unitary area of "Peterborough North Fens" which would have included most of the current district of South Holland plus parts of South Kesteven around Stamford and Bourne. However, the Redcliffe-Maud Report was rejected and was superseded by the less-incursive Local Government Act 1972. Meanwhile, following the abolition of Humberside in 1996, Lincolnshire has today returned to a state where local government is split into three parts – with the three current unitary areas of Lincolnshire, North Lincolnshire and North East Lincolnshire, replacing the historical triumvirate of Lindsey, Kesteven and Holland – albeit with very different territorial boundaries.

Finally, the 21st century has seen the continued appearance of new attractions in Lincolnshire, with one of the largest in recent times being Fantasy Island, opened at Ingoldmells in 1995. This brings us back to Billy Butlin with whom we will leave the last line – as his original holiday camp at Ingoldmells was refurbished in 1999 and now caters for around 10,000 people per week!

Quirk Alert: *Earthquakes*

Lincoln Cathedral was destroyed by an unusual earthquake in 1185. Although perhaps not that unusual, considering the earthquake that occurred at 00:56 on the 27 February 2008. With an epicentre of 2.5 miles north of Market Rasen, the earthquake recorded 5.2 on the Richter scale, the second largest onshore earthquake to occur in the UK since instrumental measurements began. It was caused by a sudden rupture and motion along a strike-slip fault, some 12 miles beneath Lincolnshire.

The two main ports on the River Witham, at Boston (left) and Lincoln (right). The latter has seen significant waterfront development during the 21ˢᵗ century around the Brayford Pool.

Some Quirky Lincolnshire Stats

To complete the Conventional Lincolnshire section, here are some unique and quirky statistics. For starters, Lincolnshire is one of the driest counties in England, while it is also Britain's principle agricultural county, with around 80% (1.7m acres) under cultivation.

Other county curiosities include Alvingham which has two churches in one churchyard and is also the only church in England dedicated to St Adelwold (Ethelwald), while St Hibald's church at Ashby-de-la-Laund is one of only four in the country dedicated to that particular Saint – all four of which are in Lincolnshire! Benniworth's church is dedicated to St Julian, also very rare, while rarer still is Scotton's dedication to St Genewys. All are surpassed, though, by Little Bytham's church, the only one in England dedicated to St Medard, a 6ᵗʰ century Bishop of Noyon. Meanwhile, Beckingham's church nave resembles the prow of a ship and Belton is probably the English church with the most monuments to size ratio. Blyton's church must be in the running for containing the most flags (a tradition started after World War I to mark the death of a mother's son in France), while Bottesford's church is home to nine deeply-splayed lancet windows, adorned with dog-tooth mouldings that are believed to be the longest and narrowest lancets in an English village church.

Sticking with churches, the church at Coates-by-Stow has an altar slab with six incised crosses, believed to be unique, as is Coningsby's church clock, which with a dial of 16.5ft (5m) is the largest single-handed clock in the world – while Appleby's church clock has no face at all; it merely strikes the hour on a big bell, and was given to the church by a farmer churchwarden who wanted the men in the fields to hear the passing hours.

Continuing with churches, the 13ᵗʰ century chapel of St Leonard's at Kirkstead is home to one of the oldest military monuments in England, a figure of a knight thought to be the 2ⁿᵈ Lord Tattershall who died in c.1212. Meanwhile, Corby church is home to one of the most extensive collections of medieval mural paintings in England, and Goxhill's church is home to a wall-painting of the crucifixion that Arthur Mee describes as "the only complete subject in any porch in England". Crowland Abbey is thought to have issued the first-ever peal of bells in 986, while Heckington's church has, according to Arthur Mee, the second finest Easter Sepulchre in England. Arthur also states that the church of St Denys at Sleaford has one of the earliest stone spires in England, and describes its 33ft by 18ft six-light window in the north transept as "unsurpassed in beauty anywhere" and its medieval screen as "one of the finest in England".

Next, Castle Bytham's church must have the only ladder to a belfry that used to be a 17ᵗʰ century maypole, while Keddington's 15ᵗʰ century wooden lectern carved in the shape of an eagle is one of only six in England. Kirkstead's 13ᵗʰ century timber screenwork is thought to be the second-oldest in the country, and Langton-by-

The White Lady of North Ormsby. No one knows why, or for how long she has been here – although the site is thought to mark the spot where a woman was once killed whilst out hunting.
PHOTOGRAPH © RICHARD CROFT.

Horncastle's church was once home to a unique chrismatory of terracotta, believed to be the only one in England and now in the British Museum. Next up, Heighington's church is the only one located in a school playground, and Caythorpe St Vincent's church has a double nave and is home to one of the oldest mulberry trees in the land, while the level of the nave floor at Gayton-le-Marsh's church is so high that the pews almost reach the capitals of the arches!

More church curiosities – the 18th century candelabrum at Frampton holds 26 candles, the parish churches of Ewerby and Grantham both have 10 bells apiece, and Friskney churchyard is home to a Georgian sentry box in which the parson would shelter in bad weather when conducting funerals. Font-wise, the oak cover at Freiston is shaped like a spire around 12 feet high and crowned with a figure of the Madonna, while the Jacobean font-cover at Skirbeck is also shaped like a tower and spire.

Another unique church feature can be found at Harlaxton, where a stairway from the tower is extended to the steeple via one of the pinnacles. Rippingdale is home to a rare 13th century monument to a deacon, Rowston's St Clement's church owns one of the smallest and slimmest steeples in the land, and Saltfleetby All Saints' church owns an extremely rare stone reredos dating from the time of Edward I (1272-1307).

Finally for churches, South Ferriby's St Nicholas' church is a rarity as its chancel faces south and its nave therefore runs from north to south – this all due to its location, perched on a steep hillside. It is thought that a landslip accounted for much of the traditional 13th century, east-west axis-build, and hence the configuration change when the church was rebuilt.

Moving away from churches, Girby Manor was the location of the discovery of one of only two known copies of the Shakespearian Quartos of 1619, Lincoln Cathedral is home to one of the four contemporary copies of Magna Carta, and the longest chestnut avenue is said to be on the approach to Grimsthorpe Castle.

Meanwhile, the deserted medieval village of North Ormsby is home to the statue of the White Lady – although no one knows who she is or how old she is – while Scothern is home to a medieval custom of ringing the "Pancake Bell" at 11:00 a.m. on Shrove Tuesday. Meanwhile, at Scotter, the Ringers' Rules can be found in black and red lettering above the tower doorway of St Peter's church and which are thought to be the oldest in existence in verse. Then there's Horncastle's August horse fair which was once the largest in the land, while Nettleton is probably home to the only First World War memorial that is, in fact, a bungalow!

Next, Lincolnshire's beer was ranked as the second strongest in the country in the 19th century, Crowland is home to the unique Triangular Bridge, and Market Deeping is home to the oldest inhabited rectory in England. Then there's Henry Winn, parish clerk at Fulletby for 76 years up to his death in 1914, aged 98, the skating championships that have been held at Baston Fen when it has frozen over in winter, and Gedney Hill, where there isn't a hill in sight for many a mile!

FINALLY: TWO NATIONAL TREASURES:

The foundations of Boston St Botolph's church (aka Boston Stump) are 36ft deep, its eight-light west window in the tower is one of the largest in the country, and its stone groining within the tower is the second-highest in England at 137ft. The Stump's medieval oak double door within the porch is also uniquely dovetailed and is also one of England's finest – as are its stalls – while the church is also home to 11 part stone, part brass memorials, more than half of the total in England. As for Lincoln Cathedral, at 57,000 square feet it is the third largest in England, measuring 481ft by 223ft at its widest point, while the central tower is 271ft high and the two west towers around 206ft. All three were once crowned with spires, too, but the central tower lost its spire in 1548 and the west towers in 1807. The cathedral is also home to a unique ten-sided chapter house.

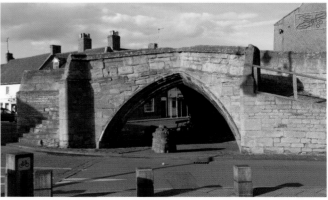

Two of the three arches of the triangular Trinity Bridge at Crowland which is also unique. It was built between 1360 and 1390 when it spanned three rivers! The "rivers" in question were the River Welland and two of its tributaries, but these were later re-routed, leaving Trinity Bridge as one of only a handful of bridges in the world that no longer span a physical obstacle. A predecessor to the 14th century bridge is mentioned in a charter of 943, but its earliest reference dates back to 716, when mentioned by King Æthelbald of Mercia. Unsurprisingly, the bridge is a Scheduled Ancient Monument and is also Grade I listed.

One section of the beautiful gardens at Belton House, which is located 2 miles north-east of Grantham. The grounds were first transformed into a park in 1690 by Sir John Brownlow and the Eastern Avenue still survives from that design.

LINCOLNSHIRE CHURCHES: THROUGH THE AGES

The lower part of Coleby All Saints' tower dates from late Saxon times

The oldest parts of St Oswald's church at Crowle date from Norman times.

St Peter's church at Creeton dates from the late 12th to the 15th century, but includes in its structure, several 10th century decorated Anglo-Saxon stones.

The oldest part of All Saints' church at Gainsborough is the 15th century tower; the nave, aisles and apsidal chancel were rebuilt 1734-1744.

Springtime in Scopwick. The village is located in North Kesteven, and the name (Scapeuic, 1086) means "sheep farm" and is derived from the Old English words scēap (sheep) and wīc (specialised farm or building or dairy farm), with the former influenced by the Old Scandinavian prefix sk-.

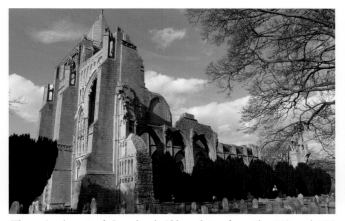

The ruined part of Crowland Abbey dates from the 11th and 12th centuries.

St Mary's church at Barnetby-le-Wold retains its Norman tower and nave.

St Peter ad Vincula church at Bottesford dates from the 13th century and includes the longest and narrowest village church lancet windows in England.

The now-abandoned Primitive Methodist church at Linwood dates from 1921, and is known locally as the Little Pink Church. See Linwood chapter on page 134 for more.

The font at St Margaret's church, Bag Enderby, includes this very rare pietà – a depiction of the Virgin Mary cradling the dead body of Jesus.

Coningsby's church clock dial is 16.5ft wide, and is the largest single-handed clock in the world. By contrast, St Martin's church clock at South Willingham is one of the smallest in the country.

Final Bonus: These photographs were, quite fittingly, the final two taken on my various tours of Lincolnshire. Here we are looking west from the Cliff at Leadenham towards the setting sun, which eventually disappears behind Brant Broughton's St Helen's church.

Quintessentially Quirky – Haxey

NAME (STATUS):	**HAXEY** (Village)
POPULATION:	4,584
DISTRICT:	North Lincolnshire
EARLIEST RECORD:	*Acheseia*, 1086 (Domesday Book)
MEANING:	Island, or dry ground in marsh, of a man called Haki
DERIVATION:	From the Old Scandinavian personal name Haki, plus the Old English word *ēg* (island or land partly surrounded by water) or the Old Scandinavian word *ey* (same thing)

The *Quintessentially Quirky* chapter is now a mainstay of Unusual & Quirky volumes, and focuses on a place in the county that encapsulates English tradition and eccentricity. And so with that kind of a brief, there was only one place to go in Lincolnshire – so take a bow you hood-chasing Boggins of Haxey…

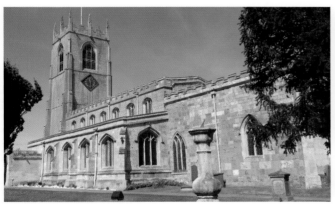

St Nicholas' church, Haxey.

The Loco, Haxey, one of the four participating pubs in the Haxey Hood.

Haxey Quirk Alert: *The Haxey Hood*

Lincolnshire offers us The Haxey Hood, a tradition thought to be over 700 years old and thus making it Britain's "oldest traditional tussle" – although the Shrovetide Footballers of Ashbourne (Derbyshire) and the Bottle-kicking, Hare Pie Wrestlers of Hallaton (Leicestershire) would probably dispute that! Anyway, The Haxey Hood is an annual event that takes place in the North Lincolnshire village of Haxey on the afternoon of 6th January, the Twelfth Day of Christmas – although if this date falls on a Sunday, the event is held on 5th January. The "game" is something of a mass rugby scrum known as "the sway", and which pushes a leather tube, known as "the hood", to one of four pubs in the parish, where it remains until the following year's game.

The official legend is that this tradition dates from the 14th century. The story goes that Lady de Mowbray, wife of John de Mowbray (probably the 3rd Baron Mowbray of Axholme [1310-1361]), was out riding towards Westwoodside. However, it was a particularly windy day, and as she crested a hill, her silk riding hood was blown away by the wind – at which point, thirteen keen-to-please farm workers in the nearby field rushed after the hood in a comical attempt to reclaim it. It was finally caught by one of the farm workers, but being too shy to hand it back to the lady, he gave it to one of the others to hand back to her. She thanked the farm worker who had returned the hood and said that he had acted like a Lord, whereas the worker who had actually caught the hood was a Fool. So amused was she by this act of chivalry and the resulting chase, that she donated 13 acres (53,000 m²) of land on condition that the chase for the hood would be re-enacted each year. Over the centuries, the twelve chasers (minus the Fool) became known as Boggins (one of whom is the Lord and another, the Chief Boggin), and the re-enactment became known as "The Haxey Hood".

As for the tradition today, for a week before the event, the Fool and the twelve Boggins tour around the villages in the parish collecting money for local charities. The crew also sing a number of traditional folk songs as they go, such as "John Barleycorn", "Drink Old England Dry" and "The Farmer's Boy" while clad in their special costumes – the only exception being that the Fool's face isn't painted at this stage. Costume-wise, the Lord and Chief Boggin are dressed in red hunting coats and top hats decorated with flowers and badges, while the Lord also carries his wand of office – a staff made from twelve willow wands with one more upside down in the centre, thus representing the twelve apostles with the upside-down willow wand representing Judas. These are bound thirteen times with willow twigs and a red ribbon at the top. The staff is supposed to represent the sword and the blood from when the game was played with a bullock's head after it had been slaughtered! As for the Fool, on the day, he wears a feathered hat decorated with flowers and rags, has his face smeared with soot and red ochre, while multi-coloured strips of material are attached to his trousers and shirt. He also carries a whip and sock filled with bran, with which he threatens anyone daft enough to get too close. Meanwhile, the Boggins wear traditional red jumpers.

As for the big day, the majority of parish folk make their way to the first of the four competing pubs – the Carpenter's Arms in neighbouring Westwoodside – where free drinks are provided for all – albeit as a token of good luck to bring the Hood home! The traditional folk songs are sung and the Fool's face is ceremonially painted. The crew and crowd then move successively to the Kings Arms, the Loco and the Duke William (all in Haxey), drinking and singing (and drinking) as they go. Then at around 2:30pm the party troop up to the church, led by the Fool – who also has the right to kiss any woman on the way! Once at the village green in front of the church, the Fool makes his traditional speech of welcome standing on an old mounting stone in front of the church known as the Mowbray Stone. During this speech a small fire is lit with damp straw at the foot of the mounting stone – a custom known as "Smoking the Fool" – and a somewhat tamer version of the earlier custom in which a substantial fire was lit with damp straw beneath a tree! I say "somewhat tamer" because the original ceremony saw the Fool suspended upside-down over the fire and swung back and forth until he was almost suffocated, before being cut down and dropped into the fire, from which he would exit as fast as he could! Worth some serious weighing up against the woman-kissing, that – but which is now academic as the custom was stopped in the early 20th century when someone forgot to damp the straw and the Fool caught fire! But anyway, the Fool then delivers a traditional speech that the crowd chant along to, as follows:

"Hoose agen hoose, toon agen toon, if a man meets a man knock 'im doon, but doan't 'ot 'im".

Translated, this means "House against house, town against town, if a man meets a man, knock him down but don't hurt him", where the houses are the four pubs and the towns are Haxey and Westwoodside.

Just before 3.00 pm (traditional kick-off time), the Fool leads the crowd to the middle of a field where the game is to be played, largely by locals, although anyone can join in. A pre-cursor game for children kicks off proceedings when twelve rolled up hessian sack hoods are thrown into the air (the sacks are rolled and sewn up to prevent them unravelling). The young combatants then have to run after a sack and try and get them off the field before being tackled. If they are tackled then they must immediately throw the sack in the air unless the challenger is a Boggin in which case the hood is "Boggined" and thus returned to the Lord who starts it off again. Those youngsters that do manage to successfully transport a hood outside of the field of play are rewarded with a small cash prize on return of said hood.

Preliminaries out of the way, it is now time for the main event. On this occasion, just one rolled hood is thrown into the air – the Sway Hood – this one made out of a two-foot length of stout leather, this being the nearest equivalent to the original "hood" which was, in fact, a freshly-slaughtered bullock's head! The object of the game is simply to convey "The Sway" towards your favoured pub! This is achieved only by pushing, pulling and rolling The Sway which often collapses – at which point, bodies are pulled out of the mud (alive, you understand) and the game recommenced. No hood-throwing or running with the hood is allowed.

Typically, there can be up to 200 competitors with a further one thousand watching, while games can last until well into the night. It is also a common occurrence for hedges and walls to be trashed, although one of the jobs of the supervising Boggins is to try and limit the damage! Needless to say, there aren't too many parked cars in Haxey and Westwoodside on 6th January, nor are there many home deliveries!

The game ends when the Sway Hood arrives (safely) at one of the pubs and is touched by the landlord from his front step. He then pours beer over the Hood and hangs it up behind his bar, where it stays until the following New Year's Eve, when it is collected by the next batch of Boggins for the following years festivities.

Far left: *These fields between Haxey and Westwoodside are awash with oilseed rape in spring. However, on January 6th, they are awash with a writhing throng of human beings forming what is known as The Sway!*

Left: *And here is the Fool making his speech while a small fire has been started underneath him!*
PHOTOGRAPH: © RICHARD CROFT.

Quirky Lincolnshire

Introducing the Shire-Ode

A Shire-Ode tells the story – in rhyming verse – of fictitious, eccentric inhabitants of the county in question. However, in so doing, it also incorporates into the flow of the verse, many place-names that can be found within that county – places which then go on to form a county almanac, of sorts. Each place appears in roughly alphabetical order, although some of the smaller places are batched up into trios known as a "Three's Up" or appear in the "Best of the Rest" section at the end of the book. The location of all of the places is also pinpointed on the map following the Shire-Ode.

As for the *Lincolnshire* Shire-Ode, this tells the tale of *Bicker, Wrangle and Wressle* and how the "Solicitors for all your needs" do pretty well out of their legal Eagle business…

Lincolnshire Shire-Ode: Bicker, Wrangle and Wressle

Bicker, **Wrangle** and **Wressle**:
"Solicitors for all your needs"
We're aptly based in **Billingborough**
Handling wills and deeds.

Our senior partners, **Mablethorpe**,
Linwood and **Penny Hill**
Have each been twice-divorced, to date
So they **Well**-know the drill.

But each one has a lovely **Holme**
Thanks to **Twenty** years of loot
Plus **Ermine Coates** and holiday boats
And a **Fleet** of Jag's to boot.

And they're not alone in **Minting** it
Cue **Cherry Willingham**
Her pockets must be very deep
As she's always **Fillingham**.

Whilst legal **Eagle**, **Austen Fen**
With **Lea** and **Melton Ross**
Each get their perks from **Will Row** work
Where **Martin Moor**'s their boss.

And even they own holiday homes
Though two are **Leasingham**
Boughton HP, with client fees;
Financially **Hameringham**.

But we've also got these two PA's
Brandy Wharf and **Donna Nook**
The insults fly, they **Howell** abuse
Being both **Bourne** common as muck.

The canteen's where they argue most
So it's called the **Bicker Bar**
Run **Bicker Gauntlet** any day
And you'll see them squabble and spar.

Quite apt, one comes from **Bitchfield**
While **Cowbit's** the others' abode
They've **Broughton** woe for many a foe;
No **Healing** down *that* road.

And with lads they're always **Leadenham** on;
Messingham about
Brandon, Bradley, Martin Dales
They've all been played, no doubt.

Thank heavens for **Mavis Enderby**
Our tea lady's so divine
With her scones and cakes and delicious bakes
And her **Tetley** tea so fine.

She talks of Mr **Rigsby**
The gent from the flat below
He's a little bit **Camp**; got rising damp
Plus he s-s-stammers a lot, you know.

Now doorman, **Boothby Graffoe**,
Who always wears **Great Coates**
Will **Greetham** with his **Hatton**
For he's quite the genial host.

That leaves our Temp from **Cleethorpes** –
Hannah with the **Aubourn** hair
And quite **Welbourn**, I'm pleased to say
As it's a **Little Common** elsewhere!

So assets, yes, we're **Holdingham**
This **Irnham**, **Burnham** brand
We've plans to suit, from branch to **Wroot**
In sterling, dollar and **Rand**!

Poppies in a field at Hameringham.

LINCOLNSHIRE LOCATION MAP FOR BICKER, WRANGLE AND WRESSLE

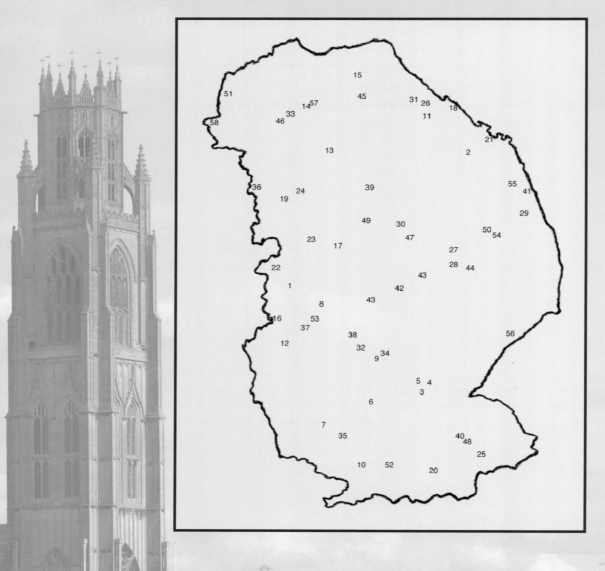

PLACE-NAME TABLE FOR BICKER, WRANGLE AND WRESSLE

1	Aubourn	16	Camp	31	Healing	46	Messingham
2	Austen Fen	17	Cherry Willingham	32	Holdingham	47	Minting
3	Bicker	18	Cleethorpes	33	Holme	48	Penny Hill
4	Bicker Bar	19	Coates	34	Howell	49	Rand
5	Bicker Gauntlet	20	Cowbit	35	Irnham	50	Rigsby
6	Billingborough	21	Donna Nook	36	Lea	51	Tetley
7	Bitchfield	22	Eagle	37	Leadenham	52	Twenty
8	Boothby Graffoe	23	Ermine	38	Leasingham	53	Welbourn
9	Boughton	24	Fillingham	39	Linwood	54	Well
10	Bourne	25	Fleet	40	Little Common	55	Will Row
11	Bradley	26	Great Coates	41	Mablethorpe	56	Wrangle
12	Brandon	27	Greetham	42	Martin Dales	57	Wressle
13	Brandy Wharf	28	Hameringham	43	Martin Moor	58	Wroot
14	Broughton	29	Hannah	44	Mavis Enderby		
15	Burnham	30	Hatton	45	Melton Ross		

Bicker, Wrangle and Wressle –
A Lincolnshire Shire-Ode Almanac

NAME (STATUS):	**AUBOURN** (Village)
POPULATION:	460 (Parish of Aubourn with Haddington)
DISTRICT:	North Kesteven
EARLIEST RECORD:	*Aburne*, 1086 (Domesday Book); *Alburn*, 1275
MEANING:	Stream where alder-trees grow
DERIVATION:	From the Old English words *alor* (alder-tree) and *burna* (stream)

Aubourn Church: St Peter's

A church existed at Aubourn at the time of Domesday Book (1086), and what was referred to as Aubourn Rectory had been given by Robert de Todeni in 1076 to the newly founded Belvoir Priory. The 11th century church was then replaced by another in around 1200 which was dedicated to St Peter, and vicars continued to be appointed here by Belvoir Priory from 1219 until 1529. However, in 1862 most of the medieval building was demolished except for the chancel, which was remodelled to become the mortuary chapel. A small square turret was also added to the north-west corner, and topped by a tiled roof.

The new St Peter's parish church was then built on a new site to the west of the village, and included some of the stone from the old St Peter's. This church was also placed mid-way between Aubourn and Haddington, thus making it better placed to serve both villages in the parish. It was designed by J.G. Hakewill of London in the early English style, cost around £4,000 and was built with a distinctive apsidal chancel and an octagonal spire that rises from its tower base to a height of 120ft.

However, this new church was not as sturdy as its 13th century predecessor, and due to water seepage into stonework which subsequently froze and split one of the walls, the church was declared unsafe for congregational use in 1968. Without the necessary funds to restore the 19th century St Peter's church, the parish church of Aubourn and Haddington was switched back to the remains of its 13th century predecessor, although the graveyard of the 19th century St Peter's continued to be used for burials. Fortunately, the older church had been restored in 1933 when a new altar and gallery for the organ were also erected, while further restoration and refurbishment has been carried out in recent years.

As for the newer, 19th century church, it is now known as the Clock Tower, thanks to its distinctive clock on the surviving tower. Parts of the church were demolished during the 1970s, and what is now a Grade II-listed building was actually only saved from total demolition by local residents who raised funds to retain the building within the parish. Indeed, the Aubourn and Haddington Parish Council have leased the building from the Lincoln Diocesan Trust since 1974, and local residents have continued to fund the upkeep of both building and clock.

Aubourn Historic Trivia: Aubourn Hall

As mentioned above, a church existed at Aubourn at the

The older St Peter's church at Aubourn dates from the early 13th century, and still retains its original priest's doorway and a lancet window.

The tower and apse are all that remain of the newer, 19th century St Peter's church. Deemed unsafe by the late 1960s, services switched back to its restored 13th century predecessor on the eastern edge of the village.

time of Domesday Book (1086), as did a fishery which was recorded as being worth 1000 eels a year. There was also an ancient mill here, known as Aubourn Mill, and rent for this watermill was paid annually to Belvoir Priory in 30 'sticks' of eels supplied by the nearby fishery. Alas, the remains of the mill were demolished in 1968, although a weir on the River Witham still marks its location. Meanwhile, at the eastern end of the village is Aubourn Hall, and which is located alongside the older of the two St Peter's churches. It was built in the early 17th century for Sir John Meres, after which the property passed to the Nevile family and has remained in their possession ever since.

The village of Aubourn is located in a valley formed by the River Witham, and has historically been a prime candidate for flooding, particularly prior to World War II. After the war, though, 8ft (2.5m) flood banks were constructed along each side of the river, thus reducing the annual flooding. Such was the confidence in these flood barriers that new housing has since been built all the way up to the flood banks! Meanwhile, the bridge that took the road over the River Witham, between Aubourn and Haddington, was Aubourn's only road link with the Fosse Way. In late medieval times this was a wooden bridge, but this was replaced by a brick-built bridge in 1790 which became of crucial importance to cattle drovers on their way to Norwich, where the cattle were sold.

Aubourn Quirk Alert: One Way and the Complaints of a Mole-catcher

Although Aubourn is a small, congestion-free country village, it is also home to a very quirky one-way traffic system. Meanwhile, one of the reasons that the "new" St Peter's church was built to the west of the village in 1862, was due to complaints from the inhabitants of Haddington, who claimed that the folk of Aubourn always got the best seats courtesy of not having to walk so far! However, the clincher for a new and larger church occurred when the squire, Henry Nevile, noted that many members of the congregation were sitting on others' knees due to all seats having been taken! And finally, talking of complaints, a number are recorded in the Lincolnshire Chronicle of the 19th century courtesy of a certain Thomas Reynolds of Aubourn. The local mole-catcher and pinder (keeper of the village pinfold), he was notoriously deaf, and also notoriously difficult to get on with – with a number of complaints featuring his brother, carts and pitchforks amongst other things!

Aubourn Hall.

The Royal Oak at Aubourn dates from the 16th century according to its website.

Far left: *This village signpost was created in 2000 to celebrate the millennium in the village.*

Centre: *One of three cast-iron water-pumps in Aubourn.*

Left: *The 19th century St Peter's church from the opposite side to the earlier photo, revealing the missing elements of the stricken church.*

Three's-Up!

	BITCHFIELD	BRADLEY	BRANDON
STATUS:	Village	Village	Village
POPULATION:	366	198	399 (Parish of Hough-on-the-Hill)
DISTRICT:	South Kesteven	North East Lincolnshire	South Kesteven
EARLIEST RECORD:	*Billesfelt*, 1086 (Domesday Book)	*Bredelou*, 1086 (Domesday Book)	*Branthon*, 1060-66; *Brandune*, 1086 (Domesday Book)
MEANING:	Probably open land of a man called Bill	Usually means broad wood or clearing	Hill by the River Brant
DERIVATION:	From the Old English personal name *Bill*, plus the Old English word *feld* (open country or tract of land cleared of trees)	From the Old English words *brād* (broad or spacious) and *lēah* (wood, woodland clearing or glade)	From the old river-name *Brant* (meaning steep or deep) plus the Old English word *dūn* (hill)

Three's Up Trivia!

Bitchfield is a small village around six miles south-east of Grantham, and actually comprises two groups of buildings. One group is known as Bitchfield and is located on the B1176, while it is connected to Lower Bitchfield by the narrow Dark Lane. The first left turn on Dark Lane is a no through road taking you to the settlement of Lower Bitchfield which also includes the parish church which is dedicated to St Mary Magdalene. The oldest element of the church is probably the Norman door inside the 14th century porch while the three round arches in the nave are also 12th century Norman; we use the word "probably" as the south wall has traces of herringbone masonry that may be Anglo-Saxon. As for the tower, that dates from the 13th century.

Finally, flowing through Lower Bitchfield is the little West Glen River, and just south of the settlement it flows by some ancient earthworks known as Camp Field.

Next, **Bradley** also has parts of its parish church dating back to Norman times – this being the lower part of the tower of St George's church. The upper half is 13th century, including the belfry (the battlements date from later), while the porch dates from the 14th century as does the font which is decorated with a Latin inscription emphasising the importance of teaching children to say their prayers!

Bradley Manor House, like the church, is also Grade II listed and has a date stone of 1686, although parts of it are believed to date back further to the late medieval period. It is thought that it was substantially extended in 1689, with further extensions built in the 20th century.

The church of St Mary Magdalene at Lower Bitchfield.

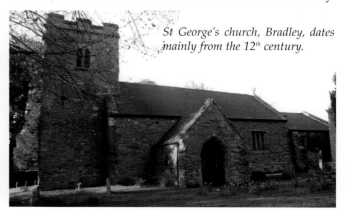

St George's church, Bradley, dates mainly from the 12th century.

Hall Lane, Brandon.

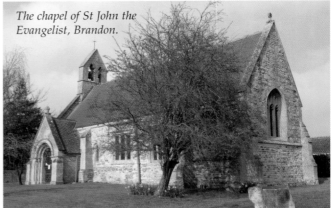

The chapel of St John the Evangelist, Brandon.

Bradley Quirk Alert:
The Black Lady and Jam!

Bradley Woods is allegedly the haunt of the Black Lady who died in the woods after her husband had left her to go to war. Their cottage was subsequently ransacked and her child taken and it is said that the Black Lady can be seen at night in the woods, wearing a black cloak and searching for her child. Meanwhile, the north window of the church is in memory of the Tickler family who lived at Bradley Manor and owned an international jam and preserve-making company that once employed 2,000 people across the Commonwealth. The window contains Latin text with the letter 'I' in the word 'Iam' being changed to a 'J' to make it look like Jam!

Finally, **Brandon** is located close to the Nottinghamshire border, around 6 miles south-east of Newark-on-Trent. Although the village is only small with a population of around one hundred, it does have a chapel of ease which is dedicated to St John the Evangelist, and which is linked to the parish church of All Saints at nearby Hough-on-the-Hill. The chapel was built in the Early English style which dates it to the late 12th and early 13th century, but also includes fragments of Saxon stonework along with a Norman door. The chapel was restored in 1872. The village is also home to Brandon Old Hall, a 16th century residence on Hall Road that was constructed with striking bands of golden ironstone, with the garden walled in the same style.

Brandon Old Hall was built in the 16th century with striking stripes of ironstone and which are retained throughout the garden wall (nearside).

NAME (STATUS):	**BICKER** (Village); **BICKER BAR**; **BICKER GAUNTLET**
POPULATION:	941
DISTRICT:	Boston
EARLIEST RECORD:	*Bichere*, 1086 (Domesday Book)
MEANING:	Settlement by the marsh
DERIVATION:	From the Old Scandinavian words *bý* (farmstead, village or settlement) and *kjarr* (marsh overgrown with brushwood)

Bicker Geographic Trivia: An Ancient Port

Located around 7 miles south-west of Boston, the village of **Bicker** sits at the southern-most point of a one-mile equilateral triangle formed with **Bicker Gauntlet** and **Bicker Bar**. The trio of places are joined by a fourth Bicker, Bicker Fen, which lies just west of Bicker Gauntlet and which is home to Bicker Fen wind-farm, complete with 13 turbines producing 26MW (2MW each), enough power for 14,000 homes.

The place-name means "settlement by the marsh". This is because in Anglo-Saxon times, Bicker was a small port sat at the head of a tidal estuary on an inlet from the Wash, and which was thus named Bicker Haven. However, whereas Bicker Haven had originally formed the outlet of the River Witham which had flowed through Bicker from the north, the river was diverted to Boston after a flood in 1014. Then in the mid-16th century, the locals began to reclaim the marsh around Bicker for pasture and without the tide to flush it out, Bicker Haven thus silted up. As a result, Bicker changed from a port to a farming village and, today, Bicker now lies around 8 miles (13 km) from the coast. Meanwhile, a mile or so to the east of Bicker is Bank House, located at the junction between the A17 and the B1181, and named after part of the former sea bank of Bicker Haven. As for Bicker Bar, the place is effectively comprised of just Bar Farm plus what has been termed the Bicker Bar Roundabout which marks the junction of the A52 and the A17.

As for the former course of the river, it is claimed that the roads of Bicker still describe it and which is thought to be a unique feature in the Lincolnshire fens.

Little more than a stream/drain today, the remnant of the former river is known as the Old Eau. Meanwhile, Bicker Fen to the north-west of the village is also the proposed landing site for a 1,400 MW power cable from Denmark called Viking Link.

Bicker Pub: Ye Olde Red Lion

Ye Olde Red Lion is a typical English pub, with low beams, open fires and real ale. It also dates back to at least 1665 when it was known as "John Drury" – although it is thought that this was actually the date when an even older pub was restored. Given it is also rumoured that the inn was once called the Mariner's Rest and/or the Sailor's Rest, the older inn may therefore have dated back to pre-1014 which was the year when Bicker ceased to be an inland port.

Bicker Church: St Swithin's

The date of the earliest church in Bicker is not known, but there was certainly one here in 1086 as one is recorded in Domesday Book, while fragments of 10th century Anglo-Scandinavian style carved stone can be found in the porch and the north and south aisles. The church today is part-Norman, part-medieval, with alterations effected in the 16th century, while further restoration was carried out in the 19th century. The original Norman church was built in the shape of a cross with a central tower, but the latter and the chancel were rebuilt in the 13th century, while the top stage of the tower was added in the 15th century. The nave is still Norman, though, with impressive arcades crowned with scalloped capitals shaped like crosses, and

The Old Eau at Bicker, remnant of the former river that once flowed into Bicker Haven to the south of Bicker.

Some of the wind turbines of Bicker Fen, with a typical fen dyke in the foreground.

Ye Olde Red Lion at Bicker has a strap line of "Since 1665" on its website. It is certainly a beautiful old English pub, with low beams, open fires and real ale!

St Swithin's church at Bicker partly dates back to Norman times.

supporting the Norman arches with their zig-zag mouldings. The Norman transepts were absorbed into the 14th century aisles.

Bicker Historic Trivia: Farming and Steam Threshing

When Bicker Haven silted up in the late Anglo-Scandinavian period, Bicker's importance diminished, and whereas neighbouring Swineshead and Donington retained their markets thanks to their location on the east-to-west trading route, Bicker did not. Nevertheless, the area continued to benefit from good quality arable land, particularly following the enclosure of the lowest-lying fen to the west in 1767, between Bicker and the South Forty Foot Drain. Arable farming is still the main industry today, particularly of vegetable crops.

Today, Bicker is also well-known locally for its annual Bicker Steam Threshing country fair which is held in early September. The event plays host to numerous traction engines and vintage tractors, as well as craft stalls and a steam organ, but the centrepiece is the operation of an old threshing machine powered by a traction engine.

Bicker Quirk Alert: Lighthouses, Yaffles, Kek and Holey Gravestones

Local Bicker legend has it that the predecessor building to Ye Olde Red Lion inn was actually a lighthouse in the days when Bicker was at the end of a tidal inlet. But while that fact is questionable, it is certainly true that the green woodpecker is known in these parts as the yaffle – and which was also the inspiration for Peter Firmin and Oliver Postgate's Professor Yaffle in the children's television programme, Bagpuss! The yaffle is also referred to in Lincolnshire as green peek and wood-hack. Meanwhile, cow parsley is referred to locally as kek!

Finally, Bicker's churchyard is home to some unusual gravestones as many of those dated between 1780 and 1830 have a characteristic hole drilled

through, usually a few inches down from the top and centrally bored. This is also a custom to be found in other Fenland churchyards, too. This is because heavy limestone or slate gravestones set in Fenland soil tended to lean after a few years of freeze/thaw cycles, and that lean became more acute as the years rolled by. This was counteracted, therefore, by drilling the hole in the gravestone, and then placing a stout wooden stake behind it. An iron bolt would then be passed and secured through the wood and the hole in the stone to give the latter more support, while the hole was lined with lead to ensure that the rusting of the iron bolt didn't cause it to expand and crack the gravestone. Of course, today, almost every stake and bolt has long since rotted away leaving just the hole. However, in Bicker churchyard there are two survivors which still have their rusted bolts in place!

A typical gravestone in Bicker churchyard, which was created between 1780 and 1830, and includes a hole drilled towards the top. See Quirk Alert for why.

NAME (STATUS):	**BILLINGBOROUGH** (Village)
POPULATION:	1,401
DISTRICT:	South Kesteven
EARLIEST RECORD:	*Billingeburg*, 1086 (Domesday Book)
MEANING:	Probably stronghold of the followers of a man called Bil or Billa
DERIVATION:	From the Old English personal name Bil or Billa, plus the Old English words *inga* (of) and *burh* (fortified place or stronghold). Alternatively, the first element may derive from the Old English word *billing* (hill or ridge), while another theory is that the place was named after the Billings tribe from northern Europe who invaded this area during the early Anglo-Saxon centuries.

The Fortescue Arms on High Street, Billingborough, dates from the 18th century.

The village pond in the centre of Billingborough.

Billingborough Pubs: The Fortescue Arms

The Fortescue Arms was built in the 18th century and was named after the local Lords of the Manor. Now encompassing several former properties, the original inn was built from stone reputed to have come from Sempringham Priory after it was sacked by Parliamentarian troops during the English Civil War. Meanwhile, Billingborough was home to another attractive pub until recently, when the former 17th century coaching inn known as the George and Dragon, was converted into five private residences.

Billingborough Church: St Andrew's

The Grade I-listed St Andrew's church dates from the late 13th and early 14th century, with later 15th century additions such as the clerestory, while at least two 19th century restorations were carried out in 1868 and 1891; indeed, the chancel was completely rebuilt during the 1891 restoration. The architecture is a mixture of Early English, and Early and Late Perpendicular Gothic and Decorated styles, of which the most striking features are its mid-14th century tower and spire. Rising from the west end of the north aisle, the tower is decorated with ornate crocketed pinnacles at each corner and which are supported by slender flying buttresses. The

St Andrew's church, Billingborough.

buttresses, in turn, are attached to the spire which rises to 150ft, while a stair turret to the upper phase of the tower is also part of the larger polygonal south-west buttress. Inside, the 14ᵗʰ century nave is particularly impressive with three large arches on the north side and four on the south side, while the pointed gabled south porch dates from around 1312.

Billingborough Historic Trivia:
Famous Residents

Eric Houghton (1910-1996), was a professional footballer who was born in Billingborough in 1910. He made 361 appearances for Aston Villa and 55 for Notts County, scoring 170 goals along the way. He also played 7 times for England, too, and scored 5 goals – a pretty formidable international goal-scoring ratio. And

as if that wasn't enough, he went on to manage Aston Villa to an FA Cup triumph in 1957, while he also played first-class cricket for Warwickshire and minor counties cricket for Lincolnshire. Meanwhile, also born in Billingborough was Robert Gordon Latham (1812-1888), a celebrated ethnologist and philologist, and son of Thomas Latham, Billingborough's resident vicar. Robert Latham went on to hold may prestigious medical and scholarly positions, but it is for his extensive written works for which he is most remembered, including a well-known text-book called *The English Language* which was published in 1841.

Finally, the local school name, Aveland, is taken from a pre-conquest Wapentake of that name, dating back to 921. The Wapentake extended from Bourne to Threekingham.

What I took to be the almshouses at Billingborough known as The Nests. However, The Nests are located opposite Billingborough Primary School on Victoria Street, and were built in 1914; the houses above look somewhat older.

The front of this 19ᵗʰ century converted grain store building reads: "HARRISON CORN MERCHANT". Research tells me that it belonged to George Harrison in the late 19ᵗʰ century – some considerable time before he took up the guitar!

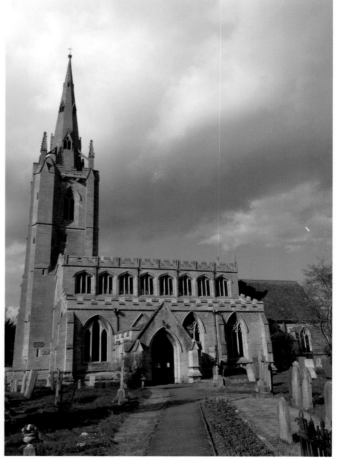

View from the south of the striking St Andrew's church at Billingborough

NAME (STATUS):	**BOOTHBY GRAFFOE** (Village)
POPULATION:	223
DISTRICT:	North Kesteven
EARLIEST RECORD:	*Bodebi*, 1086 (Domesday Book)
MEANING:	Farmstead or village with booths or shelters
DERIVATION:	From the Old Scandinavian words *bōth* (booth or shelter) and *bý* (farmstead, village or settlement). The "Graffoe" affix, is an old wapentake name, meaning "spur of land with a grove", and is derived from the Old English words *grāf* (grove) and *hōh* (heel of land or projecting hill-spur).

Boothby Graffoe Church: St Andrew's

The parish church of Boothby Graffoe is the Grade II-listed St Andrew's which was built in 1842. The 19th century church was a re-build after the previous 17th century church had to be demolished. However, the 17th century church was itself built after its medieval predecessor was demolished, with the latter having been destroyed by a freak hurricane in 1666. We know of this event, because it is recorded in the parish registers of neighbouring Wellingore which describes St Andrew's as having been "extirpated by a hurricane".

Boothby Graffoe Historic Trivia: Somerton Castle

To the west of the village are the earthwork remains of Somerton Castle. Built by Anthony Bek in 1281, a few years before he became Bishop of Durham, the castle was originally a fortified manor house with round towers at its corners. Bek gave the manor house to Edward I in 1309 and it remained with the crown for 300 years until sold by Charles I in 1628, by which stage the castle was ruinous. During 1359 and 1360 the castle hosted King John II of France and his son, Philip, who had both been taken prisoner by the Black Prince at the Battle of Poitiers. Today, one of its two remaining 45ft towers is still built into a later Elizabethan manor house, while the other ruinous tower can be found in the nearby orchard.

Boothby Graffoe Quirk Alert: Kittens in a Bag

Many followers of English comedy will know that there is an award-winning surreal comedian out there called Boothby Graffoe, although he was born James Martyn Rogers. Also a singer, songwriter and playwright, he decided on his stage-name whilst driving back to his home through Lincolnshire one night after a gig. His surreal performances include guitar-accompanied songs such as Planet Dog, Kittens In A Bag, Giraffes Don't Play Harmonicas, So It Can't Be A Giraffe, and The Consequences of Living in a Container. Having seen him live, I can highly recommend. My personal favourite is the Ballad Of The Budgie, not for the faint-hearted, and brilliantly accompanied by Nick Pynn on the violin – in a wonderfully melodic way for most of the song, but in

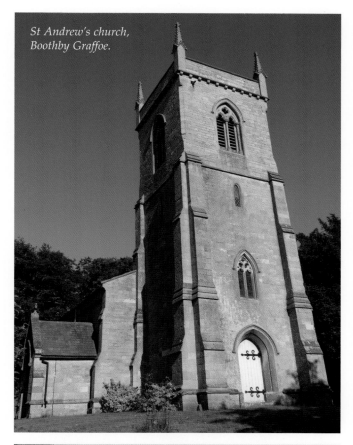

St Andrew's church, Boothby Graffoe.

Main Street, Boothby Graffoe.

a random, whacky and screechy way when the bird finally buys it! My personal favourite comedy ramble, though, is about deer in Denmark! Priceless!

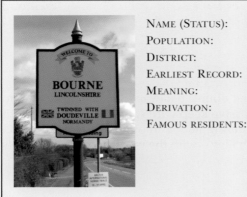

NAME (STATUS):	**BOURNE** (Town)
POPULATION:	14,456
DISTRICT:	South Kesteven
EARLIEST RECORD:	*Brunna*, 960; *Brune*, 1086 (Domesday Book)
MEANING:	Place at the spring(s) or stream(s)
DERIVATION:	From the Old Scandinavian word *brunnr* (spring or stream)
FAMOUS RESIDENTS:	Robert Mannyng (1264-1340), English chronicler; William Cecil (1520-1598), Elizabethan statesman; Job Hartop (1550-1595), adventurer; Robert Harrington (1589-1654), philanthropist; Dr William Dodd (1729-1777), clergyman and forger; Charles Frederick Worth (1825-1895), fashion designer; Sir George White (1840-1912), politician; Robert A. Gardner (1850-1926), magistrate and artist; Lilian Wiles (1885-1975), first female Met Police CID officer; Charles Sharpe (1889-1963), soldier; Raymond Mays (1899-1980), motor racing driver and manufacturer.

The Burghley Arms dates back to the 16th century and is named after the Elizabethan statesman, Lord Burghley, who was born here in 1520.

Bourne Abbey and the parish church of St Peter and St Paul.

Bourne Pub: The Golden Lion and The Burghley Arms

The Golden Lion is a Grade II listed pub that dates back to the late 18th century when it originally accommodated four separate artisans' cottages. One of them was turned into a beer house and eventually all four were converted into a tavern which opened in 1844, apparently with a celebratory pigeon shoot and dinner! Meanwhile, the Burghley Arms dates back to the 16th century. It was originally a private residence before it was converted into an 18th century coaching inn known as The Bull – a name which stuck until 1955 when it was re-named to The Burghley Arms in honour of William Cecil, trusted advisor to Queen Elizabeth I and the first Lord Burghley who was born on these premises in 1520.

Bourne Church: Bourne Abbey and the Parish Church of St Peter and St Paul

Bourne Abbey and the parish church of St Peter and St Paul is the full name of Bourne's Grade I listed parish church, that was founded in 1138. However, there was also a church here when Domesday Book was compiled in 1086, and which may have been preceded by an

Anglo-Saxon abbey. As for the 1138 Bourne Abbey, this was founded as a canonry by Baldwin fitz Gilbert de Clare for up to 14 canons of the Arrouaisian Order, which was aligned to the Abbey of Arrouaise in Artois in north-eastern France; that said, the fundamental rule of the abbey was that of Augustine and it gradually came to be regarded as Augustinian. During its early years, it is thought that *The Ormulum* was written here in 1175, an important Middle English work of biblical exegesis (an interpretation of a religious text). It is now kept in the Bodleian Library at Oxford University.

Moving into the 16th century, and the church survived destruction following its dissolution in 1536, thanks to the nave having been in use by the parish at that time, and it subsequently became the parish church. As for today, the only survivor of the Norman build is the nave, with four round arches on each side supported by huge piers with scalloped capitals. Both of the Norman aisles were widened in the 15th century which is also when the clerestory was added.

Bourne Historic Trivia: Roman Station, Saxon Stronghold, Norman Abbey...

Bourne was a settlement back in Roman Britain, almost certainly thanks to its position on the Roman road, King

Street, plus the fine-quality water supply proffered locally from natural springs – and from which the town would later take its name. The Roman settlement was also on the Carr Dyke, one of the greatest engineering feats achieved during the Roman occupation of Britain. This immense dyke stretched for 56 miles, catching the drainage from the hills, holding it and preventing it from flooding the low fens, and discharging it into the River Nene at Peterborough and the River Witham near Lincoln, whilst also providing a waterway for the transport of grain from the fens to the North. Unsurprisingly, Roman pottery has been unearthed at Bourne, and there is also a theory that there was once a Roman fort here to guard the road and waterway.

A few centuries later in around 1035, Bourne was also reputedly the birthplace of Hereward the Wake, the famous 11th century Anglo-Danish leader and key figure in the resistance to the Norman invasion of England in the area around the Isle of Ely. Although that said, the 12th century source of this information, *De Gestis Herwardi Saxonis*, refers in this connection only to Hereward's father as being "of Bourne" and to the father's house and retainers there. English clergyman, university professor, historian and novelist Charles Kingsley then used the *De Gestis* text as the basis for his lively and somewhat embellished 1865 novel *Hereward the Wake* – although there is little doubt that Hereward was a major thorn in the side of William I.

It was also not long after this episode that Bourne Castle was built, by the same Baldwin fitz Gilbert de Clare who built Bourne Abbey in 1138. Bourne Castle was a motte and double bailey castle, which was said to have had a massive keep with square towers, and with a moat surrounding its low mound and another moat enclosing the bailey – with the moats filled by Bourne's famous spring which is sourced close by at a place called Well Head. The castle's history is very sketchy, though. We know that Thomas de Wake entertained Edward III here and we also know that by the time of Elizabeth I, all that remained were the mounds and the moats that we can still see today.

The foundation of the abbey and the castle in the early 12th century was part of a general restructuring of Bourne which ensured that the current town centre was built as a new town at the entrance to Baldwin's castle, with the new main road passing between Baldwin's new castle and abbey; the pre-Norman road lies under the junction between the nave and the chancel of Bourne Abbey!

Another century on, and Bourne citizen Robert

The nave of Bourne Abbey, with the arcades here dating to the initial build in 1138. This is the view towards the tower; the reverse view is on page 33.

These earthworks in Wellhead Park are all that remains of the medieval Bourne Castle.

The Grade II-listed Red Hall, Bourne, dates from the early 17th century. From 1860-1959, it was the town's railway station booking office and waiting room.

The Bourne Eau is a 3.5 mile waterway that linked Bourne with the River Glen when constructed in 1765.

Mannyng (1264-1340) – and also known as Robert de Brunne – was a long-term canon at Sempringham Abbey, 6 miles north of Bourne. It was here that he completed the two volumes for which he is most known, *Handlyng Synne* and *Mannyng's Chronicle*. The former was a popularised religious and historical manuscript written in a Middle English dialect that was easily understood by the people of his time, and is acknowledged to be of great value because it offers an insight into the ways and thoughts of his contemporaries; moreover, it also shows us the language then in common use. Indeed, Arthur Mee covers Mannyng in his *King's England* volume of Lincolnshire, claiming that it was he who gave our language its current shape, while other sources define his works in Middle English as part of the larger movement at the beginning of the 14th century towards the replacement of Latin and Anglo-Norman. The preface of *Handlyng Synne* also contains this verse:

> For men unlearned I undertook
> In English speech to write this book,
> To all true Christians under sun,
> To good and loyal men of Brunn,
> Robert of Brunn now greeteth ye
> And prays for your prosperity.

Later in life, Mannyng moved to Sixhills Gilbertine Priory near Market Rasen, and here he wrote *Story of England*, which was largely a translation of a chronicle originally compiled by a canon of Bridlington Priory.

It is thought that a waterway to the north-east of Bourne known as the Bourne Old Eau, once connected the town to the sea in Roman times – and which in those days may have been around the Pinchbeck area. By the 19th century, though, and thanks to the Bourne Navigation Act of 1780, the new Bourne Eau was capable of carrying commercial crafts to the town from the Wash. However, passage became impossible once the junction of the Eau and the River Glen was converted from gates to a sluice in 1860.

Like so many other English towns, the railways brought prosperity to Bourne, bringing major develop-ment to the town. Improved communications also allowed the bottled water industry to develop, thus leading to easy export of the product along with the town's other rural products. Bourne's affluence was further enhanced from the corn trade boom following the mechanisation of fen drainage, and it was also in the fenland to the east of Bourne that sugar beet was first grown as an English crop, by British Sugar Ltd, and which would go on to ensure that the nation's sugar requirements were met during World War I and World War II. Talking of which, a German bomber crashed onto the Butcher's Arms in Eastgate, during World War II, after being shot down. Nine people were killed, including the bomber's crew.

The affluence first acquired by Bourne in the 19th century continues through to today, and the district as a whole has one of the fastest-growing housing markets in the country – although many of the houses in Bourne do have to pay additional drainage rates to the Black Sluice and Welland and Deepings Internal Drainage Boards. Finally, in the 21st century hydroponic food production plants have been built on the edge of the fen, while Bourne continues to bottle its own fine quality spring water, acquired from its natural springs.

Bourne Quirk Alert: White Bread Meadow, Mi Duck

Ever since 1770, White Bread Meadow has been let on an annual basis via an extremely quirky tradition revolving around an auction with a difference. Every year, the auctioneer starts a race between a set of boys who run for a specified distance. As soon as they have set off, bidding for the field begins, and whoever has secured the highest bid at the end of the race is the person who will hold the meadow for the following year, while the rent goes to buy bread for the poor.

Earlier, we talked about the huge influence that Bourne's Robert Mannyng had on the adoption of Middle English as a language in the early 14th century. What is particularly interesting, though, is that his works adopted the East Midlands dialect that was his own, and which subsequently influenced the spread of English throughout the country.

The front and rear of Baldock's Mill which was built in c.1800 as a corn-grinding water mill. Today, it has been converted by Bourne Civic Society into the town's Heritage Centre.

Three's-Up!

	BRANDY WHARF	**DONNA NOOK**	**HATTON**
STATUS:	Hamlet	Nature Reserve	Village
POPULATION:	c.20	c.3,500 grey seals	295 (Parish of Thornton Curtis)
DISTRICT:	West Lindsey	East Lindsey	East Lindsey
EARLIEST RECORD:	Unknown	*Donna Nook*, 1588	*Hatune*, 1086 (Domesday Book)
MEANING:	Brande's Wharf	Named after a ship, *The Donna*, part of the Spanish Armada, which sank off the nook of land here in 1588	Farmstead on a heath
DERIVATION:	See Three's Up Trivia	See Three's Up Trivia	From the Old English words *hæth* (heath) and *tūn* (farmstead)

This cast-iron bridge at Brandy Wharf over the River Ancholme was built by engineer John Rennie in 1831. The brick warehouse alongside dates back to the 19th century.

A small part of the vast salt marshes at Donna Nook where a c.3,500 grey seal colony breed between October and December.

Three's Up Trivia!

The North Lincolnshire hamlet of **Brandy Wharf** is allegedly derived from a religious sect of Vikings known as the *Brande*, who came over with the Danish invaders of 867. They subsequently settled here and set up a smuggling service on the River Ancholme, and the west bank pick-up point thus became known as Brande's Wharf. Today, Brandy Wharf is split down the middle, parish-wise, with the western half in the Waddingham parish (population 601) and the eastern half in the South Kelsey parish (population 604). However, if you take out the Brandy Wharf Leisure Park, the population of Brandy Wharf is probably less than 20!

Next up, **Donna Nook** can be found on the East Lindsey coast, about nine miles south-east of Cleethorpes. The salt marsh area around Donna Nook is used as a bombing range by numerous RAF bases in Lincolnshire, and the base sited here is actually known as RAF Donna Nook. There was also a predecessor RAF Donna Nook here during World War II, a radar station which tracked both low-flying intruders and German E-boats cruising offshore between 1943 and 1945. It is thought that a young Sir Arthur C. Clarke was posted here in 1943.

Despite the regular bomb-testing, a large grey seal colony thrives on the sands and dunes nearby and they actually breed here every October to December with in excess of 1,000 pups born each year. The area is managed by the Lincolnshire Wildlife Trust as the Donna Nook National Nature Reserve. The reserve covers more than 6.25 miles (10 km) of coastline, and attracts over 40,000 people a year. This has led to the Trust setting up a double wooden fence to try to stop people touching the new-born pups, for the mother may abandon the pup if she detects human or dog scent on them. Of course, the reserve isn't just a haven for seals. Deposition of material from the River Humber has resulted in extensive mudflats and saltings and the advancing dunes have trapped areas of saltmarsh behind them. As these areas have gradually become less saline, an interesting plant community has begun to develop while 47 species of bird regularly breed in the area with over 250 species recorded in total, many of which call in as part of their migration.

Donna Nook Quirk Alert:
The Donna Nook

The Donna Nook *was a 40 metre, 307 ton fishing trawler, built in 1916 at Selby in North Yorkshire. However, she was pressed into service in 1941 as a minesweeper, but was accidentally rammed and sunk by another minesweeper called the* Stella Rigel. *This was whilst hurrying to the assistance of a third minesweeper, the* Franc Tireur, *which was under torpedo attack by a German E-Boat laying mines 12 miles north of Harwich, on the night of 24/25th September 1941. Fortunately, the crew of the* Donna Nook *was saved by the* Stella Rigel!

Finally, at **Hatton**, St Stephen's church is a Grade II-listed church that was initially built in the 13th century,

but which was rebuilt in 1870 by James Fowler (1828-1892). The 1870 church was built on the same site as its medieval predecessor, using a few of the original's fragments. It has a steep-sided scissor braced slate roof and red brick walls with bands of green sandstone punctuated by stone mullioned windows. The building comprises a vestry entrance, south porch, nave, chancel and an attractive rounded apse, while the roof is topped by a stylish turret accompanied by a spirelet.

Meanwhile, the National Transmission System (NTS) has one of its 26 compressor stations located at Hatton – the NTS being the network of gas pipelines that supply gas to 40 power stations from natural gas terminals situated on the coast and then on to gas distribution companies that supply gas to homes and businesses.

Looking down the nave of St Stephen's church towards the chancel and apse.
Below: *St Stephen's church, Hatton from the south-east.*

NAME (STATUS):	**BROUGHTON** (Town)
POPULATION:	5,726
DISTRICT:	North Lincolnshire
EARLIEST RECORD:	*Bertone*, 1086 (Domesday Book)
MEANING:	Farmstead by a hill or mound
DERIVATION:	From the Old English words *beorg* (rounded hill, mound or tumulus) and *tūn* (farmstead).

Broughton Church: St Mary's

The lower parts of Broughton St Mary's church tower date back to Anglo-Saxon times, as evidenced by the lengthy stretches of herringbone masonry as well as a primitive little doorway and small windows on the south side; Arthur Mee theorises that this may have constituted the nave of the original Anglo-Saxon church. However, it was probably the Normans that gave the church its most unusual feature, the semi-circular turret fixed onto the west side of the tower which encloses a stairway to the belfry. As for the upper stretches of the tower, they date from the 15th century. In between these times, the nave (14th century) and chancel (part-13th century) were built, with the latter still including part of a Norman window, while Norman carvings can be found at the foot of the nave

arcade pillars. The clerestory and the aisles are 15th century, while the 17th century chapel was built by the Andersons, who succeeded the Redfords as the Lords of the Manor. The chapel contains a large monument to Sir Edward Anderson who died in 1660, while the chancel houses the fine alabaster 14th century figures of Sir Henry Redford and his wife.

Broughton Historic Trivia

It is believed that a settlement existed at Broughton in Neolithic times as Stone Age tools have been found in the area to the north of the town, while Bronze Age pottery was also discovered in 1956 – at a house on Ermine Street, as it happens! Of course, Ermine Street itself came next, constructed by the Romans between 45 and 75 AD; yet more archaeological finds – this time of tiles, coins and fragments of pottery – suggest that Broughton may have been the site of a Roman settlement, too.

Moving forward to the late 12th century, and Gokewell Priory was founded in the Broughton area by William de Alta Ripa, initially as a nunnery for the Cistercian order. The priory is not thought to have housed more than eight nuns during its existence, and was therefore never a wealthy institution. Nevertheless, it was still dissolved in 1536. Just over a century later in 1660, the Baronetcy of Broughton was created for Sir Edmund Anderson and survived for nine generations until the 9th Baronet, Sir Charles Henry John Anderson, died without an heir in October 1891.

St Mary's church at Broughton includes Anglo-Saxon herringbone work at the foot of the tower, and also includes the unusual semi-circular turret, fixed onto the west side of the tower (right).

Broughton Quirk Alert: All Change

In 1974, two significant things happened to Broughton. Firstly, the place achieved town status – although it does continue to run a village hall to this day! The second significant change was that, along with the rest of northern Lincolnshire, the new town changed counties and became part of the new non-metropolitan county of Humberside. However, Humberside only lasted for 22 years before it was abolished and Broughton once again became part of the ceremonial county of Lincolnshire – this time as part of the new unitary authority of North Lincolnshire. Throughout these years, the town continued to grow with new housing developments to the north and north-west of the town. In fact, it has grown to such an extent that its parish population is now in excess of neighbouring Brigg, which has been a town for many centuries longer!

NAME (STATUS):	**CHERRY WILLINGHAM** (Village)
POPULATION:	3,506
DISTRICT:	West Lindsey
EARLIEST RECORD:	*Wilingeham*, 1086 (Domesday Book); *Chyry Wylynham*, 1386
MEANING:	Homestead of the family or followers of a man called Willa
DERIVATION:	From the Old English personal name *Willa*, plus the Old English words *inga* (of) and *hām* (homestead). The affix of "Cherry" is derived from the Middle English word *chiri* (cherry-tree). NB: Middle English represents the English language from c.1100 to c.1500.

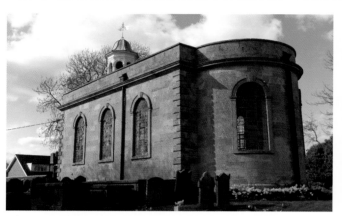

The unusual church of St Peter and St Paul at Cherry Willingham, as seen from the south-east.

The view of the church from the south-west.

Cherry Willingham Church: St Peter and St Paul's

The unusual-looking church of St Peter and St Paul at Cherry Willingham was built in 1753. The church is built of local Ancaster limestone, and sits on a little knoll above Church Lane. From the road to the west, the church appears square with a portico above the door and an attractive bellcote rising above the portico. However, the eastern end of the church is apsidal and looks like a completely different church. There was a church here before the current Georgian one, and a church is referenced here as far back as Domesday Book (1086). Inside, there is a notable marble archway-shaped monument to Thomas Becke who provided the funds for the 1753 church build, while another notable feature is the cupola which was restored to its original condition in 1967.

Cherry Willingham Historic Trivia

Stone Age and Iron Age remains have been found at Cherry Willingham, while a Roman villa was also discovered nearby. The Anglo-Saxon period is represented by a series of long and narrow fishponds running east to west just below the church, while the Norman period is represented by the entry for *Wilingeham* in Domesday Book (1086), where we learn that the manor belonged to Gilbert de Gaunt. The manor then passed to the Marmian family in the 12th century who held it until the 15th century.

The Wishing Well, one of two pubs in Cherry Willingham, the other being the Cherry Tree.

Fast-forwarding to the 18th century and the manor was purchased by the aforementioned Thomas Becke, he who built the church of St Peter and St Paul in 1753. A renowned Lincolnshire lawyer, it was also Thomas Becke who enclosed the estate and put most of the land to grass.

The mid-19th century saw Cherry Willingham become a commuter village for Lincoln and the population steadily increased – so while there were only 16 houses there in 1801, there are over 1300 today. The first school in the village opened in November 1877 with 58 fee-paying pupils, while today, the village has both Primary and Secondary schools for nearly one thousand pupils.

NAME (STATUS):	**CLEETHORPES** (Town, Seaside Resort)
POPULATION:	39,505
DISTRICT:	North East Lincolnshire
EARLIEST RECORD:	*Thorp*, 1406; *Clethorpe*, 1552
MEANING:	Outlying settlement(s) near Clee
DERIVATION:	See Cleethorpes Name Derivation section

Cleethorpes: Place-Name Derivation

As stated above, Cleethorpes means "outlying settlement or settlements near Clee". The name is derived from the Old Scandinavian word *thorp*, meaning "a secondary settlement or a dependent outlying farmstead or hamlet". The "thorpes" in question, were Itterby, Oole and Thrunscoe, initially Danish settlements from around the 9th century, and which eventually each formed part of the wider parish of Clee and which is today known as Old Clee. As for the name Clee (*Cleia*, 1086), it is derived from the Old English word *clæg*, meaning "clay".

Cleethorpes: Famous Residents

For a fairly small town, Cleethorpes is the birthplace of a number of famous people, as follows:

Kristian Adams (b.1976), cricketer; *Bill Appleyard* (1879-1958), footballer; *H. Hugh Bancroft* (1904-1988), composer; *Stephen Bennett* (b.1959), golfer; *Nibbs Carter* (b.1966), musician; *John Cockerill* (b.1961), footballer; *Peter Collinson* (1936-1980), film director; *Bob Cottam* (b.1944), cricketer; *Eorl Crabtree* (b.1982), rugby league legend; *Michele Dotrice* (b.1948), actress; *Helen Fospero* (b.1966), television presenter and journalist; *Vivean Gray* (b.1924), actress; *Chris Hargreaves* (b.1972), footballer; *Patricia Hodge* (b.1946), actress; *Gemma Merna* (b.1984), actress, model; *Carl Ross* (1901-1986), fishery entrepreneur; *Rod Temperton* (b.1947-2016), songwriter, record producer and musician; *Richard Witts* musicologist; *Darren Wrack* (b.1976), footballer; *Patrick Wymark* (1926-1970), actor.

There is obviously a lot of talent in there, including a few surprises – the cultured tones of Michele Dotrice and Patricia Hodge having hailed from Cleethorpes, for a start, as well as dear old Nell Mangle – Vivean Gray's character in Neighbours! However, my personal favourite is someone I didn't even know of until doing the research, this being songwriter, record producer and musician, Rod Temperton. Born in Cleethorpes in 1947, Temperton initially found fame as the keyboard player with 1970s funk band Heatwave, for whom he penned their three biggest hits, *Boogie Nights*, *Always and Forever* and *The Groove Line*. However, in 1979, he was recruited by Quincy Jones to write for Michael Jackson's first solo album, the multi-million selling *Off The Wall*. What this means, ladies and gentleman, is that absolute classics like the title track, *Off The Wall* and *Rock With You*, along with later classics like the mighty *Thriller* – they were all "Made in Cleethorpes"!

Of course, the list doesn't stop there. If you like your smooth soul sounds, chances are you love a song written by Rod Temperton – including one of my all-time favourite artists, George Benson – as Temperton wrote all the songs on the 1980 LP, *Give Me The Night* – including the title track and other Benson classics, *Love X Love* and *Moody's Mood*. Other artists written for include Patti Austin, Anita Baker, Mariah Carey, Karen Carpenter, Aretha Franklin, Herbie Hancock, James Ingram, Quincy Jones, Michael McDonald, Stephanie Mills, Jeffrey Osborne, Mica Paris, Donna Summer, and The Manhattan Transfer. This man was a LEGEND! Sadly, he passed away in early October 2016.

St Peter's church, Cleethorpes, built by James Fowler between 1864 and 1866.

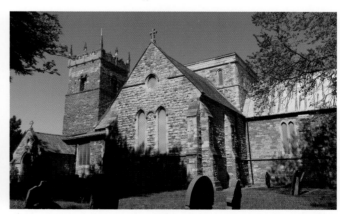

The church of Holy Trinity and St Mary at neighbouring Old Clee is a rarity in that it still has its original Saxon tower, built in around 1050.

Cleethorpes Church: St Peter's and St Mary's

St Peter's church was built in 1866 in what was then a Methodist-dominated community; the nearest Anglican parish church was at Old Clee, a mile or so to the north-west. St Peter's owes its existence to the determination of the Reverend William Price Jones. He started with a vicarage in 1852 (now part of St Peter's School), on land awarded to the vicar and churchwardens in 1846. However, it wasn't until January 1864 that a resolution was passed to build the church, at which point Louth architect, James Fowler was appointed. The church was completed two years later and was consecrated by the Bishop of Lincoln on St Peter's Day, 1866. The tower was added the following year.

As for the aforementioned church at Old Clee, this is Grade I listed and very special indeed, since the church of Holy Trinity and St Mary's dates back to Anglo-Saxon times, with the tower providing the most striking evidence. Built in around 1050, the tower doubled up nicely as an important lookout point for marauding Vikings. The 11th century tower is typically Saxon, built of rubble with roughly-dressed quoins and coupled windows in the belfry. Only the parapet is non-Saxon, dating from the 15th century. Inside, the nave is also very old. The two eastern-most arches of the north arcade date to the early Norman period with their bold roll moulding, while the western arch, which has zig-zag moulding, is slightly later. As for the south arcade, that dates from the late Norman period and the arches are again adorned with roll moulding as well as cable and billet detail. The font is also Norman, while the chancel, porch and the low tower built over the crossing are all relatively modern.

Finally, if you look hard enough between the western tower doorway arch and the Saxon keyhole window, you should be able to make out a face on a blue stone. He is known locally as the Old Man of Clee.

Cleethorpes Historic Trivia

It is known that there has been a settlement at Cleethorpes since the 6th century, although the place eventually became comprised of three outlying settlements, Itterby, Oole and Thrunscoe, each part of the wider Clee parish. By the 16th century, though, Cleethorpes had become a place in its own right, and soon developed as a fishing village, having grown to a population of 284 by the time of the first census in 1801. Shortly after this, Cleethorpes began to develop as a 19th century holiday resort, with sea-bathing and the taking of medicinal waters both fashionable pastimes. The year 1842 then saw 2,050 acres (8.3 km²) of land divided up among land owners as part of the Cleethorpes Enclosure Bill, along with the development of eight new roads. Hotels, lodging houses and inns began to appear as the resort became ever-more popular, especially when the railways opened up Cleethorpes to the working class populations of the East Midlands and Yorkshire. In fact, the Manchester, Sheffield and Lincolnshire Railway even built a mock ruin of a castle, known as Ross Castle, in 1863 as an additional tourist attraction. Named after Ernest Ross, the secretary of the railway company, the mock castle survives to this day. Meanwhile, the pier was added in 1873 and the promenade in 1885.

The town's boundaries were expanded in 1927 to include part of Humberston and the Beacon Hill area of Weelsby parish, while 1936 saw Cleethorpes granted municipal borough status. Of course, as Cleethorpes was expanding in a north-westerly direction, Grimsby was expanding in a south-easterly direction and eventually, the two towns became seamless. This led to a number of attempts by the larger Grimsby to absorb the smaller Cleethorpes, but that was all put to bed following the Local Government Act 1972, which saw both towns absorbed into the new non-metropolitan county of Humberside in 1974, and each re-badged as the Borough of Grimsby and the Borough of Cleethorpes, respectively. Both borough councils were then merged as the unitary authority of North Lincolnshire, following the abolition of Humberside in 1996, and that is how things have remained ever since, with each of Grimsby, Immingham and Cleethorpes now marketed as "Greater Grimsby" since 2009 by the North East Lincolnshire Council.

Ross Castle at Cleethorpes was built in 1863 as a tourist attraction by the Manchester, Sheffield and Lincolnshire Railway Company.

The golden sands of Cleethorpes along with the pier which was built in 1873.

View looking northwards along the promenade at Cleethorpes.

This war memorial is dedicated to the crews and ground staff of RAF North Cotes.

The gardens on the sea-front at Cleethorpes and which include a large statue of a pelican.

Interesting topiary in front of Ross Castle.

Cleethorpes Quirk Alert: Meggies, UFO's, Blundell Park and the Cleethorpes Ghost

Cleethorpes is also known in Lincolnshire by its alter-ego, Meggies. However it isn't clear why. Various theories range from a meggie being the cost of a tram fare from Grimsby to Cleethorpes, to those who served in the Lincolnshire Regiment under Captain H.W. Meggitt in the 19th century. Others think it's a rhyming alternative to Skeggy! The most likely explanation, though, is that Isaac's Hill was previously known as Meg's Island, and anyone born there became a Meggie – a fair shout given the hill was once home to two maternity homes!

Just as mysterious is the UFO that was widely spotted on 22nd September 1956 at 3pm. It hung around for a whole hour off the Cleethorpes coast, and was even picked up on the radar at RAF Manby, too. Eyewitnesses described it as a large spherical object with a glass appearance.

Next up, Cleethorpes is home to Grimsby Town's football ground, Blundell Park, thus making it one of very few English football clubs with a town or city name to have their home ground in a different community.

Finally, 1896 was the year of the Cleethorpes Ghost. Eyewitnesses described this particular phenomenon as a lady carrying an umbrella and wearing a long veil, but with holes cut out for her ghostly eyes. For some time, she was allegedly seen every night and apparently had a penchant for moaning, too, which scared the living daylights out of witnesses! However, it was later theorised that the ghost was actually a lady from Hull who had been painfully disfigured by a gas explosion. She had come to Cleethorpes for rest and recuperation but had covered herself from head to toe in a grey veil to hide her disfigurement!

NAME (STATUS):	**COATES** (Hamlet)
POPULATION:	c.5
DISTRICT:	West Lindsey
EARLIEST RECORD:	*Cotes*, 1086 (Domesday Book)
MEANING:	Place at the cottages or huts
DERIVATION:	From the Old English word *cot* (cottage, hut or shelter)

Coates Geographic Trivia

The tiny hamlet of Coates probably wins the prize for the smallest hamlet in Lincolnshire, as it is comprised of just one farm and St Edith's church. Located around 6 miles south-east of Gainsborough between two branches of the River Till, Coates is part of the parish of Stow (archaically Stow-in-Lindsey), and which includes a number of hamlets all suffixed with "-by-Stow", meaning that our hamlet here is also known as Coates-by-Stow.

Coates Church: St Edith's

Most of the oldest parts of St Edith's church date from the 15th century, although two Norman windows survive, as does the Norman font and a Norman south doorway, so the original church was likely built some-time between 1180 and 1220. One of the most intriguing features is an Early English blocked-up arch in the west wall (*shown right*) which one source rather nicely describes as an "orphaned arch" and which Pevsner suggests is early 13th century. This could possibly have once led to a long-since vanished west tower, and frac-ture lines in the north and south walls repaired with more regular stone, hint at a possible collapsed tower to the west. Alternatively, a tower may have been planned but was aborted after the completion of one arch.

Next, the pulpit is thought to date from the 15th century, which as pulpits go, is very old. It was also said to have been rescued from a barn where it had been hidden for safety! However, the most impressive part of this little church is its carved oak rood screen which,

Blocked-up arch, St Edith's church.

although much restored, still retains a lot of its 15th century work, too. Meanwhile, the rood gallery (or rood loft) is equally impressive and is the most complete example in Lincolnshire. It also retains its original framework, and is reached by the original internal stone stairway. Its survival through the Reformation is largely attributed to the Butler family who acquired the manor at around the same time, although the church's remoteness and relative signif-icance probably also helped. These factors presumably also explain why the arms of Charles I survived, too, and which can be found on the north wall of the nave, while there is also a fine brass to Anthony Butler and his wife Maria in the chancel.

The double bellcote dates from the 18th century, with one of the two bells dated 1704; the other is 15th century.

St Edith's church at Coates from the north. Note the odd mixture of windows in four different architectural styles.

The south side of St Edith's church.

Elsewhere, there are brass plates and other memorials to the Butler family along with an alabaster memorial to Brian Cooke of Doncaster who died in 1653. Finally, the altar slab, with its six incised crosses, is believed to be unique. The church was restored in 1883.

As for the dedication to St Edith, this is thought to be due to 10th century trade links with Tamworth in Staffordshire, and which has a magnificent former collegiate church dedicated to the same Saint.

Coates Historic Trivia: The Motley Crew

There are records of a church being built at Coates in the late 11th century and then given by Peter of Coates to the Premonstratensian Order at Welbeck Abbey in c.1150. A grange was then established beside what was thought to be a sizeable medieval village. The size is interesting, though, because references since the 19th century only refer to a farm and a church – perhaps suggesting that Coates was yet another medieval village that was virtually wiped out by the plague, most likely the Black Death of the mid-14th century. The reference to one farm and one church in 1842 states that George Motley occupied the farm – although sources state that he also resided in the "old hall" which had formerly been the seat of the Butler family. Whether the hall was located in Coates as well, is unclear, but further reports state that the "old hall" was demolished between 1842 and 1872 and a new hall erected in its place. Interestingly, by 1872, someone called Oldham Walker occupied the farm, although George Motley owned 200 acres of land at Coates, while the rest of what was then the parish of Coates-by-Stow was owned by Sir John William Ramsden, baronet.

Today, St Edith's church is located in the middle of a farmyard, while it is also listed in *England's Thousand Best Churches* (Penguin) by Simon Jenkins.

Looking towards the ancient rood screen and rood loft inside St Edith's church.

Looking down from the rood loft into the nave, with its old rustic pews.

The Motley Crew. Nine gravestones commemorating members of the Motley family from the 1830s to the 1890s.

The late Norman transitional south doorway.

NAME (STATUS):	**COWBIT** (Village)
POPULATION:	1,220
DISTRICT:	South Holland
EARLIEST RECORD:	*Coubiht*, 1267
MEANING:	River-bend where cows are pastured
DERIVATION:	From the Old English words *cū* (cow) and *byht* (river-bend)
PRONUNCIATION:	Pronounced by locals as "Cubbit"

Cowbit Geographic Trivia: Cowbit Wash

Located around 3 miles south of Spalding, Cowbit used to be on the busy A1073. However, the A16 has recently been re-directed from just north of Cowbit, bypassing the village to the east and then heading on down to Peterborough. As for the former A1073, that is now known as Barrier Bank which passes along the western flank of Cowbit and sits on top of an earth bank which separates the village from a flood plain to the west. The flood plain is known as Cowbit Wash and is now mostly arable land, thanks to the Coronation Channel that was built in 1953 at Spalding – a relief channel for the River Welland to control flooding in Spalding but which subsequently made Cowbit Wash obsolete as a flood plain. Before that, the River Welland used to regularly overflow and flood Cowbit Wash, and it has known to have been under water on occasion for eight months of the year, while in the winter this vast expanse of water would periodically freeze over, thus allowing general skating and indeed even fen skating championships to take place there!

From a drainage perspective, Cowbit is covered by the Welland and Deepings Internal Drainage Board.

Cowbit Church: St Mary's

The Grade I-listed St Mary's church at Cowbit dates from the 14th century when it was built by Prior de Moulton of Spalding in around 1380. The tower and chancel were added in the late 15th century (1487) by John Russell, Bishop of Lincoln; the nave was also extended at this time, while the church was consecrated and dedicated to St Mary a year earlier in 1486. The tower also includes a turret on the south side. Restoration was carried out in 1882.

Cowbit Historic Trivia: Cowbit through the Ages

The B1357 lies to the east of Cowbit, and runs along the course of a Roman road that once linked the east coast with Ermine Street. A few centuries later, swans were bred in the area, a practise which lent its name to the local court which was known as the Swan Mark. Meanwhile, a couple of miles south of Cowbit, at Brotherhouse, there is part of a shaft of a cross which is named after St Guthlac, and which once marked the boundary of the medieval lands of Crowland Abbey. Moving forward to 1798, this was when the Grade II-listed windmill on the eastern side of the village was

St Mary's church at Cowbit, built mainly in the 14th and 15th centuries.

built, while another floor was added in 1815. It was worked by wind until the mid-1930s when an engine was installed, but eventually closed in 1969. Finally, in 1867, Cowbit railway station was opened on the March to Spalding line, and offered a convenient and cost-effective export route for locally grown produce. The station closed in 1961, but the line through the village survived until 1982, and the station buildings survive to this day.

Cowbit Quirk Alert: Worth a Punt

Starting with Queen Victoria's Diamond Jubilee in 1897, Cowbit Wash has been the location of a punt gun salute to mark every coronation and jubilee, concurrent with gun salutes in London, with the latest celebrating the Diamond Jubilee of Queen Elizabeth II in June 2012.

NAME (STATUS):	**EAGLE** (Village)
POPULATION:	793
DISTRICT:	North Kesteven
EARLIEST RECORD:	*Aclei* or *Aycle*, 1086 (Domesday Book)
MEANING:	Wood where oak-trees grow
DERIVATION:	The first part derives from the Old English words *āc* (oak-tree) which was then replaced by Old Scandinavian *eik* (also oak-tree). The second part derives from the Old English word *lēah* (wood).

Eagle Church: All Saints

The Grade I-listed All Saints' church at Eagle dates from the 13th century, but all that now remains from that build is the 13th century tower; the rest of the church was rebuilt in both the 18th century and again in 1903-04. During the second rebuild, the roof was symbolically decorated with reminders that a 12th century preceptory of the Knights Templar was once founded in Eagle by King Stephen (1135-1154), although nothing of it remains today. The decorations consist internally of bosses and shields, while the respective pointed ends of the nave and chancel are decorated externally by a Jerusalem Cross and a St John Cross. The church also retains its Norman font. Meanwhile, the churchyard's stone gateway includes statues of a Knight Templar and a Knight Hospitaller, but is actually a memorial to the eight men from Eagle who didn't return from World War I.

Eagle Historic Trivia: Knights Templar

The Domesday Book names the landowners of Eagle as Roger of Poitou, Durand Malet, Odo the Crossbowman and Countess Judith. The Countess was also a niece of William the Conqueror, and widow of Earl Waltheof, 1st Earl of Northumberland (1072-1075), whom she had betrayed over his part in the Revolt of the Earls – this being a rebellion against William I by the Earls of Northumberland, East Anglia and Hereford. The rebellion failed and Earl Waltheof was executed in 1076.

Eagle was home to a 12th century house owned by the Christian military order of the Knights Templar. However, in 1312, the order was disbanded, and the house passed to another order known as the Knights Hospitaller.

The Struggler at Eagle dates back to the 18th century.

All Saints' church at Eagle, sporting a Jerusalem Cross and a St John Cross, symbolic reminders that Eagle was also the home of a preceptory of the Knights Templar, founded by King Stephen in the 12th century.

The former Eagle Wesleyan Methodist chapel, built in 1903.

The war memorial at Eagle sits at the entrance to All Saints' churchyard. As well as the eight soldiers who gave their lives during World War I, it also commemorates with statues on either side, both the Knights Templar and the Knights Hospitaller.

NAME (STATUS):	**FILLINGHAM** (Village)
POPULATION:	242
DISTRICT:	West Lindsey
EARLIEST RECORD:	*Figelingeham*, 1086 (Domesday Book)
MEANING:	Homestead of the family or followers of a man called Fygla
DERIVATION:	From the Old English personal name, *Fygla*, plus the Old English words *inga* (of) and *ham* (homestead, village, manor or estate)

Fillingham Church: St Andrew's

The Grade II-listed St Andrew's church was largely rebuilt in 1777, including a new chancel and tower. However, a church is mentioned here in Domesday Book (1086) and parts of the current church date back to a later church which was built in the late 12th century, with further parts dating from the 13th and 14th centuries. The oldest part is probably the round-headed west doorway in the tower which dates from around 1180, while both the 18th century rebuilt tower and chancel retain their 14th century arches into the nave. The latter has long-since lost its aisles, but you can still make out in the walls the 14th century arcades that once led to the old aisles, and in their place are the original 14th century aisle windows, with some fragments of mid-13th century glass. The church was further restored in 1866.

Fillingham Historic Trivia: John Wycliffe

There is evidence of a Roman settlement on the site of the current village with items being found that were possibly used for worship. Later Anglo Saxon pottery has also been found, along with evidence of an Anglo-Saxon cemetery, suggesting that settlement here may have been continuous for 2000 years.

The most famous rector of Fillingham was John Wycliffe (1324–1384), who was Fillingham rector from 1361 to 1368. Wycliffe was an early advocate for translation of the Bible from Latin, and he succeeded in translating what is now known as Wycliffe's Bible into vernacular English in 1382, two years before his death. An early church reformer and critic of the Roman Catholic Church, Wycliffe's followers became known as "Lollards", a fairly rebellious movement which preached anti-clerical and biblically-centred reforms; indeed, the Lollards were something of a precursor to the Protestant Reformation initiated by Martin Luther, John Calvin and others in the 16th century. Central to Wycliffe's beliefs were that an individual's interpretation of the Bible was the best guide to a moral life (rather than the Church's emphasis on sacraments and salvation), and that the holiness of an individual was more important than official office. He was also highly critical of the wealth, luxury and pomp of the Church. It is little surprise, therefore, that he was declared a heretic after his death, and in 1428, Pope Martin V saw that his bones were exhumed and burned, with the ashes dumped in a river.

Finally, in 1760, Sir Cecil Wray built a castellated mansion at Fillingham and called it Fillingham Castle.

Fillingham St Andrew's church.

Looking across Fillingham Lake towards Fillingham Castle. The latter was built in 1760 by Sir Cecil Wray.

NAME (STATUS):	**FLEET** (Village, Parish)
POPULATION:	2,136 (Fleet Parish); Fleet village is c.100
DISTRICT:	South Holland
EARLIEST RECORD:	*Fleot*, 1086 (Domesday Book)
MEANING:	Place on the creek
DERIVATION:	From the Old English word *flēot* (estuary, inlet, creek or stream). Neighbouring Fleet Hargate was once known as *Fleet Harbourgate* when it was a port on this very same creek.

Fleet Geographic Trivia:

Fleet is located on what is known as Delph Bank, around 2 miles south-east of Holbeach. The actual village of Fleet is very small, but the civil parish stretches from Gedney to Holbeach. The parish also includes the village of Fleet Hargate, a mile to the north of Fleet village, and which accounts for around 1,000 of the parish population. Fleet Hargate has also been designated as a conservation area by South Holland District Council, which covers six Grade II-listed buildings, including The Bull public house and another eight "unlisted buildings of local interest". The much smaller Fleet is also a conservation area, this time covering four listed buildings and six unlisted buildings of local interest. In the former category are two Grade I-listed buildings – both part of the church! The next section explains why…

Fleet Church: St Mary Magdalene

Parts of the Grade I-listed St Mary Magdalene church in Fleet, date from the late 12th century, including the nave arcades. The church is also exceptionally unusual in that its 120ft tower and spire are detached from the nave, with a gap of around 15ft between them (and hence both buildings being separately listed). Nevertheless, the tower and spire are still distinctive, with a bold stair-turret and interestingly shaped pinnacles attached to the spire by flying buttresses. First built in around 1300, both were restored in 1798 and 1843. Meanwhile, the nave dates from c.1180 to 1190 with mid-14th century additions, and was also restored in 1798 and 1843. An additional restoration between 1860 and 1862 saw the chancel rebuilt, albeit retaining its fine old sedilia and piscina with crocketed canopies.

The font dates from the 15th century, while inside the nave there is a carving of the Lincoln Imp on the north wall.

The church of St Mary Magdalene at Fleet shown from the north-west (above) and the south-east (below), demonstrating the fact that the tower is detached from the rest of the church.

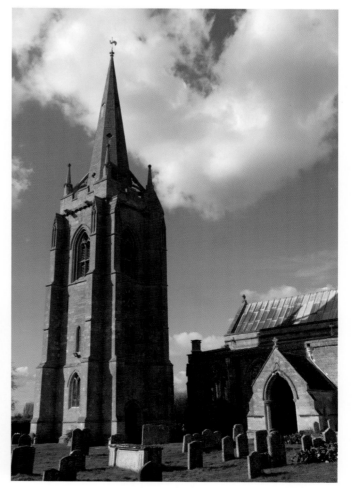

The carving of the Lincoln Imp on the wall of the nave of Fleet's church – but which is known locally as the Fleet Imp!

Fleet Historic Trivia: Creeks, the Fleet Light Railway and Terriers

Fleet's name is a fairly strong hint that, although today it is 8 miles from the sea, it once stood on a creek which emptied into The Wash. As for Fleet Hargate (formerly *Fleet Harbourgate*), until fairly recently, it sat on the A17, but has now been bypassed, with the original A17 course through the centre of the village now re-named as Old Main Road. This very road was also once part of the turnpiked Boston to Lynn road while the early 20th century also saw the railways arrive in Fleet. The village even had a station, this being on Eastgate, part-

way between modern Fleet and Fleet Hargate. The station became part of the Midland and Great Northern Joint Railway, and was served by the Fleet Light Railway, a potato railway built around 1910 to connect the Worth family farms to the M&GNJR mainline railway. The branch line closed to passengers in 1959 and to goods trains in 1965.

Finally, Fleet was the subject of the 1920 publication, *A Terrier of Fleet Lincolnshire*, based on the 11th century manuscript *Fleet Terrier* – a "terrier" being a legal document, usually a written survey or inventory, detailing lands and property in the parish owned by the Church.

The Bull at Fleet Hargate, up for sale and hopefully not about to become another victim of the 21st century pub-cull.

Looking down the nave of St Mary Magdalene's church towards the tower end of the church which is adorned with a beautiful five-light window.

Looking in the reverse direction towards the chancel.

St Mary Magdalene's octagonal 15th century font.

NAME (STATUS):	**GREAT COATES** (Village, Parish, Suburb)
POPULATION:	1,464 (Parish)
DISTRICT:	North East Lincolnshire
EARLIEST RECORD:	*Cotes*, 1086 (Domesday Book)
MEANING:	The cottages or huts
DERIVATION:	From the Old English word *cot* (cottages or huts). The "Great" affix distinguishes the village from Little Coates, which lies about a mile to the south of Great Coates.

Great Coates Geographic Trivia

Great Coates is a village and civil parish in North East Lincolnshire, located at the north-western edge of Grimsby. Nearby Little Coates was merged with Grimsby in 1928 along with parts of Great Coates parish, with the rest eventually absorbed in 1968 at which point the former Great Coates civil parish council was abolished. As for the modern parish of Great Coates, this was established in 2003 with the parish council significantly changing their name in 2008 to Great Coates *Village* Council. This new parish includes only a narrow strip of land around the village and railway station as part of the western half of the parish, but the eastern half expands eastwards towards Grimsby and includes a number of industrial areas including the Moody Lane industrial estate. It is this area of industrialisation that makes Great Coates essentially contiguous with Grimsby, with this area also containing the industrial freight line to and from Immingham Docks as well as the A180 – which was constructed in the 1950s and actually cut through the garden of the rectory of Great Coates! In fact, following the 1990s development of Grimsby's Europarc, yet another large industrial park, the Grimsby Urban Area has now not only reached Great Coates but has expanded beyond it.

Great Coates Church: St Nicolas's

First of all, the church name isn't spelt incorrectly above! And secondly, its tower is unusual in that it is constructed two thirds of rust-coloured ironstone and one third of grey ashlar. The building itself dates from the early 13th century and the nave arcades are still the originals, while the aisles and chancel were added in the 14th century. The tower was then added in the late 14th or early 15th century and the clerestory in the late 16th. The church was then restored first in 1865 by James Fowler, and then again between 1929 and 1930. Finally, the church clock dates to 1806, making it contemporary with the rectory, which was built some considerable time before a major road cut through its garden! However, that particular clock didn't become affixed to the tower of Great Coates' church until 1968; prior to that it belonged to North Willingham Hall!

Great Coates Historic Trivia: Conoco No Go

There was once a medieval manor house at Great Coates towards the southern end of the village, and it was certainly still there in October 1697 when antiquary Abraham de la Pryme recorded its features. Nothing of it survives today, though, other than the remains of its moat. As for the manor itself, this was held by John Sandale in 1313 – he being both Chancellor of the Exchequer and Bishop of Winchester. Later in the 14th century, the manor passed to the Willoughbys and then to the Barnardistons through the marriage of the daughter of Robert de Willoughby to Thomas de Barnardiston. Their son, also Thomas de Barnardiston, fought with Edward III and served as Knight of the Shire for Lincoln in 1357. The Barnardistons actually held the manor until the 17th century when it passed to the Suttons after the English Civil War.

The church of St Nicolas at Great Coates, its first two tower-stages of ironstone in striking contrast to the grey ashlar of its top-most stage.

The Reading Room, Great Coates. The building was opened by Sir George and Lady Doughty in October 1907 and was intended as a facility to enable local workers to read, learn and educate themselves.

Moving forward to the 19th century, and Great Coates found itself on the Great Grimsby and Sheffield Junction Railway, built between 1845 and 1847, with Great Coates railway station following in 1848. Other 19th century buildings include the Old Rectory and a Wesleyan chapel, while the unusually named Pyewipe Farm was also recorded and which still remains in the north-east of the parish today. The existing railway was then joined in 1912 by the Grimsby and Immingham Electric Railway which passed through the northern part of the parish, while by the 1930s, Watmough and Sons' biscuit factory was established to the north of the railway line. The company became part of Scribbans and Kemp in 1948 which eventually became United Biscuits. By the 1990s, United Biscuits employed hundreds of people, but the factory was then closed in 1995.

Following World War II, the shoreline of the Humber Estuary between Grimsby and Immingham became progressively more industrialised, including the north-eastern part of the modern Great Coates parish. This stretch included large-scale chemical plants such as British Titan Products Co. Ltd. (established in 1949, later known as BTP Tioxide, but closed in 2009) and CIBA Laboratories Ltd. (established in 1951). Meanwhile, the village of Great Coates was expanded in the 1980s and 90s with new housing estates.

One final and recent historic event is that during the first decade of the 21st century, Great Coates was almost certainly going to be the location of the Conoco Stadium, Grimsby Town's long-proposed new football stadium, so-named after a naming-rights deal with the American oil producer ConocoPhillips. Although local residents were opposed to the move, 84% of their North East Lincolnshire neighbours voted in favour of the project. However, the move – which had been on and off for around ten years – received its final nail when Grimsby Town were relegated from the Football League in 2010 for the first time in their very long history. Since then, they have constantly been in the top

five of the National League (formerly the Football Conference), and happily, they have just secured a return to the Football League, having won the May 2016 Play-Off Final.

Great Coates Quirk Alert: Free Warren, Wreckage and Waifs…and Roundhead Origins

As mentioned earlier, John Sandale held the manor of Great Coates in the early 14th century. He was also granted by King Henry V, what was termed "free warren" – this being a type of franchise or privilege granted by the monarch to a subject, promising to exonerate them from the hunting and killing of game in a forest or wood; of course, the vast majority of people in medieval England were subject to the harsh forest laws for which a breach would at the very least result in maiming of some description! However, the term "free warren" has nothing to do with rabbits; it derives from the Germanic *warian* (to take care of). The grant also applied to Sandale's heirs "forever". And in addition to free warren, Sandale was also granted the right to the manor's "wreckage of the sea and all animals called waifs, found within the said manor"! Alas, I am unable to enlarge on that – but it does conjure up some rather mind-boggling options…

Finally, we return to those other medieval landowners of Great Coates, the Barnardistons. They relinquished the manor after the English Civil War, but one book published in 1890 suggests that a member of the family unwittingly sourced the naming of the Roundheads. The book claims that certain London apprentices all had their hair cut in a round fashion, and that Queen Henrietta, having spotted one Samuel Barnardiston among them, cried out "see what a handsome round head is there". From thence on the name caught and was allegedly first used publicly by a Captain Hugle…although other sources suggest that it was by Officer David Hyde.

The railway station at Great Coates was built in 1848 and was part of the Great Grimsby and Sheffield Junction Railway.

The former Wesleyan Methodist chapel on Old Road originally founded in 1881, but now a private residence. Great Coates also once had a Primitive Methodist chapel where Station Road meets Woad Lane, and which was founded in 1895 but which no longer exists.

NAME (STATUS):	**GREETHAM** (Village)
POPULATION:	167 (Parish of Greetham with Somersby)
DISTRICT:	East Lindsey
EARLIEST RECORD:	*Gretham*, 1086 (Domesday Book)
MEANING:	Gravelly homestead or enclosure
DERIVATION:	From the Old English words *grēot* (gravel) and *hām* (homestead or enclosure)

Greetham Geographic Trivia

Greetham is situated around 3 miles east of Horncastle at one of the highest points in Lincolnshire, and thus has stunning views all around. The parish of Greetham with Somersby generally sits at between 165ft (50m) and 260ft (79m) above sea level and includes the summits of Millam's Hill (260ft/79m) and Melbourne's Hill (262ft/80m). The parish is also home to the village of Somersby where Alfred Lord Tennyson was born (see *Lincolnshire County History* for more).

Greetham Church: All Saints

The Grade II-listed Greetham All Saints' church does contain some Norman stonework from its 12th century build along with the re-set south doorway. However, much of the church that we see today is courtesy of C.H. Fowler's restoration in 1903, while the bellcote was added in 1863, and which probably replaced a former tower. The south aisle also no longer exists.

Greetham Historic Trivia

Roman artefacts have been unearthed at Greetham, while during Saxon and Viking times, the settlement was in the ancient Hill Hundred and Hill Wapentake respectively. By the 18th century, the poor were supported by income from Cross Closes, property left by Elizabeth Somersby in 1733, while 1794 was the year that Greetham's common fields were enclosed. By 1821 the village belonged to the Duchy of Lancaster, and eleven years later in 1832, Greetham House was built by Robert Dennis. Two years later, the Poor Law Amendment Act was passed and Greetham was aligned to the Horncastle Poor Law Union, while a day school was built in the village in 1870 by the Misses Dennis and was attended by 40 children.

All Saints' church, Greetham.

The tiny village green and pond at the centre of Greetham.

A series of Grade II-listed buildings on Jolls Lane, Greetham, known as The Terrace and which were once almshouses for the local poor.

View from Jolls Lane looking north-east over the Lincolnshire Wolds.

NAME (STATUS):	**HAMERINGHAM** (Village)
POPULATION:	147 (Parish of Lunsby with Winceby)
DISTRICT:	East Lindsey
EARLIEST RECORD:	*Hameringam*, 1086 (Domesday Book)
MEANING:	Homestead of the dwellers at the cliff, crag or steep hill, or homestead belonging to a man called Hamor
DERIVATION:	From either the Old English word *hamor* (cliff or steep hill) or the Old Scandinavian word *hamarr* (stone or crag), plus the Old English words *inga* (of) and *hām* (homestead). Or alternatively, the Old English personal name, *Hamor*, plus *inga* and *hām*. The name Hamor could derive from the Old English word *hamor*, which also means "hammer". A feared warlord, perhaps?

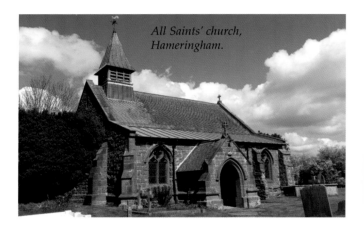

All Saints' church, Hameringham.

The centre of the tiny village of Hameringham.

Hameringham Church: All Saints

The tiny village of Hameringham is located 4 miles south-east of Horncastle, and belongs to the parish of Lunsby with Winceby, which also includes a fourth tiny village, Asgarby. As for Hameringham's Grade II-listed All Saints' church, this originally dates from c.1200, although much of it now dates from major restoration carried out in 1893 by Hodgson Fowler after the nave collapsed; Fowler also rebuilt the bell turret. However, the south arcade between the nave and aisle still dates to the 13th century with its pillars offering a striking contrast to Fowler's later arches which were constructed of green sandstone. The font dates from the 15th century while the Jacobean pulpit still has its original hourglass – designed to keep the preacher on point! The church also sports two bullet holes believed to be from the nearby Battle of Winceby in 1643.

Hameringham Historic Trivia:
Plague and Piggeries

Back in medieval times, Hameringham was located alongside the now deserted medieval village of Dunsthorpe. It is likely that Dunsthorpe fell victim to the devastating outbreaks of plague in the 14th century, which explains why its church was in ruins by 1421. The two parishes were therefore united in 1437 to become Hameringham. By the 19th century, Hameringham was home to both Wesleyan and

Primitive Methodist chapels while records from 1872 show that the parish had extensive piggeries, most owned by a William Sharpley.

The wrought-iron gate to All Saints' churchyard has a series of crosses worked into it, and which cast shadows akin to the three crosses on Mount Calvary.

NAME (STATUS):	**HEALING** (Village)
POPULATION:	2,940
DISTRICT:	North East Lincolnshire
EARLIEST RECORD:	*Hegelinge*, 1086 (Domesday Book)
MEANING:	Settlement of the family or followers of a man called Hægel
DERIVATION:	From the Old English personal name Hægel, plus the Old English word *ingas* (people of, family or followers of, or dwellers at)

Healing Church: St Peter and St Paul

The parish church of St Peter and St Paul dates from the 13th century, although the church was partly rebuilt in 1840 when the chancel was crowned with its open oak roof of trussed beams. It was then further restored in 1876 by William Fowler, who re-built the south side of the church and added a new roof and windows. Nevertheless, parts of the 13th century tower remain, including a lovely west doorway with mouldings under an ogee hood adorned with fine crockets, tall pinnacles and finials. A Methodist chapel was also built in Healing in 1906.

Healing Historic Trivia: Healing Manor and Modern Industry

To the west of Healing, archaeological evidence has been found to support the fact that the area was the site of an enclosed Iron Age settlement, and that this area continued to be occupied throughout Roman Britain, too. There was clearly still a settlement here when Domesday Book was compiled in 1086, too, although the place is confusingly referenced three times with three different spellings: *Hegelinge*, *Hechelinge* and *Heghelinge*.

In the early 18th century, Healing Manor was built, replacing an earlier manor house. Indeed, the moat of the earlier manor house still survives as part of the gardens of the final incarnation of the hall which is now known as Healing Manor Hotel. This last building was constructed in 1892, as Healing Manor, for the Portman family who had significant land holdings in and around Healing, and the house was the country estate for the Portman family for many years afterwards. In recent years the property was purchased by the local Brennan family who have turned it into a beautiful hotel and retained the former owners' name in the hotel's Portman Restaurant.

Like neighbouring Great Coates, the village began to expand in the 19th century with the arrival of the railways, and in the 20th century with the arrival of heavy industrial sites in the part of the Healing parish along the south bank of the Humber estuary. This included the appearance of the Courtaulds textile fibre plant in the late 1950s, while in 1992, an extension of Ciba-Geigy's Grimsby plant resulted in further development on the west of their site within Healing parish. Then in the north of the parish, adjacent to the river bank, are the Lenzing Tencel plant and the associated

The church of St Peter and St Paul at Healing.

48 MW Humber Energy CHP plant. Meanwhile, the 1990s also saw the establishment of another large industrial park, Europarc, at the north-eastern edge of the parish. Approximately 2,000 people are employed there today. Further housing developments in the 21st century have seen the parish population increase to almost 3,000.

Healing Quirk Alert: Healing in Healing and a Grand National Winner

In the Victorian period two neighbouring springs existed in the parish, one of fresh water which was renowned for soothing skin disorders, and the other a chalybeate (an iron spring) which allegedly helped cure disorders of the eye. Such phenomena led Victorians to believe that the village name therefore derived from its curative waters. However, the derivation is Anglo-Saxon, as outlined above.

In 1843, a horse called Cure-All was bought at the Horncastle Horse Fair for £50 after failing to reach the asking price of £240 – this on account of the fact that the horse was found to be lame when inspected by a possible buyer, Captain William Peel. However, one of Captain Peel's friends, William Loft, thought Cure-All was worth a £50 punt, and promptly arranged for the horse to be trained at Healing Manor by Christopher (Kitty) Crisp. Over the next two years, the horse was initially used as a farm hack for Loft, but when he started to show good jumping prowess during hunting with the local Brocklesby Hunt, he was put into a local race against a highly regarded chaser. Amazingly, and despite allegedly taking a wrong turn that cost him 100 yards, he only lost the race by a neck, thus bringing him to the attention of racehorse owner William Sterling-Crawford.

This is where the tale now starts to become interesting. For Sterling-Crawford already had a well-fancied horse, Rat Trap, running in the 1845 Grand National at Aintree, but when Rat Trap had to withdraw through injury, Sterling-Crawford was allowed to nominate a substitute to run in his place – and William Loft agreed to allow a lease of Cure-All to run as a nominee on condition that Loft himself be Cure-All's jockey.

The tale now starts to move from interesting to extraordinary. Firstly, because horse transportation wasn't practical in those days, the horse, trainer and groom each walked the 120 miles to Liverpool – which took them just over a week. Unsurprisingly, therefore, the horse wasn't looking his best after his travels, and was written off by experts, while the bookmakers didn't even bother to offer odds as no one was interested in backing poor, weary-looking Cure-All. Secondly, because twice National-winning jockey, Tom Olliver, and who was riding the favourite, Vanguard, commented to Loft in the paddock that his horse looked like "a Lincolnshire prize ox and would do well to complete one circuit of the course". And finally, thirdly, because the entire race was in the balance, anyway, due to heavy overnight rain followed by a sharp early morning frost, and which had left the ground dangerously hard. Indeed, Sterling-Crawford was one of the two owners who had lodged a complaint, no doubt hoping to get the race postponed, thus giving Rat Trap time to recover, plus avoiding the necessity of running the no-hoper, Cure-All. However, when he was outvoted by his fellow owners he decided he might as well give Cure-All a run out, and therefore didn't withdraw him from the race.

Of course, the rest is history, and many people were made to eat their words. In the end, the hard conditions worked in Cure-All's favour, and he actually raced past a number of tired horses in the closing stages to win the race in what was then a new record time. The history books don't record what happened after that, but presumably, having bust a gut to win and break the course record, poor Cure-All had to walk the 120 miles back home to Healing! It *is* recorded, though, that when victorious horse and trainer arrived back at Healing some seven days later, the villagers turned out in their droves to greet them and the church bells were rung in their honour. Meanwhile, Healing Manor Hotel has named the ground floor lounge the "Cure-All Lounge" to reflect this astonishing story, and plans to make Grand National day each year a special event day at the Hotel!

Healing Manor Hotel, built in 1892 as Healing Manor by the Portman family.

Three's-Up!

	HANNAH	**HOLME**	**HOWELL**
STATUS:	Village	Hamlet	Village
POPULATION:	c.60	113	509 (Parish of Ewerby and Evedon)
DISTRICT:	East Lindsey	North Lincolnshire	North Kesteven
EARLIEST RECORD:	*Hannay,* 13th century	*Holm,* 1086 (Domesday Book);	*Huuelle,* 1086 (Domesday Book)
MEANING:	Possibly island frequented by wild birds	Island, dry ground in marsh, or water-meadow	Probably mound or hillock with a spring or stream
DERIVATION:	From the Old English words *hana* (wild birds) and *ēg* (island or land partly surrounded by water)	From the Old Scandinavian word *holmr* (island, promontory, raised ground in march or river-meadow)	Possibly from the Old English words *hugol* (mound or hillock) and *wella* (spring or stream). Alternatively, the first part of the name may derive from the OE word *hūne,* meaning "hoarhound".

Three's Up Trivia!

Although the small church of St Andrew's and St Thomas the Martyr is located at the northern end of **Hannah**, it is actually the parish church of Hannah cum Hagnaby, a civil parish which constitutes the village of Hannah and the hamlet of Hagnaby. The current church dates from the mid-18th century and replaced the previous medieval church which had to be demolished – although a number of stone fragments from a 15th century doorway were incorporated into the new church. Also retained in the church porch, are a pair of carved sculptures of standing figures of six of the twelve apostles, each holding their attributes, and which may date back as far as the 13th century. It is thought that they may have been door jambs which decorated an even earlier church than the medieval one, although there are no written details of such a church. Interestingly, the carvings are of an East Anglian type, and even more interesting is the fact that they were discovered secreted above the lintel of the east window during the restoration work carried out in 1964.

In terms of structure, the church is built of greenstone with a terracotta tiled roof, and has a wooden

The church of St Andrew and St Thomas the Martyr, the parish church of Hannah cum Hagnaby.

View towards the east window inside Hannah's church.

belfry containing a single bell, as well as a three-part Venetian east window. The church was consecrated in 1753, and it was also at this time that it was re-dedicated to St Andrew and St Thomas the Martyr, having previously only been dedicated to St Andrew. St Thomas was added as he had been the patron saint of neighbouring Hagnaby Priory, a Premonstratensian abbey founded in 1175 by Agnes, widow of Herbert de Orreby.

Holme is located a mile south-east of Scunthorpe, while just to the south-east of Holme is Twigmoor Hall, the early 17th century home of John and Kit Wright. Both brothers were executed for their part in the Gunpowder Plot of 1605, the infamous conspiracy by a group of provincial English Catholics to assassinate King James I by blowing up the House of Lords. Educated at the same school in York, the Wrights had early links with Guy Fawkes, while their sister married another plotter, Thomas Percy. The authorities thus described Twigmoor Hall as: "one of the worst in her Majesty's dominions and is used like a Popish college for traitors". Prior to the Gunpowder Plot, both brothers had also been members of the Earl of Essex's rebellion of 1601, plus they were arrested several other times for reasons of national security, too.

The Grade II-listed St Oswald's church at **Howell**, dates from the late 12th century and the Norman doorway within the porch is still the original, as is the nave arcade including a carved Norman beast at the bottom of the eastern-most arch. Also in the south porch is an even older coffin-lid which is thought to be pre-Conquest (see photo on page 20), and which is decorated with three crude crosses. The bellcote and the chancel date from the 14th century, and the latter includes a sedilia on the south side, projecting aumbries on the north side and an old altar slab with five consecration crosses that Sir Nikolaus Pevsner believed was Anglo-Saxon. The font is also 14th century, as is a bust of a woman and child, while further stones commemorate

Sir Nicholas de Hebden (d.1416), his wife Katherine (d.1447) and Rector John Croxby in his 15th century vestments. Slightly later is an Elizabethan monument to Sir Charles Dymoke (d.1593), who was a 16th century MP who hailed from Howell. Finally, the church was restored in 1870 by Charles Kirk of Sleaford, who replaced the roofs of the nave and chancel. He also replaced the ancient seats and the pulpit, plus re-glazed windows and restored the floor.

Evidence of a Bronze Age round barrow has been found a mile north-east of Howell, while 1 mile to the west is the shrunken medieval village of Boughton. Meanwhile, another medieval settlement is evidenced just under the west face of the present Howell Hall, with ridge and furrow field systems a little further to the west. There may even have been a predecessor to the current Howell Hall, with ditch earthworks indicating a non-moated structure. This would likely have been occupied by the Howell family before the manor passed to the Hebden family and then to the Elizabethan and Jacobean Dymoke family. As for the current Howell Hall, this dates from the 18th century and is Grade II listed, as is the 17th century rectory at Howell.

Howell Quirk Alert: *Cue the Rector*

Howell churchyard is home to a cross for which the inscription is now indecipherable. However, it was still legible in the early 20th century and Arthur Mee confirms that it is dedicated to John Spencer, not a 20th century World Snooker Champion, but the rector of Howell from 1424 to 1448! Back in those days, Rector Spencer would no doubt have lit his church by candlelight at night – which coincidentally is exactly what the current rector does, as Howell St Oswald's is one of very few churches still without electricity, but which also lends the church an unusual and quirky atmosphere!

St Oswald's church, Howell.

The nave of St Oswald's church.

NAME (STATUS):	**IRNHAM** (Village)
POPULATION:	193
DISTRICT:	South Kesteven
EARLIEST RECORD:	*Gerneham*, 1086 (Domesday Book)
MEANING:	Homestead of a man called Georna
DERIVATION:	From the Old English personal name *Georna*, plus the Old English word *hām* (homestead)

Irnham Church: St Andrew's

The lower part of St Andrew's church dates from the late Norman period, while the north aisle and chancel date from the 14th century. The greatest treasure, however, is the 14th century Easter Sepulchre of Geoffrey Luttrell, and which includes exquisite carving and delicate tracery and foliage.

Irnham Historic Trivia: Irnham Hall

Irnham Hall passed from the Paynells to the Luttrells in around 1200, then to the Hiltons in 1418 and then to the Thimblebys in 1510, and it was they who built the current hall in around 1600. The hall's most famous resident was the aforementioned Geoffrey Luttrell, who commissioned the *Luttrell Psalter*, a celebrated medieval manuscript dating from the early 14th century. The manuscript is an illuminated psalter written and illustrated on parchment and along with the psalms it also contains a calendar, canticles (hymns or songs of praise), the Mass, and an antiphon (a call and response from a choir) for the dead. It is considered to be one of the finest visual depictions of medieval English rural life, and currently resides in the British Library

Meanwhile, Irnham Hall is home to a priest hole approached from an attic passage and is a clear indicator of the Roman Catholic faith of the Thimblebys, as is an underground passage that runs from the hall to the garden. Also discovered in 1858 was another secret room in which was found a straw palliasse bed, a crucifix and a prayer book.

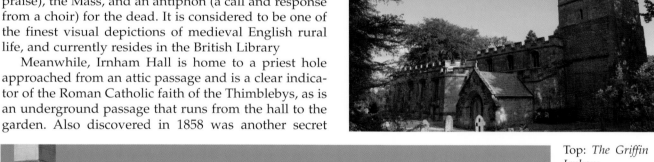

Top: *The Griffin Inn, Irnham.*

Above: *St Andrew's church, Irnham.*

Left: *Looking down Corby Road, Irnham.*

NAME (STATUS):	**LEA** (Village)
POPULATION:	1,009
DISTRICT:	West Lindsey
EARLIEST RECORD:	*Lea*, 1086 (Domesday Book)
MEANING:	Place at the wood or woodland clearing
DERIVATION:	From the Old English word *lēah* (wood, woodland clearing or glade)

Lea Church: St Helen's

The church of St Helen's at Lea is Grade I listed, but dates from a number of different centuries. The oldest part is the chancel, built in the 13th century, while the nave and chapel are 14th century and the tower late 15th. However, whereas the arch from chapel to chancel is 14th century, the arch from chapel to nave dates from the restoration carried out in the late 1840s by J. L. Pearson, as do the nave arcade and the south doorway. What is old, though, is some of the glass in the east chapel window which probably also dates from the 14th century, as do other fragments in the west window of the tower. The church also contains a number of memorials, some to the Trehamptons who owned the old manor house a mile east of Lea, and others to the Andersons who lived at the second Lea Hall. Memorials to members of the latter family include one to a 19th century rector who was incumbent for 51 years, and another to a 19th century antiquary, the 9th and last baronet, Sir Charles Anderson (d.1891). There is also a tomb with the recumbent crusader effigy of John de Braose.

Lea Historic Trivia: Heynings Priory and Cavendish Bog

Just east of St Helen's church is the site of Heynings Priory, founded in 1180 by Reynerus Evermue, lord of the manor of neighbouring Knaith. It was founded for the Gilbertine order of nuns, but was always very poor. Like all other such institutions, it was dissolved in 1539 when populated by the unfortunate prioress, Jane Sanford and her eleven nuns. Shortly afterwards in 1540, the priory was granted to Sir Thomas Heneage, then lord of Knaith manor, but when he died in 1553, both priory and manor passed by marriage to Lord Willoughby of Parham. The exact site is unknown but is believed to be at the site of Park Farm South. As for the manor of Lea, this belonged in medieval times to the

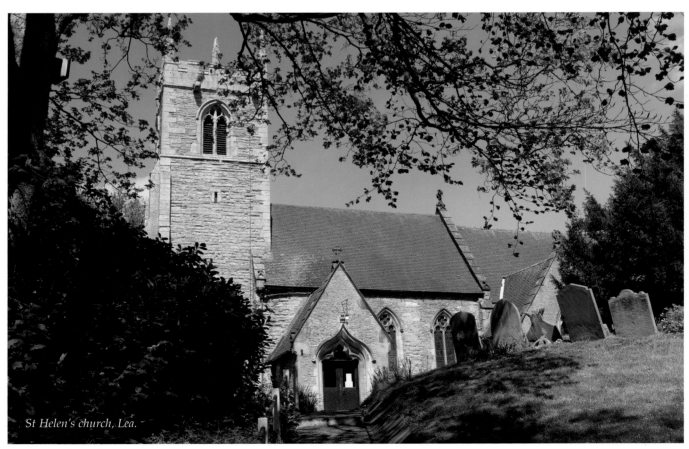

St Helen's church, Lea.

Lea Methodist chapel was previously the lodge to Lea Hall, but was purchased by local Methodists in 1950.

The village pump at Lea.

The now-combined Grade II-listed Mellow Cottage and The Old Post Office on Gainsborough Road, parts of which date back to the early 18th century.

This attractive house can be found on Willingham Road, alongside the church.

Trehampton family. It then passed to the Braose family, followed by the Nuthill family, followed by the Dallison family, before eventually passing to the Anderson family in the late 16th century where it remained for another 300 years.

Lea was the scene of a key battle during the English Civil War. It took place on July 28th 1643 and was a battle won by Oliver Cromwell against Charles Cavendish, godson of Charles I. At this stage of the war, things weren't all going Parliament's way. In neighbouring Gainsborough, they were besieged by Royalist troops from Newark Castle, a key Royalist stronghold. Cromwell had just taken Stamford, and on hearing of the siege, his army set out on the 55-mile march to take on Cavendish's forces, picking up additional troops at Grantham and Lincoln on the way. The two forces met at Lea, with the larger Royalist army ranged along a sandy plateau with marshland below and the River Trent behind – a fatal mistake, as Cromwell's forces drove them into the marshland and Cavendish was one of many Royalists killed. Cromwell then performed a sensible retreat from Gainsborough as an overwhelming force led by the Earl of Newcastle was approaching.

Newcastle took the town, but was expelled three months later when Cromwell returned with a much larger force. Two local fields are named after the battle at Lea on 28th July – Redcoats and Graves Close – while the meadow/marshland into which the defeated Royalists were driven is still known today as Cavendish Bog.

Finally, the railways arrived in Lea in 1848, courtesy of the Spalding and Doncaster section of the then Great Northern Railway.

Lea Quirk Alert: Vice-Versa

So today, it is a fairly common sight to see old chapels converted into stylish modern homes. However, here we have one that went the other way. For Lea is home to the attractive little Methodist chapel on Park Close. For many years it was the lodge to Lea Hall, but after becoming unoccupied, it was purchased by local Methodists in 1950. A porch was added to the front and a schoolroom and kitchen to the rear and the official opening occurred on 10th November 1951, when over 200 people attended. The church is still going strong today.

NAME (STATUS):	**LEADENHAM** (Village)
POPULATION:	410
DISTRICT:	North Kesteven
EARLIEST RECORD:	*Ledeneham*, 1086 (Domesday Book)
MEANING:	Homestead or village of a man called Lēoda
DERIVATION:	From the Old English personal name, *Lēoda*, plus the Old English word *hām* (homestead, village, manor or estate)

Leadenham Pub: The George Hotel

The George Hotel is an old coaching inn which probably dates from the late 18th century, and which was most likely named in honour of George III (1760-1820). Initially a two-storey building, the third tier was added in the mid-19th century at round about the same time that the railways impacted trade on traditional coaching routes.

As for the inn's most famous regular visitor, this has to be T.E. Lawrence. The pub's website claims that Lawrence (of Arabia) wrote his autobiographical account of his eastern adventures, *Seven Pillars of Wisdom* (published 1922), in what is now the restaurant, while his Brough Superia motor-cycle was a common sight in the yard of the hotel. Later in the same decade (1928) Douglas Bader was a regular at the hotel, both as a cadet at the nearby R.A.F. College, and after his return to active service in November 1939. Finally, and keeping up the aviation theme, the hotel was also regularly visited in the 1920s by Captain Walter Hinchliffe (aka Hinch). A famous aviator of the early 20th century, Hinchliffe lost his left eye in a "dog fight" with Manfred Von Richthofen (the famous Red Baron), and therefore habitually wore a black eye patch. Alas, Hinch is probably most remembered for piloting Elsie Mackay (who was his co-pilot) on a fateful flight aimed at helping her achieve her ambition of becoming the first woman to fly the Atlantic. Flying a Stinson monoplane known as *Endeavour*, the pair took off from RAF Cranwell, 5 miles south-east of Leadenham, at 08:35 on 13th March 1928. They were spotted five hours later off the south-west coast of Ireland heading west, while a French steamer later reported them as being still on course, but they are thought to be the last people to see the Stinson; they sadly weren't to be welcomed by the crowd of around 5,000 people waiting expectantly at Mitchel Field, Long Island. In December 1928, some eight months later, a single piece of identifiable undercarriage washed ashore in north-western Ireland.

Leadenham Church: St Swithun's

The Grade I-listed church at Leadenham is dedicated to St Swithun, the 9th century Bishop of Winchester who was buried after his death in 862, on his own request, outside Winchester Cathedral where men might walk over his grave. He was canonised in 912 and his remains moved to a shrine in the Cathedral – although legend has it that this work was delayed for forty days by constant rain – and hence the modern reference that rain on St Swithin's day (July 15th) means continued rain over the next forty days.

As for St Swithun's in Leadenham, there was clearly a predecessor church to the current 14th century one, as it is referenced in Domesday Book (1086). This was replaced by a new church in around 1320, and surviving today from the second half of the 14th century is the lower part of the tower and the nave. The north and south porches also both shelter 14th century doorways. The top of the pinnacled tower and the crocketed spire were added in the 15th century, with the chancel and chantry added a little later. The church then underwent a major restoration in 1830 while the pews and pulpit were replaced in 1861 by J.H. Hakewill, which was also the year that the current church clock was installed. In between these two

The George Hotel at Leadenham probably dates from the late 18th century and has had some VERY famous regulars (see above).

Leadenham Post Office and Teahouse on Main Road.

dates, the chancel ceiling was hand-painted by Augustus Welby Pugin in 1841 along with the reredos. It was also in around 1827 that early 16th century Flemish glass was purchased in Belgium by the incumbent rector and subsequently worked into the east window. Finally, the church also contains a number of 16th and 17th century monuments to the Beresford and Key families, plus 19th century monuments to the Reeve family.

Leadenham Historic Trivia: Perfect Arte
During the late 16th century, the rector of Leadenham was Dr John Dee who was incumbent from 1566 to his death in 1608. He was also an advisor to the crown on both calendar reform and astrological events during which time he wrote *The Perfect Arte of Navigation*, and was one of the founders of scientific cartography in England.

By the 18th century, much of the village belonged to the Reeve family and their family seat is still Leadenham House today, a Georgian country house built between 1790 and 1796 for William Reeve. Meanwhile, Leadenham Old Hall is a century older and was originally the home of the Beresfords, to whom there are a number of memorials in the church.

In the 20th century, the Royal Flying Corps airfield was built to the east of Leadenham in 1916 to help protect the village against Zeppelin attacks; the airfield closed in June 1919 and few traces remain today.

Leadenham Quirk Alert: The Devil's Mask
The Anglo-Saxon church at Leadenham was replaced by a new church in around 1320, as championed by Henry Burghersh, Bishop of Lincoln from 1320 to 1340. Apparently, the bishop wasn't a fan of Edward II, though, and the story goes that it was he who had the King's effigy built in the north aisle and thus facing the devil's domain, and with a devil's mask placed on a bracket above him to boot! However, when Edward II was murdered in 1327, the public wave of sympathy backfired on the bishop, and someone broke the devil's mask from its bracket and moved it to its present position over King Edward III!

St Swithun's church, Leadenham.

This Gothic octagonal canopied waterpump in Leadenham is known as the Reeve Memorial Pump. It was erected in 1867 in memory of John and Susan Reeve by their children.

Post Office Yard in the centre of Leadenham.

NAME (STATUS):	**LEASINGHAM** (Village)
POPULATION:	1,584
DISTRICT:	North Kesteven
EARLIEST RECORD:	*Leuesingham*, 1086 (Domesday Book)
MEANING:	Homestead of the family or followers of a man called Lēofsige
DERIVATION:	From the Old English personal name, *Lēofsige*, plus the Old English words *inga* (of) and *hām* (homestead, village, manor or estate)

Leasingham Geographic Trivia: North and South

Leasingham is located a couple of miles north of Sleaford and was once known as South Leasingham. This is because the hamlet located a mile north of modern Leasingham, and which is today known as Roxholm, was once also known as North Leasingham. In fact, Leasingham's civil and ecclesiastical parishes are actually a consolidation of the two parishes of South Leasingham and North Leasingham. Despite this alter-ego of North Leasingham, though, today's Roxholm includes both Roxholm Hall and Roxholm Grange. North Leasingham was also was once home to a 19th century chapel, while even further back, it also had its own Anglican church which was dedicated to St John the Baptist. However it was demolished in the 16th century and by 1841, no trace remained.

The Duke of Wellington at Leasingham.

Leasingham Pub: The Duke of Wellington

The Duke of Wellington at Leasingham was originally a thatched inn called The Sun. However, in the early 19th century it was purchased by a military captain, who renamed it The Duke of Wellington following the latter's victory at the Battle of Waterloo in 1815.

Leasingham Church: St Andrew's

Parts of Leasingham's Grade I-listed St Andrew's church date back to the 12th century. This includes the lower half of the tower which includes a Norman doorway, while on each side of the belfry is a 13th century pair of lancet windows. The south doorway is also 13th century, although the porch in which it sits is 14th century and is known as the Angel Porch thanks to the two angel carvings on its hood. Meanwhile the base and stem of the font date from the 13th century and its bowl from the 15th. Also dating from the 14th century is the chancel arch, the tri-arched nave arcade and the aisle with its piscina and aumbry. Much of the rest of the church was rebuilt during the restoration carried out in 1863, including the east end of the aisle and the chancel. The restoration was carried out during the fifty-year rectorship tenure of Edward Trollope (1817-1893) which stretched from 1843 to his death in 1893. A Victorian antiquary, Trollope was also Bishop of Nottingham from 1877 to 1893.

Leasingham Historic Trivia: Leasingham Manor and Roxholm Hall

Leasingham Manor was built in around 1550 on the foundations of a medieval house. By the 17th century, the house was owned by Sir William York, and there

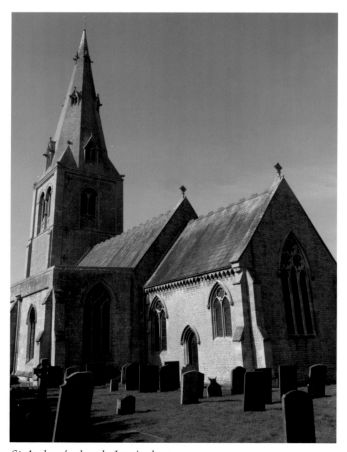

St Andrew's church, Leasingham.

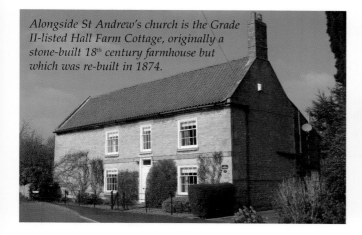

Alongside St Andrew's church is the Grade II-listed Hall Farm Cottage, originally a stone-built 18th century farmhouse but which was re-built in 1874.

The graveyard of Roxholm Chapel (founded 1871) is still in use, but the chapel itself closed in 2005.

These almshouses were given to the people of Leasingham in 1876 by their rector, Edward Trollope.

This house on Lincoln Road is located opposite the almshouses and bears the date 1655 beneath the central gable.

were rumours that he was involved in witchcraft. The house was then re-modelled in Georgian style in the mid-18th century by Sir Richard and Lady Anne Cust.

In 1871, a Congregational chapel was founded in nearby Roxholm (formerly North Leasingham) by John Montague Cole of Roxholm Hall, initially for the workers on his estate. The chapel was opened on 16th June 1871 as part of a public tea, which was attended by 180 people. However, it was re-designated four years later as a Wesleyan chapel and became part of Sleaford Wesleyan Circuit in 1875. The chapel was designed by Mr Whitaker of Dorrington, and also included a Sunday school. The chapel survives to this day, and although it closed in 2005, its neat little graveyard is still in use. As for Roxholm Hall, that is now a care centre.

Leasingham Quirk Alert: Captain's Hill, Star Date 1815

Captain's Hill takes its name from the 19th century Lord of the Manor, Captain Richard Wharton-Myddleton, who had been an ensign at the battle of Waterloo. The Captain lived at Leasingham Hall, built in 1836, and which is now Grade II listed. It was also this particular Captain who re-named the local pub from The Sun Inn to The Duke of Wellington, and which is located a little further down Captain's Hill/Lincoln Road.

Captain's Hill is named after Captain Richard Wharton-Myddleton, also of Leasingham Hall in the 19th century. Also shown above is a Grade II-listed milestone supplying distance in miles to Sleaford, Lincoln and London.

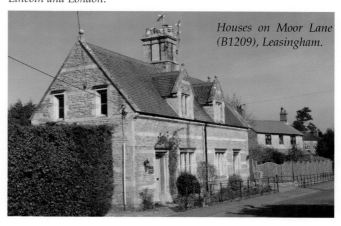

Houses on Moor Lane (B1209), Leasingham.

NAME (STATUS):	**LINWOOD** (Village)
POPULATION:	1,584
DISTRICT:	West Lindsey
EARLIEST RECORD:	*Lindude*, 1086 (Domesday Book)
MEANING:	Lime-tree wood
DERIVATION:	From the Old English words *lind* (lime-tree) and *wudu* (wood or forest)

Linwood Church: St Cornelius

Linwood's church is the only English church dedicated to St Cornelius, a 3rd century Bishop of Rome from 251 to his death in 253. St Cornelius's church at Linwood is also very old, albeit dating from almost a thousand years after the death of its saint. The oldest parts of this Grade I-listed church are therefore still partly late 12th century, although the nave clerestory, north aisle, tower and needle spire date from the 14th and 15th centuries. The chancel was part-rebuilt in 1854, while the church was further restored in 1863, and the roof was raised in 1876. Church relics include a battered 17th century chest in the south aisle, while there is also an impressive monumental brass to prosperous wool merchant John Lyndwood; the church tower was built of ironstone from a legacy left by Lyndwood after his death in 1419.

Linwood Historic Trivia: William Lyndwood

Linwood's most famous son was William Lyndwood (c.1375-1446), the 15th century bishop of St David's. He is most noted for the publication of the *Provinciale*, deemed to be an important commentary of his day upon the ecclesiastical decrees enacted in English provincial councils under the presidency of the Archbishops of Canterbury, and the beliefs of the early 15th century English clergy in general.

Career-wise, Lyndwood was ordained deacon at Oxford in 1404 and priest in 1407, while in 1408, Robert Hallum, Bishop of Salisbury appointed Lyndwood to his consistory court. By 1414 he was the principal advisor of the Archbishop of Canterbury, and by 1426, Dean of the Arches. In 1433 he became Archdeacon of Stow in the Diocese of Lincoln, and in 1442 after recommendation from King Henry VI, he was promoted by Pope Eugene IV to the vacant See of St David's. Throughout these years, Lyndwood was regularly a representative of the English clergy in their discussions with the Crown over subsidies, while he also regularly represented England abroad on diplomatic missions. He also acted as the King's Proctor at the Council of Basle in 1433, taking a prominent part as negotiator in arranging political and commercial treaties, and was Keeper of the Privy Seal from 1432 to 1443.

Linwood Quirk Alert: The Little Pink Church

Located in the centre of Linwood, is a tiny, disused chapel made of corrugated tin. This is the former Linwood Primitive Methodist chapel that also goes by the name of the Little Pink Church thanks to the fact

Linwood's church is dedicated to St Cornelius, the only one in England.

View towards Linwood Warren, an important woodland and heathland conservation area, run by the Lincolnshire Wildlife Trust Nature Reserve. It is also here that the Lincolnshire Bird Club has encouraged the recent repopulation of the woodlark.

that it glows pink in sunlight. The chapel dates from 1921 and was actually reconstructed in Linwood having been dismantled in nearby Holton Beckering. The building functioned as Linwood Primitive Methodist church from 1921 until 1959, and was then sold in 1965 after which it was used as a storehouse!

NAME (STATUS):	**MABLETHORPE** (Town)
POPULATION:	12,531 (Mablethorpe and Sutton)
DISTRICT:	East Lindsey
EARLIEST RECORD:	*Malbertorp*, 1086 (Domesday Book)
MEANING:	Outlying farmstead of a man called Malbert
DERIVATION:	From the Old German personal name *Malbert*, plus the Old Scandinavian word *thorp* (dependent outlying farmstead or hamlet)

Mablethorpe Geographic Trivia

Today, Mablethorpe is most renowned for being a seaside resort, with its numerous caravan parks, its fairground and its long and wide award-winning beach, whilst the sand train ferries visitors up and down the sea-front. However, it is also something of an energy hotspot, too, with the Theddlethorpe Gas Terminal situated a mile to the north of the town, and which supplies 5% of the UK's gas. There are also three separate wind farms in the parish owned by Ecotricity, including two turbines at Mablethorpe Wind Farm, which were the first wind turbines in Lincolnshire when they were built in July 2002.

Mablethorpe Pub: The Book in Hand

The Book in Hand dates back to at least the early 19th century when it was known to have been a thatched, whitewashed building. It was then a hotel of the same name before it became a pub. It also used to look a little more stylish, too, with two protruding bays, but they were both destroyed by a fire in 1981. As for the name, one local story claims that it was based upon a shipwreck just off the coast from Mablethorpe, and that the only survivor was the captain, who came ashore with a Bible in his hands.

Mablethorpe Church: St Mary's

There were once two parish churches in Mablethorpe, but St Peter's (to the south) was claimed by the sea in the 16th century, along with a fair slice of its parish. The surviving parish church is St Mary's, and which thankfully still sits half a mile inland, while it is reached across two bridges over the deep drain which serves rather like a moat on two of its sides – and which was presumably constructed after the first St Mary's church was abandoned in 1287 after severe flooding. As for the current St Mary's church, this is rather odd-looking – Arthur Mee describes it as looking akin to a Viking ship, given its steep chancel roof and squat tower, which could easily pass for prow and stern respectively. The oldest parts of St Mary's church date from the late 13th century, such as the south doorway and the four-bay nave arcades, while the south wall contains a late 13th century window of two trefoil-headed lights. However, much of the church was rebuilt in 1714, with other 19th and 20th century additions and alterations – for example, the chancel arch is 19th century.

As for the interior, that is as quirky as the exterior, with low slender pillars in the nave dwarfed by large arches that rise almost to the ceiling, while the tower arch appears to be somewhat lop-sided and its capitals lie only four feet off the ground! Further medieval relics survive inside, too, including the octagonal font (c.1400), a floor-stone carved with a cross, three 14th century sedilia in the chancel and a 14th century tomb with a broken helmet hanging above it. The latter is thought to belong to a knight, killed in a duel at nearby Earls Bridge, while the stone figure of his opponent (and presumably the winner of the duel) graces All Saints' church at Maltby-le-Marsh; Earls Bridge being exactly half-way between the two churches.

Ironically, it was 20th century drought rather than flood which almost did for St Mary's church, when sustained dry weather resulted in deep cracks in the

St Mary's church, Mablethorpe, and which somewhat resembles a Viking ship!

The Book in Hand at Mablethorpe is not quite what it was before the fire of 1981 claimed its front bays.

dried out clay sub-soil. This resulted in structural damage to the extent that the aisles and roof had to be supported in 1978 by new arches made of Douglas fir and mahogany.

Mablethorpe Historic Trivia:
Stories by the Sea

It is thought that much of the east coast of Lincolnshire was for millennia protected by a series of offshore barrier islands, but which were destroyed by storm surges in 1287 and 1288. Thereafter, settlements like Mablethorpe became much more vulnerable to coastal erosion. As mentioned earlier, much of Mablethorpe's parish of St Peter was lost to the sea in the late 1530s, including the parish church of St Peter. However, this wasn't the first time the parish had been inundated. According to the *Louth Park Abbey Chronicle*, St Peter's church was "rent asunder by the waves of the sea" on 1st January, 1287. The church was rebuilt during the late 13th century, but suffered further inundations in 1335, 1425, 1443, and terminally so, in the late 1530s. Accounts suggest that the church ruins remained visible until the 1870s.

vessel to safety, despite the huge seas and the fact that the lifeboat was smaller than the fishing boat and powered by one 40hp outboard engine.

The most significant "recent" storm occurred on the night of Saturday and Sunday, 31st January and 1st February 1953. Like so many other east-coast places, Mablethorpe felt the full force of the event which was caused when a combination of a high spring tide and a severe European windstorm caused a storm tide. The water level at Mablethorpe exceeded 5.6 metres above mean sea level, and thus overwhelmed sea defences, causing extensive flooding, and hundreds of people had to be evacuated from their homes.

By 1877, Mablethorpe had a station on the Louth and East Coast Railway, part of the Great Northern Railway, and this brought more day-trippers and holidaymakers from the East Midlands and Yorkshire. Shortly afterwards, in 1884, a pavilion was erected on the sand hills for visitors, while the town also held annual flower, horse, and bee shows! The Mablethorpe Convalescent House was also built in the late 19th century, as the sea air was deemed to be conducive to aiding recovery from all sorts of ailments. The house,

Mablethorpe's modern Lifeboat Station, the most recent of a line of stations dating back to the 1880s.

Late evening sunshine on the golden sands of Mablethorpe.

In the 19th century Mablethorpe became a centre for the process of breaking up old ships and selling off the parts either for re-use or scrap. Also in the 19th century, Mablethorpe became a centre for lifeboat rescue. The first lifeboat station was built in Mablethorpe in 1883, running until World War I when it had to close because of crew shortages. However, it didn't re-open after the war and Mablethorpe was without a lifeboat station until an inshore lifeboat (ILB) station was established in 1965.

Over the years there have been many heroic efforts by the lifeboat crews, such as the story from 12th April, 1998 when a D class lifeboat rescued the crew (of two) and saved the fishing vessel *Lark*. The fishing vessel had broken down, lost her anchor and was drifting towards the shore. Despite a force 7 gale, the lifeboat was launched and managed to somehow reach the fishing boat. The helmsman decided that it was too hazardous to take off the crew and managed to tow the

which was open during the holiday season, from April to November, included 75 beds and featured hot and cold salt water baths.

Naturally, a 19th century town the size of Mablethorpe had its Methodist chapels as well, with the Wesleyans building a chapel here in 1836, then a new chapel in 1869, which they enlarged in 1881. A Primitive Methodist chapel was also built in 1909. A National School was built here in 1856 and was followed by a Council School in 1906. Next, World War II saw Mablethorpe targeted by a German bombing raid, and four houses were demolished and around a dozen more suffered extensive damage. Incredibly, only six people were injured, albeit some of them seriously. More recently, in 2010, the town became home to the annual Mablethorpe Motorcycle Festival. This was in response to the fact that for over forty years, Mablethorpe has hosted motorbike sand racing each winter and spring.

Finally, it was also in Mablethorpe that Alfred Lord Tennyson (1809-1892) and his brother spent the day that their first book of verse, *Poems by Two Brothers*, was published. They were regular visitors to Mablethorpe, and it is said that the pair of them used to shout their poetry aloud towards the sea. Many years later, Alfred wrote this verse for his favourite seaside town:

Here often when a child I lay reclined:
I took delight in this fair strand and free:
Here stood the infant Ilion of my mind,
And here the Grecian ships did seem to be.
And here again I come, and only find
The drain-cut levels of the marshy lea,
Gray sandbanks, and pale sunsets, dreary wind,
Dim shores, dense rains, and heavy-clouded sea.

Mablethorpe Quirk Alert: The Beach Hut Festival and the Star of the East

Mablethorpe is the annual venue for Britain's only beach hut festival. Called the Bathing Beauties Festival, it takes place each September, and owners of the town's resident private beach huts compete in exterior design, amidst a backdrop of poetry, music, and drama. The huts are located facing the sea, high above Seaholme Road as it heads southwards out of Mablethorpe towards Sutton-on-Sea. The huts have names too, and yes, one of them is indeed called Jabba!

So, Angel of the North, Queen of the South, Spirit of the West and now, in Mablethorpe, we have the Star of the East, and what is effectively a promotional beacon. Standing at 45ft (14m) high, this multi-faceted, star-themed sculpture forms the centrepiece of a series of other sculptures that includes curved benches and a series of black granite "shadow lines" inset into the ground which radiate from the centre of the Star's supporting column. Each of the lines represents an important date in Mablethorpe's history, including the disastrous Great Flood of 1953 and the Mablethorpe meteor of 1898. At sunrise the shadow of the support-

The Star of the East, a promotional beacon that stands 46ft (14m) high.

ing column falls across the historic date lines, while at night, the Star of the East lights up, changes colour, and generally creates a lighthouse effect.

Finally, I recently read an article where someone described Mablethorpe as "the farthest corner of one of the less-visited counties" and "not only did Mr Beeching do for its railways, but it is on the end of one of the twistiest roads in Britain". This latter dig is about the A157 from Louth to Mablethorpe, and its layout is indeed odd – presumably so-structured to navigate around drains and fens.

Some of the famous Mablethorpe beach huts that take part each year in the Bathing Beauties Festival.

Three's-Up!

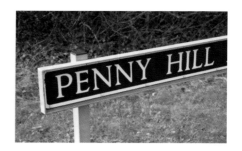

	MARTIN DALES	MARTIN MOOR	PENNY HILL
STATUS:	Hamlet	Hamlet	Hamlet
POPULATION:	866 (parish of Martin)	866 (parish of Martin)	c.100
DISTRICT:	North Kesteven	North Kesteven/East Lindsey	South Holland
EARLIEST RECORD:	*Martona*, 12th century [this is the Martin SW of Woodhall Spa]	*Mærtune*, 1060; *Martone*, 1086 (Domesday Book) [this is the Martin NE of Woodhall Spa]	19th century
MEANING:	Farmstead near a boundary, or by a pool		Unknown
DERIVATION:	The first part of the name is derived from either of the Old English words *(ge)mære* (boundary) or *mere* (pond, pool or lake), while the latter part is derived from the Old English word *tūn*, (farmstead)		

Three's Up Trivia!

Remarkably, there are five places called **Martin** located within 8 miles of each other on the B1191, either side of the North Kesteven/East Lindsey boundary! Of these five places, both Martin and **Martin Moor** appear twice on the B1191, either side of Woodhall Spa! The poor postie must tear his hair out! Anyway, we'll take them in a south-west to north-east order, starting with **Martin Moor**, which is actually not quite on the B1191, but on the B1189 just before its junction with the B1191. The settlement is very small and comprises several businesses, a couple of farms and a few houses, as well as Martin Moor Golf Club, a Koi Carp farm and Windy Bottom Animal Park!

Moving north-eastwards now along the B1191, you arrive at the first of the two **Martins**, also known as **Martin-by-Billinghay**. This is the largest of the five settlements and possesses a church, a pub (The Royal Oak), a school, shops and lots of houses. The church is a Victorian Gothic build from 1876, with the tower added in 1911, and is dedicated to the Holy Trinity. It was designed by T.H. Wyatt of London, with the build supervised by the Reverend J.W. King – although he was actually the rector of the church at Ashby-de-la-Launde for 53 years, and where he was also lord of the manor – a typical 19th century squarson! Holy Trinity church was restored between 1964 and 1966.

As for the school, this was originally founded in

Holy Trinity church at the Martin that lies to the south-west of Woodhall Spa on the B1191, and which is also known as Martin-by-Billinghay.

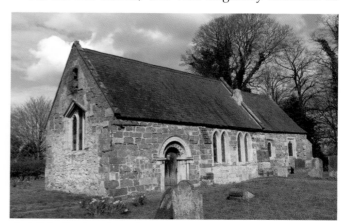

St Michael's church at the Martin that lies to the north-east of Woodhall Spa on the B1191, and which is also known as Martin-by-Horncastle.

The Norman south doorway of St Michael's church at Martin-by-Horncastle.

Inside the nave of St Michael's church.

Penny Hill Windmill on Washway Road.

Houses at the top of Penny Hill Road.

1753 and went by the name of "Mrs. Mary King's School", thanks to Mary King donating the land for it and also setting up a charitable trust. This trust was to provide a school to teach 20 poor children of the parish "reading, writing and the common prayer". The school was rebuilt in 1842 and enlarged in 1874 by the same Reverend J.W. King who supervised the building of Holy Trinity church. The school still retains Mary King's name to this day.

Next up is **Martin Dales**, an isolated collection of around a dozen houses, before you then head out of North Kesteven and into East Lindsey and the large village of Woodhall Spa. Coming out the other side, you hit the second **Martin Moor** followed by the second **Martin** – both of which are in the parish of Roughton which had a population of 644 according to the 2011 census, but which historically were part of the parish of Martin until that was abolished in 1936.

The second **Martin** is also known as **Martin-by-Horncastle**, thanks to the hamlet's proximity to Horncastle, around 2 miles to the north-east. It can be reached down the narrow Church Lane off the B1191 where you will also find the charming little St Michael's church. The church dates from the 12th century, and the Norman south doorway with its interesting mask-like decorated capitals is still the original albeit with extensive 19th century restoration. The chancel is also 12th

century and includes an early 13th century arch which is a classic example of the transition between Norman and Early English; the east window of the chancel and the window in the south wall also date from the 13th century. Most of the fittings date from the 19th century restoration (1877) except for the piscina which is the 13th century original.

A 1933 reference listing occupants of Holbeach Clough names a beer retailer and the landlady of the Pear Tree public house at **Penny Hill.** The Pear Tree was presumably located on Peartree House Road, although there is no evidence of the pub today. What is still standing, though, is Penny Hill Windmill, which can be found on Washway Road, around half a mile south of Holbeach Bank. This tower mill was built in 1826-27 on the site of a former smock mill. Today it is bereft of any sails, but it did originally have four, while in the late 19th century, the windmill had another (sixth) storey added to it and was re-equipped with six sails. The mill was still working for cereal milling until 1944, albeit on four sails by this stage, but the top and sails were then dismantled by German prisoners of war in 1945, and by 1954 all of the machinery had been removed, too.

Finally, in nearby Holbeach All Saints' church, there is the tomb of Sir Humphrey Littlebury who lived at Penny Hill Hall, and is said to have been killed during the Wars of the Roses.

NAME (STATUS):	**MAVIS ENDERBY** (Village)
POPULATION:	190 (parish of Raithby)
DISTRICT:	East Lindsey
EARLIEST RECORD:	*Endrebi*, 1086 (Domesday Book); *Enderby Malbys*, 1302; *Malvyssh Enderby*, 1430
MEANING:	Farmstead of a man called Eindrithi
DERIVATION:	From the Old Scandinavian personal name *Eindrithi*, plus the Old Scandinavian word *bý* (farmstead, village or settlement). The Mavis affix is manorial and derives from the *Malebisse* family, recorded in this region in the 13th century.

Mavis Enderby Church: St Michael's

The Grade II listed St Michael's church has been much rebuilt, but still includes a number of 14th and 15th century facets while the pillar piscina on clustered shafts in the porch is probably Norman. From the 14th century come the nave arcades and windows, while the base of the tower is still 15th century, as are the aisle windows and the font. The church was restored in 1875 by James Fowler of Louth, while most of the tower was rebuilt in 1895 by Charles Hodgson Fowler.

Mavis Enderby Historic Trivia

During medieval times, Mavis Enderby was home to a religious house which belonged to nearby Revesby Abbey, a Cistercian abbey founded by William de Roumare, Earl of Lincoln, in 1143.

Lying about a mile north-east of Old Bolingbroke, Mavis Enderby was also the family seat of John of Gaunt, whose son became Henry IV, or Henry Bolingbroke, King of England from 1399 to 1413.

In 1798, the Common Lands were enclosed at Mavis Enderby, leaving only 4 acres available for the poor. Then in 1830, a Wesleyan Methodist church was founded in the village. It remained part of the Spilsby Wesleyan Methodist Circuit from 1830 to 1932, and then the Spilsby Methodist Circuit from 1932 to its closure in 1966.

Mavis Enderby Quirk Alert: Literary Classics!

Mavis Enderby also shows up as a character in two relatively modern classics, plus one famous 19th century poem. More recently, in Chapter One of Helen Fielding's *Bridget Jones's Diary*, Bridget's mother suggests that her daughter's birthday present should be "a compact case with a pull-out handle, *with wheels attached*" – primarily "because Mavis Enderby's daughter has one!" A little further back and Douglas Adams claims in his spoof dictionary, *The Meaning of Liff*, that Mavis Enderby (n) is: "The almost-completely-forgotten girlfriend from your distant past for whom your wife has a completely irrational jealousy and hatred." Meanwhile, the village of Mavis Enderby also had a peal of bells named after it, called "The Brides of Enderby". They are mentioned in 19th century poet and

Above: *St Michael's church, Mavis Enderby.*

Left: *The medieval cross in St Michael's churchyard.*

novelist Jean Ingelow's best-known poem, *The High Tide on the Coast of Lincolnshire 1571*. This is the name given to the special peal of bells, rung out from Boston Stump to warn the townsfolk and those in the surrounding countryside of approaching danger, whether that be of pirates, of flood, or of high tides breaching the dykes. Supposedly, the name commemorates the womenfolk of Mavis Enderby.

NAME (STATUS):	**MELTON ROSS** (Village)
POPULATION:	188
DISTRICT:	North Lincolnshire
EARLIEST RECORD:	*Medeltone*, 1086 (Domesday Book); *Melton Roos*, 1375
MEANING:	Middle farmstead of the de Ros family
DERIVATION:	From the Old English words *middel* (replaced by the Old Scandinavian word *methal*) and *tūn*, meaning "middle" and "farmstead", respectively. The "Ross" part, relates to the de Ros family, who had a stronghold in the village.

Melton Ross Church:
Church of the Ascension

Melton Ross's church of the Ascension was built in 1867 following the destruction of its predecessor by fire which, in turn, replaced its predecessor which had been built in 1773. The current church does still retain a couple of relics from its predecessors though, these being a tub font in the churchyard and a holy water stoup inside. The Victorian church was designed by Ewan Christian.

Melton Ross Historic Trivia:
de Ros vs. Tyrwhit

As referenced above, the "Ross" part of the place-name relates to the de Ros family, who had a stronghold in the village, the mound of which can still be seen in what is now a farmer's field. Back in the early 15th century, the de Ros family – who owned all of the land around today's village – began a centuries-long feud with the Tyrwhit family from the nearby village of Kettleby. Apparently, hostilities began one day in 1411, when a group of horsemen rode aggressively towards a number of workers who were cutting turf for fuel near Wrawby. The horsemen belonged to Sir Robert Tyrwhit of Kettleby, and the fleeing workers were tenants of Lord de Ros, of Melton Ross – and whom Tyrwhit claimed were trespassing on his land. However, de Ros countered that it was he who held a right of common pasture for the fields in question. To settle the dispute, both parties engaged the services of Lord Chief Justice Gascoyne, who agreed to visit Wrawby and meet the two lords on the condition "that both parties bring with them what titles and other evidences are necessary to prove their cases, and be accompanied with but two friends apiece".

Lord de Ros stuck to his part of the bargain, and turned up with Lord Henry Beaumont and Lord Thomas de le Warr. Alas, Lord Tyrwhit had no intention of playing by the rules, and he showed up with around 500 armed men. Presumably, Tyrwhit had expected de Ros to do the same, and it was hardly seemly for 500 men to cut down a mere three, so no fighting took place. De Ros, however, certainly took umbrage, and sent a petition to the King, asking for "redress therein and for punishment for the offence". Unable to deny his actions to the King, Tyrwhit agreed to his punish-

Church of the Ascension, Melton Ross.

These gallows mark the spot on which James I set up the originals, designed to put an end to the bitter centuries-old feud between the de Ros family of Melton Ross and the Tyrwhits of Kettleby. They can be found on the A18 alongside the appropriately named Gallows Wood Service Station.

ment of paying de Ros "two tonnes of Gascony wine, two fat oxen and 12 fat sheep", and to also visit Melton Ross and apologise to Lord de Ros, offering 500 marks and asking "for his grace and mercy".

Shortly after the affair, Sir Robert Tyrwhit died, while his heir, Sir William Tyrwhit, was busy fighting the French where he was one of the Knights of the King's Bodyguard at Agincourt (1415), and for which he was later made Knight of the Shire of Lincolnshire in 1423. No doubt there were other incidents and skirmishes in the intervening years, but we next pick up the story two hundred years down the line in the early 17th century. For this was when open fighting is recorded as having taken place in the hunting field, in which strong words became blows, and which steadily escalated such that several of the combatants were killed. This must have been the latest of a number of such skirmishes, for the incident brought to Wrawby none other than King James I. Clearly fed up with the centuries-old feud, James ordered that a gallows be erected on the very spot where the latest bout had taken place, and he declared that in future "anyone slain in such encounters was to be considered murdered, and the perpetrators were to be hanged as an example to others." And to this day, those gallows remain on the spot, a mile or so west of Melton Ross alongside the A18 and next to the appropriately named Gallows Wood Service Station!

The level crossing that divides Melton Ross from New Barnetby.

As for the de Ros family, they had also acquired Belvoir Castle through marriage in the 13th century, and indeed it was also a de Ros who became first Earl of Rutland in the early 16th century. Meanwhile, today, Melton Ross is located a mile or so to the west of both Singleton Birch (leaders in lime production and supply) and Humberside Airport. The latter was opened in 1974, and was somewhat inevitably converted from a former RAF site, this one being RAF Kirmington.

Melton Ross Quirk Alert: Truth or Gallows Humour?

The previous section explains why the gallows were erected a mile or so west of Melton Ross, and it is documented well enough to assume that the tale is true. However, there is an alternative legend in the area. This legend suggests that a group of boys were playing what was known as "the hanging game". This is where each "player" takes a turn at hanging themselves from a tree, and the "winner" is the one who hangs by his neck for the longest time before signalling the others to "loose the noose" (well, a good game does need a good catchphrase). Anyway, the story goes that when one particular boy took his turn, all of a sudden, the Devil ran past disguised as a three-legged hare! The other boys then ran after the hare trying to catch it and in their excitement forgot all about their poor playmate who was found dead on their return. This particular legend, therefore, suggests that the gallows were erected on this spot in memory of this tragic accident.

The Grimsby to Scunthorpe railway line just east of Melton Ross where it runs alongside Singleton Birch, "leaders in lime production and supply".

NAME (STATUS):	**MESSINGHAM** (Village)
POPULATION:	3,718
DISTRICT:	North Lincolnshire
EARLIEST RECORD:	*Mæssingaham*, c.1067; *Messingeham*, 1086 (Domesday Book)
MEANING:	Homestead of the family or followers of a man called Mæssa
DERIVATION:	From the Old English personal name, *Mæssa*, plus the Old English words *inga* (of) and *hām* (homestead, village, manor or estate)

Messingham Pubs: The Crown Inn, The Green Tree Inn and The Horn Inn

All three of the above pubs get a mention in *Kelly's Lincolnshire Directory* of 1876, with the Horn Inn and the Crown Inn acknowledged as public houses even back then. However, it is thought that the Green Tree Inn was built and named after a sycamore tree, which grew in High Street and stood on the site of the village cross and which was therefore called Cross Tree – and which was also, therefore, where the great John Wesley stood and preached in the 18th century.

Messingham Church: Holy Trinity

The church of Holy Trinity was largely rebuilt between 1818 and 1821 on the site of its medieval predecessor, but did retain its 13th century nave arcades and some 14th and 15th century windows, while in the chancel the original aumbry and piscina can still be found. The tower had already been built in the late 18th century. In the early19th century, Holy Trinity church was made an ecclesiastical museum by its then-vicar, Henry Vincent Bayley (1777-1844), who was vicar of Messingham and Bottesford from 1810 to 1828. Already sub-dean of Lincoln (1805) he also became Archdeacon of Stow in 1823. It was also Dr Bayley who brought additional old glass for the Messingham church windows from as far afield as Malvern and Manchester Cathedral, while he also brought old tracery for use in the low screen, the two desks and the pulpit, the latter having originated in its entirety from Lincoln Minster, while the wooden pews came from Althorpe church.

Messingham Historic Trivia

Although Messingham is mentioned in Domesday Book (1086), and always retained a fair-sized population, it only became a large village after World War II, thanks to housing development – this mainly for the hundreds of workers at the nearby steelworks in Scunthorpe. Two centuries earlier, a Methodist church was founded in Messingham in 1772, and John Wesley – born in 1703 around 7 miles to the west in Epworth – is known to have preached in Messingham at around that time. However, it wasn't until 1821 that the current Wesleyan Methodist Church on church Street was founded. Later, a Temperance Hall was built in Messingham in 1875, while a Primitive Methodist church was also founded in the village, eventually closing in 1951. Gravel from Messingham was also

Holy Trinity church, parts of which date to the 13th century, but the majority of which was rebuilt between 1818 and 1821.

The war memorial in the centre of Messingham.

The old junior school building at Messingham.

used in roadbuilding in the 19th century but the quarries around the village eventually became exhausted during the 20th century. However, in the 21st century, they have been re-used, thanks to the Messingham Sands Fishery angling complex to the west of the village and the Lincolnshire Wildlife Trust Messingham Sand Quarry Nature Reserve to the east.

NAME (STATUS):	**MINTING** (Village)
POPULATION:	286
DISTRICT:	East Lindsey
EARLIEST RECORD:	*Mentinges*, 1086 (Domesday Book)
MEANING:	Settlement of the family or followers of a man called Mynta
DERIVATION:	From the Old English personal name, *Mynta*, plus the Old English word *ingas* (people of, family or followers of, or dwellers at)

The Sebastopol Inn at Minting.

St Andrew's church, Minting.

Minting Pub: The Sebastopol Inn

The Sebastopol Inn at Minting is an award-winning pub for cuisine today, but also has an interesting history. Parts of the building date back to the 16th century, but it was the Beer House Act of 1830 that hugely influenced its future. This is because for the payment of two guineas, this Act enabled a householder or ratepayer to acquire a license to turn their private home into a public house, and this is exactly what happened here in 1836 when farmer George Cartwright became the first landlord, brewing his own ale. The inn was initially known simply as "the beerhouse", but shortly after the Crimean War of 1853-1856, the story goes that a soldier was at "the beerhouse" celebrating his return from the war which had claimed the lives of over 21,000 British soldiers. Alas, later that night, he fell into a dyke and drowned. During the inquest, the coroner insisted that a pub name was required for his records and "the beerhouse" just wouldn't suffice. As the soldier's connection with the Siege of Sebastopol (1854-1855) kept cropping up, this was the name that was adopted – although the English spelling of the place-name has since changed to Sevastopol.

Interestingly, although it was quite common in the 19th century to name public houses after major events, it is thought that there is only one more in the UK that has the same name, this being at Windsor. As for Farmer Cartwright, he actually had competition from Farmer Winn who combined a butchers shop and brewery with his beer house, which he named the Axe and Handsaw, and which survived until 1926. By the 1960s, the Sebastopol Inn also included a Tankard Room with a collection of over 150 tankards from around the world, and an Armoury with a collection of around 50 swords and ancient firearms!

Minting Church: St Andrew's

St Andrew's church was almost completely rebuilt in 1863 by Ewan Christian, although an old 13th century arcade does survive between the nave and aisle. In addition, parts of the stem of a 13th century churchyard cross have been set into the east wall of the nave, one part showing the Crucifixion and which is dated 1210, and the other carved with trailing leaves. Finally, the east window is 15th century with three cusped lights, while an ancient octagonal font was found under the altar in 1930. The church is Grade II listed.

Minting Historic Trivia: Minting Priory

Minting Priory is thought to have been founded by Ranulf de Meschin (1070-1129), the third Earl of Chester, sometime in the early 12th century. The priory housed Benedictine monks and was originally a land grant to the Abbey of St Benoit sur Loire at Fleury in France (founded c.640). However, although the grant was made before 1129, the earliest written reference to the priory is much later in 1213. Indeed, church records suggest that there were issues of morality at Minting Priory. One letter in 1238 from Bishop Grosseteste to the Abbot of Fleury states that: "The monks at Minting have lately been found to be living luxuriously with harlots, they have enriched themselves, known no obedience to the rule, and have been given much to eating and drinking, not being ashamed to eat meat, even on Wednesdays."

Anyway, by the 14th century, the priory belonged to the Crown, and presumably suffered thanks to it being dependent on a French mother house given that England was in the middle of the Hundred Years War. The Benedictine Minting Priory was eventually dissolved in 1414, and then granted as a grange to the Carthusian priory of Mount Grace in North Yorkshire in 1421. Nothing survives of Minting Priory today other than some earthworks in the centre of the village.

In terms of other Minting history, the Wesleyan Methodists built two chapels here in 1838, while a school followed in 1851 but which was superseded by

another built in 1876. Finally, in the 20th century, Minting was one of a handful of Thankful Villages, so-named because it did not suffer any fatalities during World War I.

Minting Quirk Alert: Pumas and Ducks

Minting has been the location of several sightings of puma-like animals over the years. It is also the home of Lincolnshire's own "dialect champion", a farmer called Farmer Wink (real name Robert Carlton), who has produced videos about rural life, narrated in his broad Lincolnshire accent, and who has a regular slot on BBC Radio Lincolnshire. Typical local vocabulary quirks include diphthongs such as pronouncing the Lincolnshire town of Louth as Low-uth. Others include "duck" as a term of endearment, "mardy" meaning upset or angry, "mowt" (pronounced mout) for might, "frit" meaning frightened, and the standard greeting of "now then!"

As for the Sebastopol Inn, given its age, it will hardly come as a surprise to find that it has its resident ghost, this being a mystery lady regularly seen in an upstairs window, while doors are wont to open and close when no-one is around!

Left: *These earthworks in the centre of Minting are all that remains of the 12th century Minting Priory.*

Below: *Fields of oilseed rape on the outskirts of Minting.*

NAME (STATUS):	**RAND** (Village)
POPULATION:	157 (parish of Goltho)
DISTRICT:	West Lindsey
EARLIEST RECORD:	*Rande*, 1086 (Domesday Book)
MEANING:	Place at the border or edge
DERIVATION:	From the Old English word
	rand (border or edge)

Rand Church: St Oswald's

Rand's Grade II-listed St Oswald's church dates from the early 14th century, although the nave and chancel were both rebuilt in c.1820 and 1862 respectively, the latter by R. J. Withers. However, the arch between them is still the 14th century original, as is the tower (bar its battlements); the head moulds of the east window are also early 14th century. The church is also home to a number of fine monuments including portions of six brasses found in the vestry in 1890. However, the oldest monument is the late 13th century effigy of a lady that can be found under a recessed arch in the north wall of the chancel, and which is thought to have been inspired by the Angel Choir in Lincoln Cathedral. (There are further monuments to the Metham, Harrington, Leigh and Fulnetby families.) Finally, there is also an elaborately decorated stone coffin-lid inside the church that is believed to date from between the 10th and 12th centuries.

Rand History: James Harrington

James Harrington (1611-1677) grew up in Rand before his family moved to Upton in Northamptonshire. Harrington is thought to have accompanied Charles I to Scotland in 1639 in connection with the first Bishops' War, but later financially assisted Parliament with loans in 1642 and 1645 during the English Civil War. These actions demonstrate his divided sympathies and, having survived the war, he became a political theorist of classical republicanism. He is best known as the author of the controversial work, *The Commonwealth of Oceana*, which was published in 1656, and which propounds an ideal constitution, designed to facilitate the development of a utopian republic.

Rand Quirk Alert: Bees and Ducks

Today, Rand is the location of Rand Farm Park as well as the Beehive Business Park which is dominated by the corporate headquarters of E. H. Thorne Beehives Ltd. This family-run company is world-renowned as one of the best manufacturers and suppliers of beehives as well as all items of bee-keeping equipment. The company has been manufacturing beehive equipment for over 100 years, while their catalogue was the first full colour beekeeping equipment catalogue in the English speaking world. The wedge type frame for hives and which is the most popular form world-wide, was developed in nearby Wragby by E. H. Thorne many decades ago, and products such as plastic honey

St Oswald's church at Rand, accompanied by the cast of a famous Alfred Hitchcock film!

The entrance to Thorne Corporate Headquarters (above) and its landscaped grounds (below). This family-run company is world-renowned as one of the best manufacturers and suppliers of beehives and of bee-keeping equipment.

extractors, feeders, bee escapes, spacers, wax moulds and mobile observation hives were all introduced by the company, too. The company also produces and exports honey labels to over 70 different countries, while "Bees on a Budget"' kits are ideal for small-scale bee-keepers and Beginners Kits are ideal for those who are new to the practice. Meanwhile, bee on your guard! The sign (top right) greets all visitors at both ends of the village!

Three's-Up!

	RIGSBY	TWENTY	WRESSLE
STATUS:	Hamlet	Hamlet	Hamlet
POPULATION:	c.20	c.75	c.60
DISTRICT:	East Lindsey	South Kesteven	North Lincolnshire
EARLIEST RECORD:	*Rigesbi*, 1086 (Domesday Book)	*Old Twenty Foot Drain*, 1826	Unknown
MEANING:	Possibly farmstead or settlement where rye grows	Named after the 17th century Twenty Foot Drain	Something twisted, perhaps referring to broken ground or a winding river
DERIVATION:	From the Old Scandinavian words *ryge* (rye) and *bý* (farmstead, village or settlement)	As above	From the Old English word *wræsel*, meaning "something twisted"

Three's Up Trivia!

Rigsby is a tiny hamlet in the parish of Alford on the eastern edge of the Lincolnshire Wolds, with fine views towards the coast. The hamlet only comprises a couple of houses, a farm and the Rigsby Wold Holiday Cottages, plus a Grade II-listed church which is dedicated to St James. The original church probably dated from Norman times, and was certainly converted to a Chapelry by Robert de Welle in 1195, and given by Gilbert de Rigsby to the Gilbertine Priory of St Katherine at Lincoln to which it belonged for over 300 years. However, the current church was an almost complete rebuild in 1863 by James Fowler of Louth – although he did rebuild it in a Norman style, using local Ancaster stone. One of the few survivors from the original church is the west doorway on its inside, while the original Norman chancel arch also survives. One element that definitely hasn't survived, though, is the original church roof, which was thatched and supported by wooden props! As for the rebuild in 1863, this cost £685 and was funded by all of the labourers in the Parish of Rigsby with Ailby, who each contributed a week's wages.

Next up, **Twenty** is located in Bourne North Fen, 3 miles due east of Bourne and at the southern end of what is known as the Black Sluice Level – the latter named after the sluice at Boston via which this land is drained to the sea. The Black Sluice Internal Drainage

St James's church at Rigsby.

The tiny hamlet of Rigsby.

Board maintains a small electric pumping station at Twenty. The hamlet is therefore surrounded by rich land reclaimed from wetland which was formerly freshwater fenland interspersed with marine creeks and marshland. The references to "black" reflect the fact that the land here is rich in agricultural silt and black freshwater.

A relatively modern place, Twenty takes its name from the Twenty Foot Drain, a drainage scheme put in place in 1638 by Robert Bertie, 1st Earl of Lindsey; indeed the hamlet marks the spot where in the first half of the 19th century, the North Fen Drove crossed the 17th century Twenty Foot Drain. Lindsey's drain actually ran from south of modern-day Twenty to Dowsby Fen, 5 miles north of Twenty. From there it headed off eastwards to Gosberton High Fen, Risegate Eau and Bicker Haven before draining into the estuary of the River Welland.

Regarding the Earl of Lindsey's Twenty Foot Drain, it was actually sabotaged during the English Civil War, and it wasn't until an Act of Parliament was passed in 1765 that the drain was properly utilised when it was incorporated as a feature into the aforementioned Black Sluice scheme. The Twenty Foot Drain actually survived until the 20th century, when parts of it – including the stretch at Twenty – were filled in. However, its course can still be easily traced upstream from Dowsby Fen.

Today, the village of Twenty is little more than a handful of houses yet it once had its own railway station on the line between Bourne and Spalding.

Opened in 1866, the station was used to transport products from the locality such as the black, humic soil. In the 20th century, though, both the line and station were closed to passengers in February 1959.

Finally, **Wressle** is a hamlet in the parish of Broughton in North Lincolnshire. It is thought that a settlement has existed in this area since Neolithic times and New Stone Age tools have been found in this area, particularly on the commons near Wressle.

It was also on a site just north of Wressle that it was reported in the Scunthorpe Telegraph in June 2013, that drilling for oil was about to commence, with Egdon Resources U.K. Ltd receiving temporary planning permission from North Lincolnshire Council along with environmental permits for drilling and testing operations. The site was initially thought to have the potential to yield between 200 and 300 barrels of crude oil per day, which would have been worth around £4.5 million a year. Drilling took place during July and August 2014 with a well drilled to a total depth of 7,350ft (2,240m). Test operations then took place between January and March 2015, indicating that 710 barrels of oil could be acquired per day (bopd) from three separate reservoirs, although by October 2015, that estimate had been lowered to 500 bopd for just the Ashover Grit reservoir. Should the go-ahead be received from the Oil and Gas Authority, North Lincolnshire Council and the Environment Agency, the Wressle well will involve only conventional drilling for oil and not the process of hydraulic fracking for shale gas or oil.

Twenty Pumping Station is located at the western entrance to Twenty.

The bottom of Station Road at Twenty where its former railway station was on the Spalding to Bourne line, opened in 1866. The station closed in 1959.

NAME (STATUS):	**WELBOURN** (Village)
POPULATION:	647
DISTRICT:	North Kesteven
EARLIEST RECORD:	*Wellebrune*, 1086 (Domesday Book)
MEANING:	Stream fed by a spring
DERIVATION:	From the Old English words *wella* (spring) and *burna* (stream)

Welbourn Church: St Chad's

St Chad's church at Welbourn is Grade I listed and includes a tower which dates back to the 12th century, although its battlements date from the 14th century, while the octagonal, crocketed spire dates from the 15th century. Much of the rest of the church was built between these two dates, including the 14th century porch, nave and aisles, the build of which were probably overseen by the treasurer of Lincoln and who was also known as John of Welbourn. The impressive clerestory followed in the 15th century, but the original chancel was replaced in 1854 while the church was further restored in 1884.

Welbourn History: Welbourn Castle

Back in Roman times, Ermine Street passed across the eastern Welbourn parish boundary, although interestingly, Roman earthworks have been recorded on the north-western edge of the village. These are thought to be the remains of a Roman encampment, possibly a marching camp.

In the centre of Welbourn on what is known as Castle Hill, you will find a series of earthworks and buried remains which mark the location of the medieval Welbourn Castle, a scheduled ancient monument. Thought to date from the 11th or 12th century, the castle was what is known as a medieval ringwork, a form of fortified defensive structure, usually circular or oval in shape, but actually D shaped in this particular case. The castle would have been protected by the wide ditches and massive bank on the north, east and west sides, while the south and south-western approach was protected by a lighter double bank and stream.

A little later, in 1288, a survey of the Barony of Bayeux provides a detailed picture of the estate in the late 13th century. There was a walled court surmounted by a small tower plus a ditch. In the court was a hall with two chambers, a kitchen, a brew house, a granary, a stable, an ox house, a cow shed, a sheep fold, trees and garden. This sizeable collection of buildings served a large arable farm of 340 acres with another 48 acres of meadow and pasture, along with two water mills.

The 13th century also saw Welbourn granted a weekly market as well as an annual six day fair following the Feast of St Chad. As for the 14th century, the arrival from Europe of the Black Death in 1349 took nearly half of Welbourn's population and decimated farming and other trades. At this time, the village of Sapperton lay to the south of Welbourn. However, it is believed that it was in

The Joiners Arms at Welbourn.

St Chad's church at Welbourn has a strangely convex 15th century spire, supported by a tower which dates back to the 12th century.

Some of the remaining earthworks of Welbourn Castle which was built in the 11th or 12th century.

Looking down the eastern side of Welbourn Castle earthworks which reveals a long stretch of the castle moat.

The village pond on Beck Street, with the village hall behind. The pond is fed by a spring that is at least 700 years old.

Welbourn Manor, now a care home, but which includes elements that date back to the 13th century.

the mid-14th century that the village was abandoned – presumably due to the plague – and hence its definition today as a "deserted medieval village".

Welbourn was later hit by another disaster when the village was all-but destroyed by a freak storm in October 1666. One account states the following: *"On the 13th there was the strongest whirlwind or earthquake, or both, in Lincolnshire that was ever heard of. In the town of Welbourn near to Newark, of 80 stone houses only three were left standing, the timbers being so disposed that none can tell his own"*.

In the late 16th century, there was a fortified manor house in Welbourn owned by Sir John Popham (1531-1607), who was Lord Chief Justice of England from 1592 to 1607. During his tenure, Popham presided over some famous trials, including the Jesuit, Robert Southwell, Sir Walter Raleigh (1603) and the conspirators of the Gunpowder Plot, including Guy Fawkes (1606). In fact, in 1587, even before his tenure of Lord Chief Justice of England, Popham had been involved with the trial of Mary, Queen of Scots at Fotheringay, and which resulted in her execution. As for his manor house, nothing remains today.

Onto the 19th century, and a Wesleyan Methodist chapel was built on High Street in 1839. The village school followed in 1865, built by the Countess of Buckinghamshire. It was enlarged in 1884 by which stage it accommodated 164 pupils, while the current Welbourn Primary School is resident on the same site.

Sticking with the mid-19th century, Sir William Robertson (1850-1933) was born in Welbourn at the old post office which was situated on The Green. Young William left the village school in 1872 at the age of twelve and eventually enlisted as a trooper in 1877. He went on to become the first and only British Army soldier to rise from the rank of a private soldier, to the rank of field marshal and Chief of the Imperial General Staff, attaining the latter post between 1916 and 1918 during World War I.

Welbourn Quirk Alert: Forge of Nature

Today, Welbourn is still home to a working forge and blacksmith's workshop which dates back to 1864. Welbourn Forge has served the needs of farmers and tradesmen in the area for over 150 years and the forge is still fired on the first Saturday of each month. The forge also exhibits old photographs, displays and memorabilia…as well as a restored earth privy!

Looking down the nave of St Chad's church towards the chancel.

NAME (STATUS):	**WELL** (Estate Village)
POPULATION:	166 (Well Parish)
DISTRICT:	East Lindsey
EARLIEST RECORD:	*Welle*, 1086 (Domesday Book)
MEANING:	Place at the spring or stream
DERIVATION:	From the Old English word *wella* (spring or stream)

Well Geographic Trivia

Well is a small village and civil parish situated on the eastern slope of the Lincolnshire Wolds, a mile or so to the south-west of Alford. The village is also part of the estate of Well Vale Hall, which faces the village, set in its 170 acres of parkland. Meanwhile, the chalk spring after which Well is named, still rises near the village today and becomes one of the sources for Anderby Creek which, in turn, empties into the North Sea.

Well Church: St Margaret's

Well's Grade I-listed Georgian parish church is dedicated to St Margaret, and can be found in the grounds of Well Vale Hall. It was built of red brick in 1733 by an unknown architect, and was unusually built in the style of a Palladian temple along with pillars, a portico and a distinctive bell tower. The church was later altered in the late 18th century, and restored in 1959.

Well Historic Trivia: A False Lord (?) and Well Vale Park

In terms of very early history, three contiguous Celtic barrows were found in the parish, while in 1725, two urns containing six hundred Roman coins were found. There is also a story doing the rounds that the manor of Well was held by a Richard de Wells at the time of the Norman Conquest, thanks to his service as a baker to the king – but which one, we don't know. This story originates from a book written by Thomas Allen in 1833, called *The History of the County of Lincoln, From the Earliest Period to the Present Time*. However, there is no mention of a Richard de Wells in Domesday Book. As well as the assets of the village, Domesday Book lists the Lord of the Manor at the time of the survey's compilation (1086) and at the time of the Conquest (1066), and the latter is listed as Tonni of Lusby. The Lord of the Manor in 1086 is then listed as Rademar, with the tenant-in-chief being Gilbert de Ghent. It is also unlikely that anyone called "Richard" (a French name) or with a "de" (French for "of") in their name would have owned an English manor before the Norman Conquest – so perhaps this de Wells character was William I's baker and was thus allocated Well in 1066 – and then changed his name to the manor he owned which was a common practise of post-Conquest Norman lords. All conjecture, of course!

Moving on, Well Hall Park (now also known as Well Vale Park) was first formally laid out in the 1720s following the damming of Well Beck to create two lakes (known as Upper and Lower), although it is likely that a formal garden had already been laid out here in the early 18th century. It was also during this period in around 1725 that the existing early 17th century house was extensively enlarged and remodelled by James Bateman, with the house located due south of the bridge dividing the two lakes. Today, an open lawn slopes down to the lower lake to the east of the hall, and reveals outlines of early 18th century terraces perhaps constructed at the same time as the two lakes.

The house later passed through marriage to the Dashwood family and was further enlarged by Francis Dashwood in the late 18th century while further changes were made by Guy Elwes in 1925, when parts were

St Margaret's church, Well, with its paladian temple-like design.

View towards Well Vale House from St Margaret's church.

rebuilt following a fire – although that fire had occurred many decades earlier in 1845! Today, the Grade II-listed house is a private school. Also Grade II listed is the Well Vale Park Coach House, built in c.1733, and the ashlar

gate piers, built in around 1730 in the form of obelisks with fluted circular bases with lions' heads.

Finally, to the east of the village is Well cricket ground, which also serves nearby Alford.

Well Vale House and the western (upper) of the ornamental lakes, constructed in the 1720s by the damming of Well Beck.

The Grade II-listed Well Vale Coach House, built in 1733.

The centre of the village of Well.

NAME (STATUS):	**WRANGLE** (Village and Parish)
POPULATION:	1,397
DISTRICT:	Boston
EARLIEST RECORD:	*Werangle*, 1086 (Domesday Book)
MEANING:	A crooked stream or other feature
DERIVATION:	From either the Old Scandinavian word *vrengill* or the Old English word *wrengel*, both meaning "bent or crooked"
FAMOUS PEOPLE:	Joseph Gilbert, astronomer who served on Captain Cook's second expedition when he discovered New Caledonia

Wrangle Geographic Trivia: Silt

Wrangle is located around 8 miles north-east of Boston, and both its geography and history mirror those of Bicker, with both villages having converted over the centuries from a port to a farming village. Wrangle was certainly a medieval port, serviced by Wrangle Haven, one of a number of tidal creeks which formed during the Bronze Age, about 2,500 years ago. At that time, Wrangle Haven was the third biggest harbour on this part of the English coast, after Bicker Haven and The Haven at Boston. However, Wrangle Haven eventually silted up, a process hastened by artificial enclosure for pasture which meant that the tide no longer flowed off the marsh twice a day to keep Wrangle Haven open. As a result, Wrangle now lies around 3 miles from the coast, while economic activity has changed accordingly – from fishing and salt manufacture up to the middle of the 17th century, to a prosperous wool trade and farming on reclaimed land.

Wrangle Church: St Mary and St Nicholas

The church of St Mary and St Nicholas is Grade I listed, with parts still dating to the 12th century. Certainly between 1154 and 1189, the church was affiliated to Waltham Abbey in Essex, with the latter supplying Wrangle's church with its priests. Indeed, records state that the glass of the original 12th century east window included a Latin inscription which read: "Tomas de Wyversty, Abbot of Waltham had me made". The church was moved to the Diocese of Lincoln when Waltham Abbey was dissolved in 1540.

Today's church still includes the 13th century nave and its arcades, and south doorway. The chancel is mainly 14th century when parts of the church were restored, and it retains its original sedilia, double piscina and aumbry, while 14th century glass survives in the north aisle, too. The clerestory dates from the late 14th century, the porch from the 15th century and the font is dated 1724. The chancel was then restored again between 1875 and 1878 by Ewan Christian, while the church roof and seats were repaired in 1896. The church also contains a number of monuments to the Reade family who were Lords of the Manor from the 14th century to the late 17th.

Wrangle Historic Trivia: King's Hill

It is thought that when the Romans occupied Wrangle, the settlement was actually an island in The Wash, and was almost certainly the location of a Roman salt works. It was also around these times that sea enclosure and land reclamation resulted in the settlement being connected to the mainland to the west. It is thought that the Saxons – also drawn here by salt production – then began to systematically enclose and drain areas of the coastal salt marsh as a means of extending their agriculture eastwards. Indeed, coastal ecologists have identified four eras of enclosure for agricultural land reclamation: during Saxon times, from the medieval period

The Angel Inn at Wrangle which is over a century old. Its predecessor once stood on the banks of a creek in the days when Wrangle was a port!

The church of St Mary and St Nicholas at Wrangle.

up to 1700, from 1800 to 1900, and post-1950.

In the north-west of the Wrangle parish at what is known as King's Hill, there are some impressive earthworks which pinpoint the location of a medieval moated motte and bailey castle, and which is a scheduled monument; certainly, the motte and bailey earthworks have been little altered over the centuries, a real rarity in Fenland country. It is thought that the castle was associated with a manorial estate established during the 11th and 12th centuries, and one theory is that this was actually a fortified grange affiliated to Waltham Abbey along with Wrangle church. During the 13th and 14th centuries, though, the castle belonged to the Earls of Lincoln As for the name, this comes from the fact that the property

The war memorial in the centre of Wrangle.

passed to King James I in the early 17th century. Later records from 1911 also show that King's Hill was a lot larger than it appears today, with farming having encroached over the last century or so, and earthworks to the east, west and south having been ploughed out – probably erasing evidence of outbuildings or animal pens. Today we can still clearly make out the mound of the motte, to the north, which measures around 196ft (60m) in diameter and stands around 6.5ft (2m) high, and with the flat top containing evidence of the earthwork remains of former buildings such as the keep. Then to the south of the motte, the remains of the bailey measure 196ft (60m) north to south in diameter and 230ft (70m) east to west, while the bailey site is only 3ft (1m) high – and which also still shows evidence of former buildings, almost certainly domestic and agricultural.

During 20th century excavations of the King's Hill site, Roman and medieval pottery was found, both in 1937 and 1959, with the latter dig at the north end of the

site also uncovering a Roman kiln site. Then in 1960, Roman pottery was found, including Samian and colour-coated ware, along with medieval pottery.

In the late 13th century, the manor still belonged to the Earls of Lincoln, and Henry de Lacy (3rd Earl), held a market at Wrangle every Saturday. Meanwhile, in the late 16th century, Wrangle Manor was held by Queen Elizabeth I, whereas by contrast, in 1676, the manor passed to a commoner, Thomas Woodcock. As for Wrangle Hall, this was the seat of the Reade family from the 14th century until the late 17th century. However, much of the house was dismantled in around 1806, and the remainder renovated some time on the 1830s. The house was also associated with an ancient chapel here, and which was still present in a field opposite the hall in the 18th century. It is likely that this was the St Peter's chapel referenced at Wrangle in 1342. As for the present Wrangle Hall, this is relatively modern, built on the site of its predecessor which was eventually demolished in 1935.

Finally, in the church, an American flag and a brass plaque commemorate the crew of a US Liberator bomber that crashed on Wrangle Common in 1944. All but one crew member died in the accident.

Wrangle Quirk Alert: The Quick-Thinking Vicar

Aside from Wrangle once having been a port, did you know that many of the original 14th century stained glass windows of St Mary and St Nicholas's church were demolished by Puritans during the English Civil War? Thankfully, one of them was saved thanks to the vicar having the presence of mind to remove it – and to then bury it in the vicarage garden!

Some of the earthworks at King's Hill, site of a medieval motte and bailey castle located in the north-west of Wrangle parish.

NAME (STATUS):	**WROOT** (Village)
POPULATION:	455
DISTRICT:	North Lincolnshire
EARLIEST RECORD:	*Wroth*, 1157
MEANING:	Snout-like spur of land, although one other reference (Stonehouse) suggests it means "out of England" – perhaps referring to the place when it was an island prior to surrounding land reclamation
DERIVATION:	From the Old English word *wrōt*

Wroot Geographic Trivia

Wroot is located in the Isle of Axholme on fenland that is surrounded by banks, drains and channels as well as the canalised River Torne. Prior to the 1620s, Wroot was very much an island surrounded by wetlands, and was famous for celery and rhubarb growing. The village's geography meant that it could only be reached by boat before the land was reclaimed around it – see *Wroot Historic Trivia* for how that was achieved.

Wroot Church: St Pancras

Very little remains of the original 14th century church at Wroot as it was largely rebuilt first in 1794 and then again in 1879, but original relics include a Norman stone coffin, a chalice dating to 1510 and a bell dated 1260, the oldest in the Diocese. Someone who knew the medieval church very well, though, was Samuel Wesley, rector of both Epworth and Wroot – and the father of the great John Wesley who was born in Epworth 4 miles east of Wroot. In fact, young John assisted Samuel at Wroot for two years as curate, between 1726 and 1728, and a stone at the entrance to the churchyard commemorates this fact. It is also thought that two of John Wesley's sisters are buried in Wroot's churchyard although their graves are not marked. St Pancras' church also claims the second oldest bell in the Diocese of Lincoln, while it also attracts pilgrims from all over the world due to the Wesley connection. Inside the church there are framed pictures illustrating the Wesley history.

As well as the 1794 and 1879 church rebuilds, local legend also has it that a much older timber church was burned down on the same spot in around 1348 when the Black Death had begun to ravage England. That legend also has it that the fire took the whole village as well, and was actually a deliberate measure to attempt to contain the spread of the disease. However, the village was then rebuilt further to the north whereas the second church (the 14th century one) was built on the same spot as both its predecessor and its two successors.

Wroot Historic Trivia: The Drainage of Hatfield Chase and the Wesley Family

In the late 12th century, Roger de Mowbray was Lord of the Manor of Wroot. However, on his death, he left his possessions at Wroot to "God and the monks of St Mary's at York". The manor was later confiscated by Henry VIII in the 16th century, while over a century later Charles II sold the land to the Dutch drainage engineer, Cornelius Vermuyden as part of his scheme to drain Hatfield Chase (see *Lincolnshire County History* for more on this). Prior to the drainage, Wroot had been something of an island on slightly higher ground surrounded by wetlands. However, the drainage came at a cost for the people of Wroot, as the ownership issue dramatically reduced their common pasture in the fens, which they depended on for pasturage, and for peat which they burned as fuel. Furthermore, part of the Epworth parish commons that included Wroot, had

The Cross Keys is Wroot's only pub, and was listed in Kelly's Directory *of 1885.*

Wroot's church is dedicated to St Pancras and was built in 1879.

already been part-enclosed by the Lord of the Manor in the 14th century. So while the richer members of the community challenged the project in court by lawsuits, groups of commoners rioted against the enclosures in 1627. It did neither faction any good, though, and the legal debate over the drainage and enclosures actually went on until the 18th century.

As already mentioned, Samuel Wesley was rector at Wroot in the early 18th century, occasionally living there, too. However, the living obtained from the small parish was unsupportive for Wesley, who allegedly described the place as "little better than a swamp". Wesley's daughter, Mehetabel, was also not overly complimentary about the village when she wrote of the inhabitants of Wroot to her sister Emilia:

The Wesleyan Methodist church at Wroot, founded in 1870 over a century after John Wesley himself worked in the village.

Fortune has fixed thee in a place
Debarred of wisdom, wit, and grace –
High births and virtue equally they scorn,
As asses dull, on dunghills born ;
Impervious as the stones their heads are found ;
Their rage and hatred steadfast as the ground.
With these unpolished wights, thy youthful days
Glide slow and dull, and Nature's lamp decays :
Oh what a lamp is hid 'midst such a sordid race !'

Samuel Wesley's son, John Wesley, was curate at Wroot from 1726 until July 1728, after which he became Moderator of Lincoln College, Oxford. Ironically, it was 1870 before the Methodist chapel was built on High Street, some one hundred years after the Wesleys lived there. Also built in 1879 was the village school, which originally held around 100 children. It was built on the site of a former Free School, founded and endowed in 1706 by Henry Travis, and which was to provide instruction in English, Church catechism and Christian religious principles – and indeed, one of the teachers there was, of course, John Wesley. Children were to be selected for the schools by parish parsons and church-wardens, and when they left – at the very late age for those days of seventeen – they received a book entitled *The Whole Duty of Man.*

What is known as the Wesley Beacon which commemorates village links with the great John Wesley.

The Best of the Rest

AUSTEN FEN	Status:	Population:	District:	Earliest Record:
	Hamlet	c.40	East Lindsey	Unknown
Austen Fen Trivia:	**Austen Fen** is located on the Louth Navigation which was completed in 1770 and runs from Louth to Tetney Haven, and thus accommodated barges shipping products between Louth and Grimsby. The barges made good use of the large, early 19ᵗʰ century wharf-side warehouse at Austen Fen, which survives today with its three storeys and nine bays. Austen Fen is also the location of Austen Fen East and West pumping stations, which pump water into the Louth Navigation from the surrounding fens and which are owned and operated by the Lindsey Marsh Internal Drainage Board.			

BOUGHTON	Status:	Population:	District:	Earliest Record:
	Hamlet	c.10	North Kesteven	*Boughton*, 1334
Meaning:	Usually farmstead of a man called Bucca or where bucks are kept			
Derivation:	From the Old English personal name *Bucca* plus the Old English word *tūn* (farmstead), or the Old English words *bucca* (male deer or goat) and *tūn*.			

BURNHAM	Status:	Population:	District:	Earliest Record:
	Hamlet	c.30	North Lincolnshire	*Brune*, 1086 (Domesday Book); *Brunum*, c.1115
Meaning:	Place at the springs or streams			
Derivation:	From the Old Scandinavian word *brunnr* (spring or stream) in a dative plural form			

CAMP	Status:		District:	Earliest Record:
	Military training camp		North Kesteven	N/A

ERMINE	Status:	Population:	District:	Earliest Record:
	Housing Estate	5,736	Lincoln	*Ermine*, 1950
Derivation:	Named after Ermine Street, the Roman road which today divides East Ermine from West Ermine			
Ermine Trivia:	The **Ermine** estate to the north of Lincoln was built in the 1950s and is home to just under 6,000 people. The estate is split into two parts, East Ermine and West Ermine, and which are divided by the A15, or Riseholme Road as it known for the dividing stretch. The parish church is the Grade II-listed St John the Baptist, built in 1963. It was built by local architect, Sam Scorer, in a striking modernist style, which includes a paraboloid aluminium roof, a hexagonal floor-plan and a striking east window by Keith New.			

The warehouse at Austen Fen, built in the early 19ᵗʰ century on the Louth Navigation.

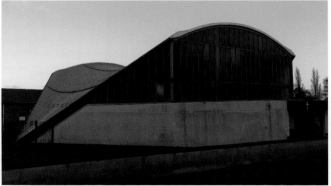

The unusual and striking St John the Baptist church is located in Ermine East.

HOLDINGHAM	Status:	Population:	District:	Earliest Record:
	Estate	2,774	North Kesteven	*Haldingeham*, 1202
Meaning:	Homestead of the family or followers of a man called Hald			
Derivation:	From the Old English personal name *Hald*, plus the Old English words *inga* (of) and *hām* (homestead)			

LITTLE COMMON	Status:	Population:	District:	Earliest Record:
	Road	c.50	South Holland	N/A
Little Common Trivia:	**Little Common** is a narrow no-through road (called Little Common Lane) heading north out of the village of Holbeach Clough. You also turn into Little Common from a west-to-east-aligned road known as Roman Bank, named after a dyke constructed in the 14th century to reclaim land, and which was constructed along the same course as a sea-bank constructed by the Romans around a thousand years earlier.			

TETLEY	Status:	Population:	District:	Earliest Record:
	Hamlet	c.100	North Lincolnshire	*Tetley*, 1316
Meaning:	Possibly island or woodland clearing belonging to a man called Tæte			
Derivation:	From the Old English personal name *Tæte*, plus either of the Old English words *ēg* (island) or *lēah* (woodland clearing)			
Historic Trivia:	Read's *History of the Isle of Axholme* states: "At a short distance from Crowle is Tetley, which from remote times was the property of the family of Stovin; for George Stovin, who lived in the reign of George I, declared he was the eighth or ninth descendant who had possessed that property. Several residences have been erected on the same site; and at a short distance from the house [Tetley Hall] is a small burial ground, containing several sepulchral memorials of the Stovin Family."			
	Tetley eventually passed to Henry Lister Moore, who built the present Tetley Hall. As for the Stovins, it would appear that the first of note was William the Conqueror's "Chief of the Bowstringers".			

WILL ROW	Status:	Population:	District:	Earliest Record:
	Road	c.20	East Lindsay	N/A

The entrance to Little Common Lane.

A quirky signpost on Little Common Lane indicating that the house to the left is Common Field Cottage. The signpost also points north to "The Wash".

Bibliography

Books

Arthur Mee, *The King's England: Lincolnshire* (Hodder and Stoughton, 1970)
Stewart Bennett, *A History of Lincolnshire* (Phillimore & Co. Ltd., 1999)
Stephen Wade, *The A-Z of Curious Lincolnshire* (The History Press, 2011)
A.D. Mills, *Oxford Dictionary of British Place Names* (Oxford University Press, 1991)

Information Panels and booklets at:

Alkborough: Julian's Bower
Aubourn
Bag Enderby: St Margaret's church
Barholm: St Martin's church
Barlings Abbey
Belton House
Bicker
Cleethorpes: Ross Castle
Coates: St Edith's church
Crowland Abbey
Deeping Gate
Fleet: St Mary Magdalene church
Grantham
Grimsthorpe Castle
Haxey
Howell: St Oswald's church
Leasingham: St Andrews church
Lincoln
Market Deeping
Minting
Moulton Windmill
Old Bolingbroke: Bolingbroke Castle
Somersby: On The Trail of Tennyson
Somersby: St Margaret's church
Stamford: Stamford Castle
Stamford: St Leonard's Priory
Stow: St Mary's church
Thornton Abbey
Tupholme Abbey
Welbourn: Welbourn Castle
Winceby
Woolsthorpe Manor

Websites

http://en.wikipedia.org/wiki
http://greatenglishchurches.co.uk/
https://historicengland.org.uk/
http://neighbourhood.statistics.gov.uk/
http://parishes.lincolnshire.gov.uk/
http://redlionbicker.co.uk/
http://www.aboutbritain.com/
http://www.axholme-fhs.org.uk/

http://www.axholme.info/
http://www.bonby.org/st-andrew-s/
http://www.bottesfordhistory.org.uk/
http://www.bourneunitedcharities.co.uk/
http://www.bradleyvillage.co.uk/
http://www.britishlistedbuildings.co.uk/
http://www.caistor.net/
http://www.caitlingreen.org/
http://www.castleuk.net/
http://www.cleethorpestouristboard.co.uk/
http://www.cowbitvillage.co.uk/
http://www.crowlandabbey.org.uk/
http://www.doddingtonhall.com/
http://www.domesdaybook.co.uk/
http://www.egdon-resources.com/
http://www.ermine-estate.org.uk/
https://www.flickr.com/
http://www.gatehouse-gazetteer.info/
http://www.genuki.org.uk/
http://www.geograph.org.uk/
http://www.greatcoatespc.com/
http://www.greatfen.org.uk/
http://www.grimsbytelegraph.co.uk/
http://www.healingmanorhotel.co.uk/
http://www.heritagegateway.org.uk/
http://www.historicengland.org.uk/
http://www.lincolnshire.gov.uk/
http://www.lincolnshirewolds.info/
http://www.lincstothepast.com/
http://www.lincstrust.org.uk/
http://www.louthleader.co.uk/
http://www.marketrasenmail.co.uk/
http://www.megalithic.co.uk/
http://www.messinghamparishcouncil.co.uk/
http://www.moultonwindmill.co.uk/
http://www.myprimitivemethodists.org.uk/
http://www.mysteriousbritain.co.uk/
http://www.pastscape.org.uk/
http://www.pubisthehub.org.uk/
http://www.rodcollins.com/
http://www.royaloakaubourn.co.uk/
http://www.scunthorpetelegraph.co.uk/
http://www.skegness.net/
http://www.southhollandlife.com/
http://www.spaldingtoday.co.uk/
http://www.stamfordmercury.co.uk/
http://www.stjohnthebaptistparishchurch.org.uk/
http://www.stone-circles.org.uk/
http://www.stpeterscleethorpes.org.uk/
http://www.thegeorgeatleadenham.co.uk/
http://www.thesebastopol.com/
https://www.thorne.co.uk/
http://www.village-links.co.uk/
http://www.woldsandtrentmethodist.org.uk/
http://www.workhouses.org.uk/